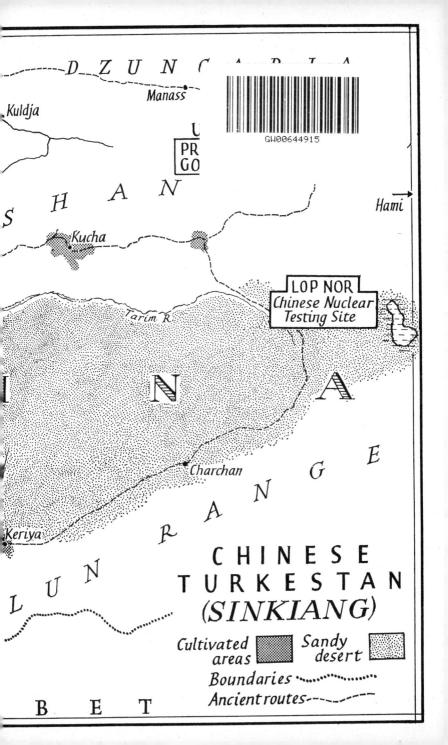

Macartney (left) and Francis Younghusband (centre)
with the Amban of Yarkand (between them) in 1890

MACARTNEY AT KASHGAR
NEW LIGHT ON BRITISH, CHINESE, AND RUSSIAN ACTIVITIES IN SINKIANG, 1890-1918

MACARTNEY
AT KASHGAR

New Light on British,
Chinese, and Russian Activities
in Sinkiang, 1890-1918

C. P. Skrine and Pamela Nightingale

HONG KONG   OXFORD
OXFORD UNIVERSITY PRESS
1987

Oxford University Press

Oxford New York Toronto
Petaling Jaya Singapore Hong Kong Tokyo
Delhi Bombay Calcutta Madras Karachi
Nairobi Dar es Salaam Cape Town
Melbourne Auckland

and associated companies in
Beirut Berlin Ibadan Nicosia

First published by Methuen & Co. Ltd. 1973
This edition reprinted, with permission, in
Oxford Paperbacks 1987

ISBN 0 19 584156 5

Printed in Hong Kong by Golden Crown Printing Co., Ltd.
Published by Oxford University Press, Warwick House, Hong Kong

Contents

Preface   *page* vii

Introduction by Sir Clarmont Skrine   viii

1 Travellers to Kashgar   1

2 Rival Empires   17

3 The Opening Moves   33

4 Assault on the Pamirs   50

5 The Pamir Settlement   67

6 The Struggle to Survive   85

7 The Russian Ascendancy   102

8 The Move into Sarikol   124

9 Diplomatic Adjustments   137

10 Recognition and Reforms   152

11 Revolution in Kashgar   173

12 The Chira Crisis   188

13 The Contest for Sinkiang   208

14 The New Regime   232

15 War and Counter-Intelligence   248

Bibliography   265

Index   268

Illustrations

PLATES

Frontispiece: Macartney and Francis
Younghusband with the
Amban of Yarkand in 1890

Between pp 116 and   The market place at Kashgar
117:   The Mir of Hunza with his
sons

Chu, Taoyin of Kashgar,
1917–1923

Between pp 132 and 133:   The Macartney family in 1913

Macartney with his son Eric in
1913

The British Consulate-General
in Kashgar after it was rebuilt
in 1913

MAPS

Endpapers: Chinese Turkestan (Sinkiang)
pp x and xi: Central and Eastern Asia

The maps were drawn by Mr William Bromage

Preface

This book is an account of the career of Sir George Macartney who spent twenty-eight years from 1890 to 1918 as the sole British representative in Sinkiang, China's most westerly province. It does not pretend to be a history of the area or of the complicated Central Asian diplomacy of Russia, China and Britain during that period. In its most complex part this has been covered from the British side by G. J. Alder in *British India's Northern Frontier, 1865–95*. Instead the authors have concentrated on the record of a career remarkable not so much for spectacular achievements as for dedicated service and objective reporting in one of the most remote and lonely posts ever maintained by the British government. From it emerges a shrewd and objective account of Russian and Chinese power in Sinkiang in a period which was crucial for the fate of the province. Now that Russia and China are again in dispute over Sinkiang Sir George Macartney's analysis of their objectives and policies before 1918 has a fresh significance.

This book is written chiefly from the Political and Secret Records in the India Office Library which contain the Kashgar diaries and correspondence, supplemented by Foreign Office material in the Public Record Office. Sir George Macartney left no collection of personal papers, but the authors are indebted to his son, Mr Eric Macartney, for information about his family and for photographs of his father. They are also grateful to the Librarian and staff of the India Office Library and Records.

Introduction
by Sir Clarmont Skrine

This book stems from an account I wrote in 1966 of the repercussions in Sinkiang of the Chinese revolution from the point of view of the British Consul-General in Kashgar. My memoir was too short for a full-length book and Mr Anthony Forster of Methuen agreed to an expansion of it into a biography of Sir George Macartney who founded the Kashgar Consulate-General and worked there alone for twenty-eight years.

My work on the biography was cut short by illness in 1967. Luckily I was able to secure the services of Dr Pamela Nightingale, a graduate of Newnham College, Cambridge, as a collaborator. This is the book which she has now written.

For me the story is particularly enthralling because I arrived in Kashgar in 1922, only four years after Macartney retired. The Consulate Guard which had been conceded to Macartney by the government of India in his last year had just been replaced by eight mounted but unarmed locally recruited orderlies. Many of the characters who were active in Macartney's time were well known to me, notably the infamous General Ma Titai who continued to flourish until 1924 when his palace was stormed and he himself paid the price for his tyranny.

I now realize that the picture I drew in my book on Sinkiang was sadly incomplete. The little town of Bai, twenty-five marches north-east of Kashgar and roughly half-way to Urumchi, was the nearest I could approach, in the limited time at my disposal, to the provincial capital. We in Kashgar knew little of Yang Tseng-hsin, the provincial Governor in Urumchi. Indeed he must have been a somewhat shadowy figure to Macartney. I depended for Urumchi news on reports of intelligence agents of doubtful veracity, valuable but infrequent letters from members of the China Inland Mission, and on the talk of rare visitors from the provincial capital, usually travellers passing through on the 4,000-mile trail from the China coast to India. Few of these had actually seen or talked with the formidable Governor. We certainly supposed that his position was impregnable. In my last report from Kashgar in 1924 I expressed the opinion that the Governor's removal from his post by the central government was extremely unlikely. I did not take into account the danger Yang lived in from the envy, hatred and malice, not of the Muslims he ruled, but of his own countrymen. Assassins hired by a trusted friend laid him low on 7 July 1928 and with him destroyed the peace and relative prosperity of the New Dominion he had nursed and protected so long.

It was not until the 1930s that news began to seep out, showing what a remarkable governor Yang Tseng-hsin had been. We now know that his statecraft was responsible for the survival of peace and order in Sinkiang throughout and after the turmoil of the Chinese Revolution. Macartney came to the fore at the same time. He was in a position of influence during the Chinese Revolution and his diplomatic skill was equally invaluable later when repercussions of the Russian Revolution were felt in Kashgar.

Macartney's dispatches and diaries throw a fitful light upon the sequence of events that led to and followed Yang's accession to power. They also reveal Macartney's wise diplomacy. How strange the working of Fate, by which a Christian diplomat collaborated almost unconsciously with a Confucian mandarin in saving his province from the alternatives of foreign domination or chaos.

CENTRAL &
EASTERN
ASIA

Urumchi–Peking.....1,500 m.
Yarkand–Urumchi....680 m.
Yarkand–Delhi.......640 m.
Yarkand–St Petersburg–
......(Leningrad).....2,500 m.
Yarkand–London—
.............3,500 m.

for detail see
end paper maps

Orenburg

Caspian Sea

Krasnovodsk

Tashkent

Bokhara

Kokand

Samarkand

AFGHANISTAN

KABUL

Srinagar

KASHMIR

LADAKH

PERSIA

INDIA

Karachi

ARABIA

Bombay

DELHI

Indian Ocean

R U

M O

Urumchi

Hami

SINKIANG

Kashgar

Yarkand

Lop
Nor

Charchan

Khotan

G

H

C

T I B E T

NEPAL

Lhasa

SIKKIM

BHUTAN

Bay
of Bengal

ONE

Travellers to Kashgar

In the late summer of 1890 two young Englishmen sat with their hosts to be photographed in Yarkand, an oasis town of Chinese Turkestan. Their impeccable European clothes and sun helmets were in bizarre contrast with the blue silk jackets, pork-pie hats and long robes of their Chinese hosts, and the assorted garb of their Turki attendants. Dominating the group with his military bearing and imperious gaze was Captain Francis Younghusband, then twenty-seven years old, but already a veteran explorer of Central Asia. His was a figure that could have been photographed anywhere in the British empire in that last decade of the nineteenth century; his stiff carriage and stern expression gave an air of supreme self-confidence, even arrogance, which not even his status as a guest of the Manchu empire could subdue.

In contrast, the Amban, or chief magistrate of Yarkand, sat in the group with his hands resting on his knee and looking composedly at the camera. He too had assurance, but of an older Confucian mould. He represented the Manchu imperial power which only thirteen years before had reconquered Eastern Turkestan and named it Sinkiang, the 'New Dominion'. As one of the élite of Chinese scholar-officials the Amban belonged to a civilization that stretched back for thousands of years and still looked on the world outside China's borders as barbarian. Despite the humiliations of the past fifty years and their surrenders to foreign powers the Chinese retained a sense of cultural superiority which showed itself in the dignity and firmness behind the Amban's courteous treatment of his guests.

Younghusband and the Amban typified in their own way the two imperial traditions, the one new and aggressive, the other ancient but tenacious. Although separated by great distances in outlook and origin these two powers had now come to meet along the mountain ranges that divided the Indian from the Chinese empires. It was the expansion of the British-Indian empire that

1

had brought Younghusband to Yarkand on a mission from the Indian government. With him as assistant and Chinese interpreter had come the other Englishman in the photograph, the twenty-three year old George Macartney.

There seemed little at first to distinguish Macartney's figure from that of Younghusband. He sported the ubiquitous moustache of the period, but faced the photographer with less assurance. His reserve was apparent in the sidelong glance of his eyes, deep-set above high cheekbones. Like the Amban his face had something of the detached and analytical qualities of the scholar, but unlike Younghusband Macartney's appearance revealed a certain modesty, even diffidence of temperament. No one looking at these three figures would have guessed that in the person of George Macartney the two traditions of China and Great Britain did in fact meet. Only Macartney's command of the Chinese language gave any hint that he had mixed parentage, a Scottish father and Chinese mother, and that he had been born and brought up for the first ten years of his life in Nanking.

Macartney's father, Halliday Macartney, was descended from the same branch of the Scottish family that had bred the eighteenth-century diplomat, George Macartney, who was made a peer in 1775, became a governor of Madras, and was then sent on an important mission to the Emperor of China. Despite his ancestry Halliday Macartney did not begin his career in particularly rich or influential circumstances. He studied medicine and went out to the Crimean War as an assistant surgeon. Later, his regiment took him to China where he found he preferred fighting to healing. He resigned his commission to join the Chinese army under General Charles Gordon which was engaged in putting down the Taiping rebellion. He achieved some distinction in this service and in 1864 decided to make his home in China with the ambition of gaining an influential position in the Manchu court. First, though, he married a near relative of Lar Wang, a Taiping prince, who had been one of the leaders of the great rebellion. Macartney had taken part in 1863 in the storming of the last Taiping stronghold, Suchow, when Lar Wang had been killed and Macartney had taken his womenfolk under his protection. He chose one of them as his bride and married her according to the Chinese rite in December 1864. Two years later in January 1867 their eldest son George was born, and subsequently they had two

2

other sons and a daughter. Very little is known of Halliday Macartney's Chinese wife as she did not mix with his European friends. But she was said to be attractive and intelligent, and the family lived together in Nanking until 1876 when Macartney returned to London as secretary of successive Chinese ministers at the Court of St James. His wife stayed behind and died two years later in Nanking.

The first ten years of George Macartney's life were thus spent in the society of Nanking where his father was the founder-manager of China's first arsenal. He grew up speaking English and Chinese and was old enough before he left to have absorbed a good deal of Chinese culture and to have become familiar with most aspects of Chinese life. This part of his education continued informally in London through his father's position as secretary and interpreter at the Chinese legation. He never lost his fluency in his mother's tongue and it became apparent that he had a gift for languages. He was sent to Dulwich College but instead of going on to an English university he went to France and took a degree at Caen University in 1886. Two years previously his father had married a Frenchwoman as his second wife. Besides speaking fluent French the young Macartney also learnt some Russian and German, and eventually he was to add Persian, Hindustani and Turki to his repertoire. With his background and linguistic ability it seemed inevitable that he should have a career in the East, and he sought a British consular post in China. But he failed to achieve his ambition; perhaps his background and French university were too unorthodox, or his reserve created a bad impression. Instead he had to sail for the East in the comparatively lowly post of Chinese interpreter in one of the subordinate services of the government of India.

It seems unlikely that George Macartney took with him to India the typical attitudes of the young English recruits of the time. The Indian civil service then and for some time afterwards drew on the cream of the public schools and universities, and its members had not only intellectual ability but an *esprit de corps* which made the service almost a caste. Young men went to the East imbued with a sense of national superiority and convinced of their ability and therefore of their right to rule. The idea that their Asian subjects might prefer self-government to good government did not cross their minds and had hardly yet occurred to the educated

3

classes amongst those they ruled. Young Englishmen unashamedly went to India to pass on the benefits of a superior civilization compared with which Asian society as they saw it was backward, inefficient, often cruel, and corrupt. They took with them the public school caste loyalties and the public school tradition of *noblesse oblige*. English society in India reproduced and often distorted these attitudes; beliefs in social and cultural superiority turned into assumptions of racial superiority and of the divine right of the English people to rule over coloured races. In the small world of the club and drawing-room where the women had often only gossip to while away their exile, any stepping over the lines of caste and convention was not treated kindly. Every detail of a man's career and his antecedents could be discussed and judged at leisure, and little escaped public knowledge.

It was not a world designed to make the young George Macartney feel at home. Throughout his life people who did not know him intimately commented on the depth of his reserve and on his reticence about his personal affairs and achievements. Partly this was a matter of temperament, inherited from his father, but no doubt it was increased by the circumstances of his life. Uprooted at an impressionable age from the Chinese world into which he was born, and separated from his mother, his transfer to an English public school must have come as a cultural and mental shock. The scholarly bent of his mind and his dislike of all forms of sport cannot have made things easier for him. When added to this was the consciousness of mixed parentage in a society where marriage to a non-European usually cut one off from one's fellows, there might have been the makings of lifelong psychological problems. That these did not arise, or that George Macartney was able to overcome them says much for his father's upbringing and his own stable character. Fortunately he was blessed with a very even temper which made it easy for him to get on with people. Few could quarrel with so quiet and modest a man.

Nevertheless, when he sailed for the East in 1887 at the age of twenty Macartney must have felt something of an outsider among the usual complement of passengers to India. He had then spent half of his life in China and half in Europe, and it must have seemed that he belonged completely to neither world. The sense of apartness had been there from childhood. His mother had never mixed with his father's European friends – whether by her prefer-

4

ence or his father's choice is not clear. Halliday Macartney's own attitude to his Chinese masters was itself ambiguous. A friend said of him that although people dubbed him 'a Chinaman at heart' he believed that Halliday Macartney 'inwardly despised and disliked the natives, though he did not care to see them unjustly attacked, and thus appeared at times as their champion'. What attitude he passed on to his son is nowhere explicit, but George Macartney always showed the greatest respect for the feelings and interests of the Chinese although he saw with clear eyes the weakness and corruption of their government. It seems that this would also be a just description of his father's attitude. Certainly Halliday Macartney was not a man to give his life in serving a people whom he held in contempt. But he did not bring his Chinese wife with him to London, and his son, no doubt, found it best not to mention her at school. He was to maintain this silence about his mother throughout his life, even to his own children. In London his father's circle was cosmopolitan rather than English and Macartney's choice of a French university further emphasized the difference between him and his fellow recruits for service in India.

It was therefore a silent and perhaps disappointed young man who left England to take up an appointment with the Burma Commission. But before he could begin the work assigned to him he was transferred to serve as Chinese interpreter with the Indian military expedition to Sikkim which in 1888 freed that border state from Tibetan control. Macartney's general ability as well as his proficiency in Chinese earned him a favourable report and led to his appointment a year later as interpreter to accompany Younghusband to Sinkiang.

The two men had set out from Kashmir and trekked eastwards to Leh, the only town of Ladakh, and then northwards over passes 16,000 to 18,000 feet high into Chinese territory and the ancient city of Yarkand. The journey took four months and won for Macartney the friendship and esteem of Younghusband. When they parted a year later the great explorer acknowledged his debt to his companion:

We had been together a year now, and the greater part of the time by ourselves. It does not always follow that two men who have never seen each other in their lives before can get on at a stretch without a break and with scarcely a change of society. I felt myself especially fortunate, therefore, in having for a companion a man who was not only a first-class Chinese scholar and tactful in dealing with the Chinese but who was also willing to give and take, as travellers have to be.

Macartney, on his part, had the greatest admiration for Younghusband and the year he spent in his company was probably the most formative in his life.

Not only was Yarkand the place where happily Macartney was photographed at the very outset of his career, but it was here, too, within a few days of their arrival that he met a Russian officer, Captain Gromchevsky, whom Younghusband had tracked down on the Pamirs the year before. The meeting at Yarkand was symbolic. There on Chinese territory Macartney met for the first time the representative of a power whose expansionist aims he was to try, at times single-handed, to keep from absorbing Sinkiang. In that first meeting, though, with the affable Russian there seemed little threat. Younghusband's relations with Gromchevsky were friendly. He wrote in one of his books that he found the Russians individually 'the most charming people in the world. In spite of their reputation for prevarication they are frank and they are kindly and warm-hearted.' But neither he nor Gromchevsky were under any illusions about each other's designs in Sinkiang. Each knew that the other would strain every nerve and use every trick to protect and extend his government's interests in this remote province of Central Asia. For Younghusband this meant popular acclaim for explorations and encounters on the Roof of the World; for George Macartney it was to mean years of patient watching, largely unknown and unrecognized, over the varying fortunes of the contestants in the 'Great Game'.

Younghusband's first meeting with Gromchevsky in 1889 was the signal that the contest had begun in earnest between Russia and Britain for the control of the mountain passes into India. From the time of Trafalgar India had been protected by the British navy from all threat of invasion by sea, but Britain's European enemies had seen opportunities for trouble-making in India's long northern border with Afghanistan and China. Napoleon had proposed a combined Franco-Russian expedition against this frontier as a way of striking at his enemy in a vulnerable place, and Russian columns had actually started off towards India, but without proper maps and equipment had not got very far. Nevertheless the strategy had not been forgotten by the Russians.

What might have seemed an unlikely adventure or a mere paper exercise at the beginning of the century had to be taken seriously by the 1860s when the great Russian drive into Central Asia and the Far East was well under way. With their ambitions in Europe blocked by Britain the Tsar and his generals turned to the east for compensation. They saw in Central Asian conquests not only prospects of unlimited Russian aggrandizement but a chance to threaten Britain through the back door of her Indian empire. Sabre-rattling near the northern Indian frontier where the British had only thirty soldiers to defend each mile could make the politicians in London more pliable. If the Russian Foreign Office should exercise a restraining hand the War Office could go over the Foreign Minister's head to the Tsar. And if the War Office should prove faint-hearted there were always generals ambitious for a cheap victory and the loot of a Central Asian town. Once a conquest was made, prestige and the pride of the Romanovs demanded that it be kept.

Once the Russian drive to the east had begun it was not easy to call a halt. Traders and settlers would push farther afield and come into contact with other Central Asian tribes. There would be problems of raiding and disputes which called for Russian intervention, and again the army would move forward. In this way, one after the other, the khanates of Central Asia collapsed like so many cards before the Russian advance; Bokhara in 1868, Khiva in 1873, Kokand in 1875, and Russia then was in contact with India's turbulent neighbour, Afghanistan. The sabre-rattling began in earnest. During the 1878 crisis in the Near East Russian columns were ordered to march to Wakhan and the Chitral passes, and they were only turned aside by the Congress of Berlin. What would have happened if the Congress had not intervened was a speculation which must have given the Viceroy some anxious thought.

Britain's first efforts to control Afghan affairs had ended in the disasters of the first Afghan war when a whole British expeditionary force was slaughtered and only one man lived to tell the tale. So fiercely independent and jealous were the Afghans and so turbulent in their domestic politics that their borders offered unlimited scope for intrigue and aggression to a hostile power. British policy swung between two extremes in its efforts to meet the danger. The adherents of the 'forward policy' believed in active intervention, with military support where necessary, to give India favourable allies on her frontier, while the protagonists of the 'close border' or 'masterly inactivity' doctrine believed in a cautious maintenance of the *status quo*. Diplomacy was their weapon, and in 1870, with Gladstone in power and opposed to military adventures, the British government tried to solve the Central Asian problem by negotiating spheres of interest with the Russians. The British agreed to give Russia a free hand with the Turcomans of Transcarpia in return for recognition of the British 'special interest' in Afghanistan and Baluchistan. This would protect the land routes to India from the west. But the problem was to decide the northern boundary of Afghanistan, which would be the dividing line between the two spheres of interest. What followed was a classic example of the folly of border-making by drawing lines on maps.

The natural frontier between Afghanistan and the Russian sphere of interest was the river Oxus, but in the easternmost section of its course, instead of flowing conveniently from east to west, the river described an immense capital Z, of which the upper and lower strokes each ran for 140 miles west by south. To make matters worse the upper parts of the river were fordable at low water and in places bridgeable so that its valley had become the home of isolated mountain people who had settled on both banks. This was especially true of the long northward reach where the principalities of Shignan and Roshan which straddled the river were feudatories of Afghanistan, while that of Darwaz, further north, paid tribute to Russian-controlled Bokhara. The Russians probably knew something of this complicated geography but the British negotiators were entirely ignorant and had to accept whatever maps the Russians chose to show them.

It is not surprising then that after two years of haggling and frustration the British Foreign Secretary, Lord Granville, agreed with his Russian counterpart, Prince Gortchakov, on a delimitation of the frontier which was 'so ambiguous and contradictory as to be almost incomprehensible'. At the last minute the British had accepted a Russian proposal that this section of the frontier should be simplified by drawing a straight line from the eastern end of Lake Victoria on the Great Pamir to the junction of the Kokcha river with the Oxus. Ten years later this makeshift arrangement gave the Russians plausible grounds for claiming several inhabited valleys on the right bank of the Oxus ruled by the chiefs of Roshan and Shignan who were feudatories of Afghanistan. Most serious of all was the discovery that the straight line that had been drawn on the map did not penetrate far enough to the east to meet the Chinese frontier. It left a gap of 60 miles between Afghanistan and the Chinese province of Sinkiang.

One result of these flaws in the Granville-Gortchakov Agreement of 1873 was that not only did it give to Russia nearly 1000 square miles of territory to which she had neither historic nor ethnic right but it further vexed Anglo-Afghan relations. The Amir refused to surrender his claim to the valleys on the right bank of the Oxus although he was pressed by the Viceroy, Lord Mayo, to do so. His relationship with Britain deteriorated and when in 1878 he received a Russian mission at his capital the second Afghan war with Britain followed. The outcome was that the strongest Afghan of his generation, Abdurrahman Khan, was helped by the British to power in Kabul. The new Amir hated the Russians for the treatment he had received when he had been a prisoner in their hands, but his own and his subjects' fierce independence made him hostile to anything that looked like an encroachment by the British. Until the flaws of the 1873 Agreement were removed there was a serious possibility that the Amir's anti-Russian feelings would lead him to clash with the Russians in Shignan and Roshan as he had already clashed with them and lost at Panjdeh. It was certain that the Russians would not lose any chance of provocation and once fighting had broken out there was no knowing what strategic advantages they would gain.

But the most dangerous situation was that created by the gap that had been left between the demarcation line and the Chinese frontier of Sinkiang. For here on the high and inhospitable plateau of the Pamirs, which has been aptly called the Roof of the World, a corridor of unclaimed territory existed which allowed the Russians free access to the south through the passes of the Hindu Kush into the hill states of India. It was here in a climate three months spring and nine months winter, in valley-bottoms 10,000 to 13,000 feet above the sea and empty of settled humanity that the next round of the Great Game was to be played. For this Younghusband and Macartney had come to Sinkiang.

The British government's interest in the country beyond its mountainous northern frontier had waxed and waned throughout the second half of the nineteenth century. There had always been a trickle of Indian trade from Kashmir and Leh over the cruel Karakoram Pass to Yarkand. The traders had carried opium, cotton, piece-goods, spices and hardware on the backs of pack animals over eleven major passes, only two of them lower than Mont Blanc, and had returned by the same route with *charas* (marijuana), China tea, silk, carpets, gold and silver. But so long and hazardous was the journey, and so heavy the losses among the animals that there was little likelihood of any great increase of the trade. The market was restricted, and besides their natural geographical advantages, the Russians had obtained trade privileges on the border in 1851, and permission ten years later to build a factory near Kashgar.

Then an event occurred which roused the interest of the government of India. A revolt broke out among the Muslim people of Eastern Turkestan against their Chinese overlords, and a Kokandi adventurer named Yakub Beg used the situation to establish himself at the head of the insurgents. He drove out the Chinese and founded an independent Muslim state with his capital at Kashgar. Further, he refused to recognize the Russian treaty rights and put a stop to Russian overland trade with China. He appeared friendly towards the British and when Lord Mayo became Viceroy in 1869 he thought he could use Yakub Beg's kingdom in his policy of establishing independent buffer states between the British and Russian empires. Mayo also believed that British goods could move in to fill the market which was closed to the Russians.

But Yakub Beg was not strong enough to keep the Russians permanently at bay and he only averted their advance on to the Kashgar plain in 1872 by signing a commercial treaty which allowed them to establish agents in any towns they chose, gave Russian merchants freedom of passage and set a maximum of $2\frac{1}{2}$ per cent for import duties. The Russian success inspired the British to send the Forsyth Mission to Kashgar in 1873 to ask for similar privileges. Yakub Beg at first conceded them but then from fear of the Russians refused to ratify the agreement. Sir Thomas

Forsyth and his companions returned disillusioned about the prospects of increased trade but they had been made aware for the first time of the dangers of a Russian advance across the Pamirs and through the passes to Hunza, Yasin and Chitral.

In 1877 it looked as though the government of India would achieve its ambition to station a British representative in Kashgar when Yakub Beg asked for one to be sent. But the request proved to be only a last desperate throw on his part, for three years earlier an army had started moving across the breadth of China in one of the longest marches since Mongol times. The Chinese had not forgotten their old province in Turkestan and slowly but irresistibly they returned to reconquer it. By December 1877 they were in Kashgar city and Yakub Beg was dead. Once more Eastern Turkestan was Chinese and became Sinkiang, the New Dominion. The Chinese, though, did not attempt to expand their frontier westwards and there remained the unclaimed corridor between Sinkiang and Afghan territory. Only now it was not two but three empires that confronted each other across the snows and silence of the high Pamirs; and the change did not bode well for Britain.

Some of the effects of the change became apparent when Ney Elias visited Yarkand on behalf of the government of India in 1880. Although he had permission from Peking to travel in Sinkiang, Elias met with difficulties and frustration. The Chinese permitted the Indian trade with Yarkand only on sufferance and imposed import and transit duties on it at will. The Russians dominated the commerce of the province. When Lord Dufferin tried to secure equal status for the British and sent Elias to Sinkiang again in 1885 to ask for a permanent British representative there the Peking government refused to send anyone to negotiate with him, and he had an unfriendly reception. Not only did the Chinese bear a grudge against Britain for recognizing the rebel Yakub Beg but relations were made worse by the Burma dispute and the ill-feeling over the Sikkim negotiations.

By 1889 the government of India was not so much concerned with commercial advantages as consumed by anxiety about the northern frontier and particularly the security of the passes into the Indian hill states. The surveyors of the Forsyth Mission were not the only people to discover that the Russians could pass through unclaimed territory on to the Pamirs. In 1880 Colonel

Kostenko, a member of the Tashkent General Staff, drew the attention of his Russian colleagues to 'this belt of no-man's-land' which, he went on to say, 'will sooner or later have to be included in the Russian dominions, which will thus be in immediate contact with the range forming the watershed between the Oxus and the Indus'. In 1883 three Russian explorers covered most of the Pamirs as far east as the approaches to Roshan and Shignan, and the same year there was evidence of Russian intrigues with the Indian state of Chitral.

Worse was to come. There were five small Muslim states on the border of Kashmir which were potentially fertile soil for foreign intrigue. Two of them, Hunza and Nagir, were of more than doubtful loyalty to their suzerain, the Hindu ruler of Kashmir. Since the only access to them was by a precarious mountain track into the 12 mile long gorge which they shared their activities were difficult to control. Their narrow valley could not support the population, so raiding the Leh–Yarkand route and slave trading supplemented their income. A complicating factor was that the chiefs of Hunza paid formal tribute to the Emperor of China and acknowledged him as their suzerain. The Chinese exercised no administrative control over 'Kanjut' as they called Hunza. Nevertheless they looked upon the state as part of their empire, and the Mir or chief of Hunza had a hereditary landholding in the Yarkand district which had been granted by the Chinese for his past help in putting down a rebellion. However, when Yakub Beg came to power he put a stop to the Hunza raiding and this blow to their economy forced Hunza and Nagir to turn to Kashmir for help. In return for an annual subsidy they acknowledged the Maharaja of Kashmir as suzerain and pledged themselves to stop raiding on Kashmir soil. Kashmir also seized the opportunity to occupy a fort which commanded the entrance to the Hunza–Nagir gorge.

It was not long before ambition and intrigue in the two small states brought about a critical situation for the government of India. Safdar Ali Khan, the son of the Mir of Hunza, murdered his father and had himself acclaimed as Mir. He then conspired with a cousin in Nagir to eject the Kashmiri troops from the fort they had occupied in the valley, and he turned to China for support. The Chinese Foreign Office presented a note to the British Minister in Peking complaining that the Kashmiris had attacked

Kanjut. This intervention by the Chinese complicated for the government of India what was already a difficult problem – the protection of Kashmir's northern border from possible Russian infiltration. In June 1888 the Viceroy wrote to the Secretary of State summing up the situation:

> Though a petty state of no military strength, Hunza is not without importance. From Chinese Turkestan it can be reached by a pass or passes unexplored, and immediately to the north, across the Killik Pass, lies the gap between Afghanistan and China. By pushing through this gap, in however insignificant numbers, or by becoming the successors of China in Kashgar . . . the Russians might at any time, if the suzerainty of Kashmir were not previously established, acquire very inconvenient rights or claims over Kanjut. The country is, no doubt, rough and difficult, but the embarrassment caused by its turning to Russia would none the less be material. . . . For these and other reasons we cannot recognize Chinese rights in Hunza.

The Viceroy might summarily dismiss Chinese rights but it was obvious that the Maharaja of Kashmir could not maintain any effective control over Hunza. The Kashmiri army was a collection of men without any trained officers or organization and it reflected the incompetence of the state administration. Safdar Ali continued to raid the Leh–Yarkand route, and, most ominous of all, in 1888 he received as guests into his kingdom a party of Russians, who called themselves a scientific expedition, and who were led by Captain Gromchevsky. The Russians had spent that season exploring the Pamirs and had found their way through the passes into Hunza where Gromchevsky had serious discussions with Safdar Ali in which it appeared that Russian arms were the chief subject.

This was too much for the government of India and they moved at last with some decision. The Maharaja of Kashmir was superseded and his authority was entrusted to a state council. The army was reorganized and British officers were brought in to train it. A British Agency was established at Gilgit and work was begun on a road which connected Srinagar, the capital of Kashmir, with Gilgit. Gromchevsky's arrival in Hunza convinced the government that they must know more about the passes through the Hindu Kush and about their feasibility as military routes for a Russian invasion. The man appointed to explore them was Captain

Francis Younghusband who had recently completed a pioneer journey of more than 4000 miles across the Gobi desert to Kashgar and India. In 1889 Younghusband had explored all of the passes east of the Baroghil and found two easy routes from the Pamirs into Hunza. He also discovered that the upper course of the Yarkand river where it flowed through the Raskam valley was fertile enough to support a small military force all the year round, a discovery whose significance was underlined when he intercepted there Gromchevsky and a party of Cossacks, back again after their visit to Hunza the previous year. For two nights Younghusband and Gromchevsky had camped together exchanging their experiences in broken French. Both knew they were playing a big game and scarcely tried to conceal it. They parted in a friendly spirit but Younghusband conspired to lead Gromchevsky astray in his explorations and caused the Russian party to lose their horses.

Younghusband's discovery of what he thought were easy passes from the Pamirs into Hunza, combined with new evidence of Safdar Ali's hostility, convinced the government of India that something must be done to try to close the Pamir gap and keep the Russians off the passes. Ney Elias had recommended after his 1885 journey that the Afghans and Chinese should be persuaded to close up their territories to a common frontier across the Pamirs which would only leave the Russians the possibility of violating it by an act of aggression. The government seized on this plan in 1890 and again picked Younghusband to survey the limits of Chinese claims on the Pamirs and to persuade them to make their claims effective. Because of the diplomatic side of his mission Younghusband needed a Chinese interpreter, and so it was that George Macartney accompanied him in 1890 to Yarkand.

Younghusband's discussions with the Amban of Yarkand were hopeful. The Amban claimed that the border of his district on the Pamirs extended at least as far west as Somatash in the middle of the Alichur Pamir and that the nomad Kirghiz of the region paid grazing taxes to the Chinese magistrate of Sarikol. A few months previously the Taotai of Kashgar had sent an armed party to establish a frontier post at Somatash where there was a stone commemorating the Chinese conquest of the region 150 years before. But unfortunately a stronger force of Afghans had turned the Chinese out of Somatash under the pretext that it was part of the

14

Afghan province of Badakhshan. Nevertheless the stone remained for Younghusband to see the truth of the Chinese claim and the Amban offered to arrange guides and an escort for a tour of the Pamirs. Permission had first to be sought from Kashgar, and while Younghusband and Macartney awaited a reply from the Taotai Gromchevsky arrived in Yarkand. The Russian had been exploring the northern border of Tibet but no doubt he had heard of Younghusband's journey, and when the two Englishmen left Yarkand after a fortnight's wait he followed to report to his Consul on their movements. The Pamir round of the Anglo-Russian contest had begun.

On 25 September 1890 Younghusband and Macartney arrived with their escort of Chinese soldiers at Tashkurghan, the headquarters of the Chinese border district of Sarikol. The district embraced the Taghdumbash Pamir, the only one of the eight Pamirs that was occupied by the Chinese. Of the others the Wakhan was in Afghan territory and the rest formed the unclaimed area that was the object of so much interest. Over these Macartney and Younghusband now travelled surveying the country which was to be the scene of disputes, invasion and conflict for the next three years.

The Pamirs covered a total area of 23,000 square miles and embraced mountain ranges of lofty heights which ran from east to west and formed the watershed between the Oxus and the Tarim basins. The name 'pamir' properly belonged not to the mountains but to the chain of valleys between them which had been scooped out by glaciers and then filled with their alluvium, so that they resembled Scottish moors, covered in snow for seven months of the year, but bearing patches of grass and flowers in the summer. Exposed to constant high winds and extremes of temperature the Pamirs could only supply summer grazing to a few nomad Kirghiz families. But on their easternmost edge between the double chain of mountains that linked the Alai range with the Karakoram ran the fertile Sarikol valley and the Taghdumbash Pamir. Here round Tashkurghan the land supported a small population of farmers and nomadic cattle breeders, and provided a fertile corridor through which the Russians could gain access to the passes to Hunza and Gilgit.

It was the disputed area west of Sarikol that concerned Younghusband on that visit, and from Tashkurghan he and Macartney marched in a wide detour through the Taghdumbash and the Little and Great Pamirs to Somatash on the Blue Lake, 120 miles west of Tashkurghan. The place was uninhabited but they found a small dilapidated fort and a large stone in two fragments. No one could decipher the worn letters but it was obviously the stone referred to by the Amban, and on the strength of this Younghusband decided that the Alichur Pamir belonged to China. He then proceeded to sketch out a common boundary between China and Afghanistan on the Pamirs which on paper would have disposed of the gap between them. In fact it was an impossible frontier for either to hold, let alone defend, against the Russians, and Younghusband's intervention led only to Somatash becoming the focus for a three-cornered dispute between the Chinese, Afghans and Russians which lasted for three years and twice led to bloodshed.

In 1890, though, Younghusband felt satisfied that he had solved the Pamir problem, and from Somatash he and Macartney marched by stages in bitter cold until they came to the point where, crossing the last pass, they could look out over the 1000 mile long plain of the Tarim Basin. On 1 November 1890 they came within view of the long brown walls of Old Kashgar. The Taotai had allotted them a single-storey house and garden called Chini Bagh (Chinese Garden) outside the walls of the city overlooking the river. When he and Younghusband crossed its threshold Macartney could have had little suspicion that it was to be his home for the next twenty-eight years.

TWO

Rival Empires

When Macartney looked down on the plain of the Tarim Basin from the heights of the Pamirs and surveyed the world where he was to spend the rest of his career he saw what appeared to be an endless desert stretching away to the east, one of the driest regions in the whole of Asia. On the north, west and south the desert was enclosed by lofty mountain ranges; the Tien Shan or Celestial Mountains to the north, the Pamirs to the west, and the Kunlun–Karakoram complex forming the border with India to the south. From this last range ran the Yarkand river which under the name of Tarim flowed eastwards when it reached the plain until it lost itself in the swamps and sands of the Lop Nor district south of Kucha. Smaller glacier-fed streams also flowed into the plain and, where they broke through the skirts of the mountains, patches of oasis like jewels strung on a necklace circled the desert. The old silk route on which Marco Polo had travelled to China linked Kashgar, the most westerly oasis, with the southern towns of Yarkand, Karghalik, Khotan, Keriya and Charchan, and then ran east by Lop Nor into the heart of China. A similar historic road ran north along the foot of the Tien Shan linking Kashgar with Aksu, Kucha, Turfan, Hami and Urumchi, the capital of Sinkiang.

The desert with its encircling oases and mountains formed Kashgaria, the southern half of Sinkiang, and the only part of the province that Macartney was to know well. Beyond the Tien Shan lay the northern part known as Dzungaria, but nearly 1000 miles separated its northern boundary, the Altai mountains, from the Pamirs in the south, and even the capital, Urumchi, was the same distance from Kashgar. Urumchi could and did make its will known in Kashgar but in a province bigger than Britain, France and Germany combined the Governor could only be a distant figure, and the southern oasis towns largely lived in a world of their own.

In this world water was the mainstay of economic life. A

complex system of canals and drainage channels drew on the mountain streams and irrigated the loess soil, making up for the mere 2 inches of rain that fell each year. Wherever water could be brought to the soil there was an amazing fertility. Canals and country lanes ran between lines of willow and poplar. Low farmhouses built of mud bricks, each with its tree-shaded courtyard and veranda, were dotted between fields of corn and cotton. Everywhere there was an abundance of vegetables and fruit trees. In the fruit season the stalls of Kashgar overflowed with peaches, melons, pomegranates and grapes, which could all be bought by the trayful for the equivalent of a few coppers. Food of every kind was plentiful and cheap. Even the climate suited the Arcadian scene. Although the temperature went down to zero in winter and the ground froze to a depth of 18 inches there was little snow and the sun shone nearly every day of the year. The high mountain ranges round Kashgar gave protection from the Central Asian winds and the summer heat never reached Indian standards. The most trying occurrences were the dust-storms in the early summer when the wind blew with hurricane force for about twenty-four hours and left an atmosphere clouded with dust for days afterwards. It was an easy, healthy life for the people and the only serious infectious diseases were typhoid and smallpox. Despite the lack of medical care the mortality rate was not high.

The general ease and plenty perhaps explains the lethargy of the native Turki people who made up the great majority of the population. Although Muhammadans they had none of the fanaticism of other groups of their coreligionists, and apart from sporadic rebellions, which were usually led by outsiders, they were content to be governed by the Chinese. Their language was a Turkish dialect, and many had fair skins and almost European features. Good tempered and hospitable, but unenterprising, they were content to live as small cultivators and traders, indifferent to politics apart from quarrels over water supplies. They were, said Younghusband, 'the essence of imperturbable mediocrity'. Provided they were not overburdened by taxes they were apathetic about the fate of Kashgaria. It was reported that when the Chinese were advancing on Kashgar after the downfall of Yakub Beg the Kashgarians who were in Yakub's army merely stripped off their uniforms and went out to cultivate the field as though nothing extraordinary had happened.

Each oasis town took pride in its independence and neither race nor religion seemed capable of combining them into a national unit. The nomadic Kirghiz tribes of the mountains also had their separate way of life. They were not averse to joining in a rebellion if there was a chance of looting the towns, but generally they had little to do with the politics of the oases. They paid grazing taxes for the pasturage of their flocks and moved from Russian to Chinese or Afghan territory at will depending on the demands made on them by the local officials. The only martial element in the population was provided by the Tungans. They were Chinese in dress, manners and customs, and Muhammadan in religion, and were thought to be Turkish in origin. They were strong in Kansu and in the northern part of Sinkiang, particularly round Urumchi and Turfan, and were destined to play an important part in the history of the province.

The oases varied greatly in size. Some were mere villages but the more important ones supported large fortified towns. Yarkand with a population of about 60,000 was the chief commercial town and the headquarters of the Indian traders, but the centre of government was at Kashgar with its smaller population of about 40,000. Travellers commented on the monotonous appearance of these Central Asian towns with their narrow, dark and dirty streets, and the houses, looking identical, built of mud bricks with flat roofs. The Chinese had added their own new city to each town of any importance. They were hardly more distinguished in appearance and were built round the *yamen*, or government office, and the barracks for the troops. In the Kashgar oasis the Chinese had built their new city $2\frac{1}{2}$ miles to the south of the old Muhammadan town. Both had moats and thick crenellated walls pierced by iron gates which were shut at sunset. The main streets in the old town led to the large market square in which stood the chief mosque. On market days the whole area was choked by a press of animals and gaily clad country people laden with their wares. Chini Bagh, which was to be Macartney's home for so many years, lay on the north side of the city immediately outside the walls and on a high cliff overlooking the river. The Russian Consulate, a building in the European style, was also outside the walls near the Andijan Gate.

From their separate quarters the Chinese dominated the local population by a splendid show of power. The massive gateways of their buildings and the pomp which surrounded the Taotai whenever he was carried through the streets in his sedan chair impressed the simple population. Younghusband acknowledged the effect: 'The deep booming of the gongs through the stillness of the night, the blaring of the trumpets, and the noise of the cannon, nightly remind the inhabitants of these towns of Turkestan that the conquerors, who have returned again and again to the country, are still among them and still on the watch.' As a matter of policy the Chinese kept themselves aloof from their subjects. Only the Chinese language was spoken in the business of the *yameı* and a strict compliance with Chinese procedure and customs was enforced. The officials never relaxed into any familiarity with the people but maintained a racial exclusiveness as marked as that of the British in India. Unlike the British they made no attempt to pass on their culture to the 'turban heads' as they called the Turki population. Nothing could shake their belief in the superiority of Chinese civilization over the rest of the world, but they were content that it should be respected from a distance. Government in their eyes meant the collection of taxes and the maintenance of law and order and had nothing to do with improving the education and morals of the people. This they left to the Muslim religious leaders who were chosen by the people but whose appointment had to be confirmed by the Chinese.

This *laissez-faire* attitude on the part of the Chinese met with the approval of their subjects whose own views on government were similar. Provided their religious practices were not interfered with, and taxation did not go beyond certain limits, they did not object to their alien rulers. Conservative to a degree, they did not welcome even the smallest efforts to improve their condition. It suited both the Chinese and the leading members of the Turki community to work together to maintain the *status quo*. The Chinese were realists enough to see that if they could manipulate the natural leaders of the population the masses could be safely ignored. At the same time rich Muslim traders and landowners were aware that an alliance with the conquerors was to their advantage. As tax collectors for the Chinese they took their own percentage of whatever was raised while the Chinese buttressed their position in the local community. The alliance worked well and once Russia had annexed Kokand in 1875 there was little internal threat to Chinese rule. The Kokandians had used their shadowy rights and religious influence over Kashgaria to inspire insurrections against the conquerors, but after the Russian annexation these activities came to an end and the Turkis lapsed into their habitual indolence.

In this one instance the Russian advance into Central Asia made it easier for the Chinese to maintain their hold on Sinkiang, but when it came to facing Russian aggression the Chinese dragon was a paper one only. The 7000 or 8000 Chinese troops in Sinkiang were adequate to maintain law and order and to put down minor troubles, but as a military force they provoked only derision. English travellers thought them good at gardening. Their comforts appeared to be well attended to, but military discipline was non-existent and 'officers and men formed a species of happy family party'. The officers' most striking trait in the eyes of an English observer was their cowardice. Unlike the civil officials they had little education, and most could barely read or write. There was a Chinese saying, 'You don't make a nail out of good iron or a soldier out of a good man.'

The soldiers had a miscellaneous assortment of weapons but they never cleaned them and they were corroded with dust and dirt. There was occasional rifle practice, but since there was no firing range it took the form of pot shots at whatever struck the soldiers' fancy. Training and manœuvres consisted of the performance of 'complicated but senseless evolutions to represent screws or dragons' accompanied by hideous grimaces and yells which were meant to terrify the enemy. There were no supply, administrative or medical services and many of the units existed on paper only so that the officers could draw the pay of non-existent troops. On one occasion the Kashgar commander-in-chief was ordered to march his two regiments out of the city, but since only one existed he ordered the troops to march out of the city one day, to return singly under cover of night, and then march out again the next day.

This Gilbertian state of affairs in the army had its parallel in the civil government, for both were run on an accepted basis of venality and corruption. After the reconquest of the province from Yakub Beg the administration fell into the hands of a group of Chinese families who, as the central Manchu power declined, were able to make themselves into a hereditary civil and military service. They paid large sums of money for entry into the lower ranks as an investment, and as there were no more than 200 higher posts in the province the investments yielded returns only by moving officials from post to post. The official's concern, therefore, was to make as much money out of his charge as quickly as possible, and the inevitable consequence was that he had little time or attention for local problems. The responsibility for this state of affairs lay with a system that looked on its officials merely as remitters of taxes and paid them virtually nothing for doing it. The salaries were so low as to barely exist and the officials had to provide and pay their own staff. It was therefore expected that they should tax their district as heavily as possible, send the usual sum to Peking, and, after the Turki collectors had taken their percentage, pocket the rest.

It was not only the tax system that was corrupt. Bribery and venality pervaded all public business and the administration of justice. Probably the worst offenders were the Turki officials who were given a good deal of scope for oppression. These officials, or Begs as they were called, were appointed and dismissed by the Ambans, but since the Chinese did not learn the language and customs of the Turkis the Begs had a great deal of power in their hands. They collected the taxes and acted as magistrates in petty cases, so they were more directly in a position to squeeze the people. The Amban was the equivalent of the Indian District Officer and acted as judge, revenue collector, governor of the gaol, registrar of land transfers, and coroner. Above him was the Taotai, the equivalent of the Indian Commissioner. There were four Taotais in the province in charge of forty districts between them, and above them was the Futai, the Governor at Urumchi, who was appointed directly by the Emperor.

Although this system of government had its glaring defects the extraordinary thing about it was that it worked. The people were reasonably prosperous and contented and showed no desire for representative government. Despite the corruption, which was understood and accepted in Asia, the really worthless Chinese official was the exception. George Macartney was to declare after nearly twenty years' experience that 'quite a large proportion of mandarins in Turkestan do strive to rule equitably and in a manner most conducive to the welfare of the natives'. Their virtues were their own, he added, and their faults those of the system. But even the system aimed at keeping discontent to a minimum. If money was the Amban's first concern, his second, on which the first really depended, was the preservation of peace and quiet within his district. His superiors held him personally responsible for any disturbance. Conscious of their military weakness the central government would always make the local official the scapegoat rather than risk direct conflict with their subjects. So the Ambans took care to keep the grain tax at 25 per cent of the crop, and even the most venal of them would make concessions rather than allow the grievances of his district to reach the Taotai's ears. The result was that taxation was lower than in Yakub Beg's time and in the Turkis' opinion it was lower than in Russian-occupied territory. They had no economic reason for wanting the Chinese replaced by their own or other rulers.

Thus the Chinese government maintained its rule over Eastern Turkestan by a mixture of suppleness and laxity and by a confidence born of its ancient civilization. Their government had the merit of keeping the country at peace. If they did nothing to develop its resources they did not hinder the irrigation of new land and the growth of trade. A slow but steady improvement in the standard of living was perceptible as the years passed after the Chinese reconquest. Cruelty was commonplace in the maintenance of law and order but the Turkis shared the Chinese indifference to physical suffering and accepted maimings as punishments for minor offences. It was not from the Turkis that change would come but from the weakness of the moribund Chinese empire and the discontent of its Chinese subjects.

All this lay in the future, though, when Macartney and Younghusband arrived in Kashgar. Peking's hold over Sinkiang appeared precarious in 1890 but the threat then seemed to come from the north, from schemes afoot in St Petersburg. Throughout the bazaars and along the caravan routes of Central Asia it was known that the most important man in Kashgar was not the Taotai but M. Petrovsky, the Russian Consul who had arrived in Kashgar in November 1882 after the signing of the Treaty of St Petersburg.

The Treaty was the price the Chinese had to pay for recovering Kuldja, which they had lost when Yakub Beg had expelled them from Kashgaria. The Russians had occupied Kuldja and the strategically important Ili district, immediately north of the Tien

Shan, under the pretence of maintaining order in the region. By this move they acquired the granary of western China and commanded the passes through the Tien Shan into Kashgaria. When China defeated Yakub Beg she demanded the return of this territory, but under the terms of the Treaty of Livadia Russia exacted a heavy price. Peking refused to ratify the agreement and sentenced to death the envoy who had negotiated it. Russia and China were on the brink of war until Peking was persuaded by Britain to resume negotiations. The outcome was the Treaty of St Petersburg, signed in February 1881. It was hailed as a diplomatic victory for China, but although the Russians agreed to evacuate almost the whole of the Ili region and the passes through the Tien Shan they kept the western part of the territory they had seized. Even more important were the trade concessions Russia secured. A free trade zone 30 miles wide was granted her along the frontier and two-thirds of the duty on land-borne goods was remitted elsewhere. She was allowed to establish two consulates immediately, one of them at Kashgar, with a further five to follow. Finally, the Chinese had to pay an indemnity of 9 million roubles. The Russian troops withdrew but their shadow stayed over Sinkiang.

The man who arrived in Kashgar at the end of 1882 to take up the post of Russian Consul appeared with his wife and son, a secretary and an escort of forty-five Cossacks. But the character of M. Petrovsky was such that even without his Cossacks he was capable of winning the title which was soon accorded him of 'virtual ruler of Kashgar'. A man of strong ambition and dominating personality, temperamental and vain, he was capable of preposterous rudeness and bitter enmity, but he could also when he wished be a charming and witty host, urbane and astonishingly well informed about the world's affairs. Younghusband and other English travellers were impressed by the Consul's knowledge of India culled from his collection of parliamentary blue books and the annual *Moral and Material Progress Report* published by the government of India. Petrovsky was critical of the democratic concessions and liberal tendencies of the government of India which he condemned as weaknesses. When Ralph Cobbold, an English traveller, was in Kashgar in 1898 he found the Consul one of the best informed men he had ever met, and Younghusband was impressed by his collection of scientific instruments and his interest in earthquakes and astronomy. No one could doubt

Petrovsky's ability and energy but as a diplomatic representative his character was marred by his supreme egoism and his vengeful nature. Many of his Russian colleagues disliked and feared him. It was a bold man who dared cross him, even in small things, for Petrovsky would pursue him with unremitting spitefulness and intrigue. Such was the man who bullied and terrified Kashgar from the Taotai downwards into submission to his will. The Chinese hated him but were helpless. They well knew that Sinkiang lay within the power of Russia and at her whim could be swallowed up.

It was not only the force of the Consul's personality that made him formidable. He had behind him the policy of the Russian government which looked on Sinkiang as an unofficial colony. The Governor-General of Turkestan, who was in charge of Kashgar policy, was responsible not to the Russian Foreign Office but to the War Minister and the Tsar, so that military rather than diplomatic interests governed Russian decisions. Petrovsky boasted of the latitude that his government allowed their representatives compared with the restrictions imposed on British-Indian officials by Simla and Whitehall. Moreover, if the Chinese officials in Kashgar should make difficulties the Consul could telegraph to the Russian Minister in Peking who would bring the necessary pressure to bear on the Chinese government. But this was seldom necessary as the Consul's temper was sufficient threat by itself. He boasted to Ralph Cobbold in 1898 that the Taotai did whatever he told him and should he prove obdurate a threatened whipping was enough to change his mind. How much truth there was in this last story is doubtful, but it says a great deal about the Consul's attitude to his Chinese hosts.

Petrovsky's power did not rest solely on his own personality or on the threat of the Cossacks over the border. The Treaty of St Petersburg opened the way for Russian merchants to dominate the trade of the province. They included the Andijanis, Russian subjects from the newly conquered khanates of Central Asia. Under Petrovsky's zealous protection they were increasingly filling the bazaars of Kashgaria with cheap Russian machine-made goods. As the Russians pushed ahead with their road and railway building programme the cost of transporting goods from Russia was reduced and so competition became more difficult for the Indian traders who year by year made the painful trek over the

Karakoram. By 1900 the cost of transport from Russia was only half that of goods sent over the passes from India. The towering figure of M. Petrovsky was but a reflection of his country's economic and military domination of Kashgaria.

Younghusband was not enthusiastic about his stay in Kashgar. After riding for hundreds of miles in late autumn 12,000 to 15,000 feet above the sea most people would welcome the comparative warmth of a house at a mere 4400 feet, but Younghusband seemed to suffer from heat and claustrophobia at Chini Bagh. He insisted on pitching in the garden one of the felt-covered circular tents of Central Asia called in Turki an *aq-oi* and in Russia a *yurt*, which he had bought from a Kirghiz headman in the mountains. He used it for sleeping in the whole of his time at Kashgar. What depressed him most was the haze of thin loess dust, what he called 'the impalpable dust from the desert which for ever shrouds Chinese Turkestan and makes it a dreary, though interesting, country to live in'. But his view was jaundiced by the boredom which he felt throughout his eight months of comparative inactivity at Kashgar.

The boredom was relieved by visitors to Chini Bagh. Many came to take advantage of the dispensary which was set up by the Indian hospital assistant who had accompanied Younghusband and Macartney. He proved to be an able doctor and even the Chinese sought his services. Traders also came from places like Kashmir, Ladakh, China, Afghanistan, Bokhara, Ferghana and even Constantinople. Younghusband and Macartney gossiped and talked politics with them through interpreters. Younghusband wrote of them:

> All were intelligent men, courteous if they knew that courtesy would be shown them, and a visit from any of them was always a pleasure. They discussed politics constantly as their trade depended so much on the political situation. . . . The Central Asian question is therefore of great interest to them; every movement in the game is watched with keenness, and the relative strength and probable intentions of the two great powers, whom they regard as struggling for the supremacy of Asia, are freely discussed by them.

The nature of this struggle was not obvious at first when Younghusband and Macartney called at the Russian Consulate. They found Petrovsky friendly and hospitable and he and his secretary, M. Loetsch, appeared to welcome their company during the long winter months. Petrovsky talked freely and openly about matters of high strategy as one civilized European to another in a land peopled by ignorant Asiatics. One December day he opened his mind to Macartney and made no secret of his fears, or hopes, about the future of Kashgaria. The Kirghiz of the mountains to the west, he said, were not at all afraid of the Chinese; on the contrary, the Chinese feared *them*. If anything should happen to disturb the peace of the plains, or if the government appeared insecure, the Kirghiz might easily come down and loot the towns as they had done before. The Kirghiz only needed a strong and trustworthy leader, someone who by birth as well as ability commanded the respect of the Muslim population. There were two candidates for the crown of Kashgar, but unfortunately neither was suitable material. Beg Quli Beg, who was the son of Yakub Beg, was too dishonest and too maladroit in his intrigues to command much influence, and Hakim Khan, the descendant of Kashgar's patron saint, Hazrat Apak Khoja, was of too weak a character to lead any movement. Both, the Consul added, were living in Russian Turkestan under government surveillance.

The implications of Petrovsky's confidences were not lost on Macartney. The Russian liked to boast but there was usually a purpose behind his revelations. Macartney took the point that the Russians had 'at their disposal ample means for making mischief in this country, and for even bringing about a revolution'. It was a warning to the English intruders against meddling in Russian preserves, but it did not shake Younghusband's confidence. He was sure he could fulfil his mission.

Thanks to Macartney's services as interpreter and his knowledge of Chinese customs he and Younghusband established friendly personal relations with the Taotai and his officials. Macartney was almost certainly helped by his father's position in London and by the fact that Halliday Macartney had accompanied the Marquis Tseng as secretary and aide in his successful negotiation of the Treaty of St Petersburg. The Pamir question quickly arose. The Taotai wrote to Younghusband within a few days of his arrival complaining that an Afghan chief with eleven men had expelled the Chinese from their fort at Somatash on the Alichur Pamir. Since the Afghans were supposed to be under the influence of the government of India the Taotai asked Younghusband to intervene. Younghusband responded immediately: this was the chance to gain recognition for the Pamir boundary he had drawn in which he had allotted the Alichur Pamir to China. He wrote to the Afghan governor of Shignan to say that the Chinese claimed Somatash and he hoped that the Afghans would issue orders without delay to withdraw their men from the place. Younghusband told the Taotai what he had done and expressed his conviction that out of friendship for China the government of India would take the necessary steps to guard the frontier in future. This was going far beyond any intention of the government of India and when the Amir of Afghanistan indignantly reported Younghusband's action to his superiors they were embarrassed and disowned his claim. But Younghusband's approach to Central Asian politics had a soldierly simplicity. He had settled Chinese rights on the Pamirs and all that remained was to see that the Chinese enforced them.

In the spring of 1891 Younghusband heard rumours that the Russians were making preparations on their frontier and that the Governor-General of Turkestan was going to visit the Alai valley in southern Ferghana that summer. This was enough for Younghusband. There was nothing to show that the Russians would move towards the Pamirs but he found it easy to believe the Turkis when they said that a Russian Governor-General had never yet moved to the frontier without making war. It was all useful material in his campaign to get the Taotai to act. Accordingly in April he called on the Taotai and told him of his conjectures of a possible Russian move on to the Pamirs. He pointed out how ill defended the Chinese frontier was and how the Afghans might seek to forestall the Russians by making advances there themselves.

The Taotai's reaction was just what Younghusband hoped for. He sent men to the Russian frontier to report on the preparations that the Russians were making, and when they returned he sent General Chang to Murghabi and Somatash with thirty soldiers. Younghusband was satisfied. He thought this action would be sufficient to deter any Russian move and it gave proof of the Chinese occupying the frontier he had assigned to them. The Chinese also busied themselves in adding a 12 foot thickness to the walls of Kashgar, and their military officers spoke freely of the chances of a collision with the Russians, the outcome of which they considered would be entirely in their favour.

Younghusband had many doubts on that score. His professional training made him acutely aware of the deficiencies in the Chinese forces. But what it had not prepared him for was an adversary like M. Petrovsky. When it came to tracking down opponents over impossible country, exploring unknown passes, and enduring physical hardships, Younghusband had few rivals, but in Kashgar he was out of his element. Unlike Macartney he was depressed by what he referred to as 'the Consul's constant low intrigues'. Although he was aware that something was going on behind Petrovsky's urbane front Younghusband probably did not suspect the depths of his designs. The friendly reception that Petrovsky gave the two Englishmen masked the fact that he had been eagerly lapping up the rumours that had gathered round their tour of the Pamirs. In a country where, as Macartney was to find many times over, the appearance of a handful of men crossing a pass could be magnified into a hostile invasion, the activities of Younghusband and his companion were easily distorted. No rumour was too wild for Petrovsky. There can be little doubt that he sent his superiors highly coloured reports suggesting that the two Englishmen were stirring up the people near the Russian frontier and that the British were planning to attack across the Pamirs or to occupy them in force. The Russian military officers in Turkestan were always eager for action and undoubtedly Petrovsky's reports were seized on with relish. In the spring of 1891 General Vrevsky, the Governor-General of Turkestan, conferred with the Minister of War, and the Governor-General's intention of visiting the Alai frontier was announced.

Petrovsky's activities did not stop at rumour-mongering. In 1898 he boasted to the English traveller, Ralph Cobbold, that while Younghusband was pressing the Taotai to occupy the Chinese frontier the Taotai was passing on to Petrovsky all that Younghusband told him. Petrovsky, wrote Cobbold, 'related this fact with evident relish, and he expressed himself as being greatly amused at the fact that the Indian government had decorated the explorer in recognition of his political services.' Petrovsky went on to say that acting on the Taotai's information he 'took steps to render the Russian occupation effective before the Chinese troops were half-way to the Pamirs'. He ridiculed Younghusband's work in Kashgar and the policy of the government of India in sending an explorer ignorant of the Chinese language and unacquainted with the duplicity of the Chinese character to conduct such a delicate mission.

It is unlikely that Petrovsky was lying when he boasted that he knew of Younghusband's conversations with the Taotai; the timing of the Russian activity that followed suggests accurate intelligence. But the implication of his remarks, that his own superior knowledge of the Chinese language and character was responsible for the Russian coup, does not carry much conviction when Younghusband himself noted with surprise that Petrovsky's knowledge of China was limited to his stay in Kashgar, and that he did not speak or understand Chinese. So far from the Taotai's betraying Younghusband's advice it was against all his interests to invite Russian activity on his frontier, for the worst possible 'face' for a Chinese governor was to lose a piece of territory, no matter how small. The Taotai was an old man and in Younghusband's opinion was weak and past his best but he had done much good service in Chinese Turkestan in the past and he was not the man to betray his country's interests. It was easy enough, as Macartney explained 'in a country like China where, during an interview with an official, you see a whole crowd of people standing about the doors, peeping through the windows and listening to all that is said', for Petrovsky to discover what Younghusband was discussing with the Taotai. If he needed precise details there was always the Taotai's secretary at hand, according to Younghusband's estimate 'a thorough scamp, who was subsequently removed for gross bribery'.

Not only was Petrovsky able by these methods to counteract Younghusband's designs for the Pamirs but he started a new intrigue to poison the Taotai's mind against Younghusband and Macartney. Petrovsky and Gromchevsky had been in touch with Hunza before the two Englishmen had arrived in Kashgar and they knew about the British road building activities in that quarter which appeared to threaten Hunza's independence. It was not difficult to make the Taotai think that the British as much as the Russians were directly threatening his territory. Britain could not match Russia's land power but her naval strength had already humiliated China and only five years previously she had summarily annexed Upper Burma, a country larger than France and one over which the Chinese claimed suzerainty. Britain was trying to penetrate Tibet which also owed allegiance to China, and in 1888 British forces had driven Tibetan troops out of Sikkim.

It was not surprising, therefore, that the Taotai was concerned about the British advance towards Hunza. In February he told Younghusband that he would like to see three frontiers delimited: that between China and Afghanistan on the Pamirs, that between China and the Ladakh district of Kashmir, and that between Kanjut (Hunza) and India. Younghusband did not take this last suggestion seriously. He mentioned it in a letter to the government of India only as an instance of the amazing Chinese ignorance of geography; they evidently thought Hunza was north of the Hindu Kush. But he was wrong. The Taotai doubtless knew that Kanjut was beyond the passes but that fact was not relevant. 'Face' knew no barriers and as long as tribute came regularly from a barbarian chief his country belonged to China, no matter how high the passes over which that tribute had to come. Therefore although Younghusband studiously avoided raising the subject of Hunza with the Chinese it was not far from the Taotai's mind when he considered the clash of British and Russian interests over the Pamirs.

The conflict, which hitherto had been covered by a façade of politeness, first showed signs of coming into the open in July 1891 when Petrovsky's behaviour towards Younghusband changed abruptly for no apparent reason. It was then that there arrived in Kashgar a young lieutenant named Davison who was on leave from his regiment in India. He was almost destitute and asked Younghusband for help. He had taken it into his head, without any previous experience of mountaineering, to cross the Mustagh Pass in emulation of Younghusband's feat, but he had lost his way and most of his possessions. Somehow he had struggled to Yarkand where he borrowed money and went on to Kashgar. Younghusband decided to take him back to India with him, but before they left he took him to pay an informal friendly visit to the Russian Consulate. They called out of office hours and to Younghusband's astonishment Petrovsky refused to receive either of them. The next day a Cossack brought round a note from Petrovsky intimating that in diplomatic circles the proper time for calls was in the morning, and he presumed that an insult was intended. Younghusband apologized and explained, but Petrovsky was not appeased. Relations between Chini Bagh and the Consulate had not been restored when Younghusband and Davison started on their journey back to India.

There was more behind Petrovsky's behaviour than irritation at a breach of etiquette. As Ralph Cobbold found to his discomfort, the Consul was always ready to suppose that English travellers were spies. Davison's unorthodox journey following on the revelation of Younghusband's designs must have started the Consul on wild speculations about its purpose. The presence of another British officer in Kashgar suggested dangerous activity of some kind, and when it became known that he and Younghusband were leaving together for the Pamirs Petrovsky's most fertile imaginings seemed on the point of realization.

Younghusband, on the contrary, believed that his mission was accomplished. After the Chinese had sent soldiers to their boundary he thought it improbable that the Russians would send any troops on to the Pamirs. But in view of the Russian Governor-General's visit to the Alai he considered it prudent to return to India by the Pamirs instead of by the Karakoram and he asked the government of India for permission to use this route. In the same letter he proposed that Macartney should stay behind on special duty in Kashgar until affairs were more settled. The government of India's consent to both these proposals came in July, and on the 22nd of the month Younghusband and Davison left Kashgar for the Pamirs. A rumour had already reached them that a Russian party had started in the same direction from Margillan and the two Englishmen hastened to watch its movements.

Behind them as the sole representative of British interests in Central Asia they left George Macartney, who was then twenty-four years old.

THREE

The Opening Moves

Macartney remained only one day in Kashgar after Young-husband and Davison had left. He then moved to Yarkand, 120 miles to the south-east which was the best centre for keeping in touch with affairs on the Pamirs. Here, too, there was no Russian Consul to spy on his doings. Ten days later he received a dispatch from Younghusband, dated 4 August 1891, in which he reported that a Russian party of more than 120 cavalry and infantry under a Colonel Yonoff had reached the Pamirs ahead of him and had divided its forces. The infantry had marched westwards to the Alichur Pamir while the cavalry continued southwards towards the Hindu Kush passes. Younghusband sent Davison to follow the infantry and report on their movements while he himself hurried to the south along the Taghdumbash Pamir to reach the passes before the Russians.

This was the last Macartney was to hear of Younghusband until he received through intelligence agents the sensational news of Younghusband's expulsion from the Pamirs and the arrest of Davison by the Russians. What had happened was that Young-husband had shadowed Yonoff's Cossacks to a lonely spot called Bozai Gumbaz near the source of the Oxus and more than 150 miles from the Russian frontier. There he found ten Cossacks guarding a supply dump and twenty-four horses. The Colonel with the rest of the party had gone farther on foot to cross the Khorabort Pass which took them into British territory. Young-husband had pitched his camp and awaited their return. On 13 August Colonel Yonoff and his detachment returned from their reconnaissance and Younghusband boldly asked them into his tent for drinks. Yonoff was a quiet and friendly man and he made no secret of his party's movements. Not only had they crossed into British Yasin but they had returned by way of the Baroghil Pass into Afghan Wakhan. The few and badly armed Afghan frontier guards had tried to stop the Cossacks but were simply brushed aside.

There was more to it than a four days' reconnaissance on the wrong side of the Indian frontier, serious though that was. It seemed that the invaders claimed for Russia not only the whole Pamir plateau, apart from Chinese Sarikol and the Taghdumbash Pamir, but also the right-bank valleys of the upper Oxus inhabited by Afghan settlers of Shignan and Roshan. Yonoff said he had been ordered by the Governor-General to annex all the Pamirs except the Taghdumbash, the status of which had not been decided. Russia claimed the plateau because its Kirghiz inhabitants came from the territory of the former khans of Kokand, to whom they used to pay tribute. As Kokand now belonged to Russia the Pamirs were also Russian. The Russian claim to Shignan and Roshan was based on the Granville–Gortchakov Agreement of 1873. According to this the northern boundary of Afghanistan ran in a straight line from the Victoria Lake to the junction of the Kokcha river and the Oxus. Lord Granville's chickens had come home to roost with a vengeance.

Despite these revelations Younghusband had enjoyed a friendly supper with the Russians that evening and the next day the whole detachment rode off northwards to return to its base. But at eleven that night they returned and Colonel Yonoff courteously informed Younghusband with many apologies that the Governor-General of Turkestan had ordered his removal from Russian territory. Younghusband refused to go, saying that Bozai Gumbaz was Afghan territory, not Russian, but the Colonel was firm and Younghusband had to submit. Further, he was required to sign a declaration that he would not leave the area by any of twenty-one named passes, which meant that he could only return to India by the Hunza routes or by the Karakoram. Younghusband scrupulously kept his word but he was in no hurry to return to India. He pitched his tent near the northern mouth of the Killik Pass where he could keep an eye on any further Russian movements towards Hunza and could also wait for Davison.

Davison appeared, to Younghusband's great relief, on 4 October. He too had had an adventurous time. He had stayed with the Russian infantry commandant at Somatash until Yonoff and his Cossacks had returned from Bozai Gumbaz when he had been placed under open arrest. Yonoff had summoned the Kirghiz of

Alichur and a certain number of dissident Shignis and had announced that they should regard themselves as Russian subjects, not Afghans or Chinese, as the Tsar was annexing the whole of the country between the traditional frontier of Chinese Sarikol and the river Oxus. He followed this up by ordering the Chinese General Chang and his escort to leave 'Russian territory' with veiled threats of what would happen should they return. He took away the General's flag and, worse, the Somatash stone, China's only tangible evidence of her right to the Alichur Pamir.

The Russians returned to the Alai by way of Roshan, evidently reconnoitring the trans-Oxus territories they intended to take from the Afghans. When they arrived at Margillan Davison was placed in the care of an Englishman named Elliot who held the post of Third Secretary of the British Embassy in St Petersburg. He was travelling with the Governor-General on his Alai tour. From Margillan Davison was escorted by Cossacks to the Chinese frontier at Irkeshtam. He reached Kashgar on 18 September and then rode to meet Younghusband. On 5 October they started together for Gilgit.

The news of the invasion of the Pamirs and the ruin of Younghusband's hopes of excluding the Russians from the passes would have shaken most young men left in Macartney's position. But his first official report which he wrote on 13 September showed unmistakably what metal he was made of. It was remarkable for its detached observation, reasoning, and coolness of judgement. Macartney reported that the Chinese were raising extra cavalry at Kashgar in preparation for further Russian encroachments on the Pamirs in the spring. But he had heard of the presence of Mr Elliot of the British Embassy on the Russian Governor-General's tour and he thought it unlikely that the Russians would have tolerated his presence if they had seriously intended to annex the Pamirs. 'That the Russian central government, knowing that a military occupation of the Pamirs and the surrounding country might involve two great European Powers and probably the whole of Europe in a war, should have given their consent to such an occupation, seems incredible.' In Macartney's view the alarming results of the *promenade militaire* on the Pamirs were due more to an excess of zeal on the part of the local military authorities than to any premeditated plan of the Cabinet of St Petersburg. The Russian intention, no doubt, was to show that they would not acquiesce quietly in whatever disposition of the Pamir frontiers it pleased the Indian and Chinese governments to make. He thought Younghusband's expulsion was intended to force a protest from the British government which would lead to a negotiated settlement. He expected further trouble, though, in the spring.

Had Macartney been present at Bozai Gumbaz when Colonel Yonoff told Younghusband about his mission he would probably have been less optimistic about the motives and objective of the Tashkent General Staff. At that early stage in his career he knew little of the methods by which the Imperial government evaded responsibility for acts of blatant aggression on the part of their generals in Transcarpia and Turkestan. Time after time, in spite of solemn assurances from St Petersburg that no further conquests would be ordered or approved, a Chernaev or a Kaufmann would storm some Central Asian city and present his imperial master and the world with a *fait accompli*. Younghusband, who had seen Yonoff's map of the Pamirs with the new Russian frontier marked, and who had heard Gromchevsky and Yonoff's officers talk of advancing on Afghanistan and India, believed that the Russians had made a deliberate attempt to annex the Pamirs and that they wanted them for hostile purposes.

Younghusband summarized his views on Russian objectives when he reported to the government of India on his mission. His considered opinion was that although the Russians could walk into Kashgar whenever they chose it was unlikely that they would take this extreme step as there was no obvious frontier for them to hold. They would be plunged into a campaign with the Chinese which would force them to subdue all the towns as far east as Hami. The Russians themselves calculated that this operation would take two years and would cost them a vast amount of money, while the country could not possibly repay the expense of occupation. Younghusband also discounted the threat of a large-scale Russian invasion of India along the Pamir route. The nearest cantonment at Osh was 400 miles from the Hindu Kush and apart from the first hundred miles of the route it would be almost impossible to procure local supplies for the troops. Transport difficulties and the need to protect the line of supply would limit the number of troops who could reach the Hindu Kush to about 1000. Of these probably only 500 would be available to attack Gilgit. The road over the Pamirs and through the Hindu Kush passes would not be too difficult in the summer, but on the Indian side of the passes all the routes leading to Gilgit were execrable. Snow on the passes would limit the campaigning season to three months and since the British had strengthened their garrison at Gilgit it was unlikely that the Russians could seize the place before they had to return to their base.

It was therefore unlikely that the Russians would gain much military advantage by advancing across the Pamirs, but the possession of them would be useful politically. Demonstrations of force there by Russian troops would make for uneasiness in the Hindu Kush regions. British officers would have to keep turning out the hill tribes to take precautionary measures against the Russians and this would not make the British more popular. The Russian Consul at Kashgar was already in touch with most of the chief men in the valleys south of the Hindu Kush and if the Russians should occupy the Pamirs no doubt these communications would increase. Any discontented chief would be bound to look to the Russians for help in his quarrels. For these reasons the British government should do everything possible to help the Chinese to hold the Pamirs. But Younghusband recognized that if the Russians chose to invade with force neither the Chinese nor the British could stop them unless pressure could be brought to bear elsewhere.

Before Younghusband's report arrived the government of India was already planning its own reply to the Russian move on the Pamirs. In May 1891 Hunza and Nagir had both been giving trouble as a result of British road making between Gilgit and Nomal. They had started their slave raiding again and had been narrowly prevented from capturing the fortress of Chalt. In July a small mission from Safdar Ali of Hunza had arrived at Kashgar with letters to the Taotai. The envoys ignored Younghusband but they visited the Russian Consul and then disappeared into Russian territory on the excuse of buying white hawks. At the beginning of October they returned by way of the Alai with eight Russian rifles and a further ten pony-loads, of which two at least contained gunpowder. They had been hiding on the Pamirs for a considerable time in order to avoid Younghusband whose presence prevented them from crossing the Taghdumbash. Earlier, one of their number had returned to Hunza with letters for the Mir from the Governor-General of Turkestan. It was not known what promises these might contain. In view of the Russian expedition to the Pamirs Colonel Algernon Durand of the Gilgit Agency wrote early in September to the government of India recommending that Hunza and Nagir should be brought completely under British control and that the British position at Gilgit should be strengthened. He proposed asking Hunza and Nagir for permission to build roads through their country. If the rulers refused then British troops should enter their territory, depose the Mir of Hunza, and appoint one of the younger sons of Nagir as heir to the throne instead of his ill-disposed eldest brother.

By 25 October the government of India had decided that there was a real threat of Safdar Ali's introducing a Russian force into Hunza and they accepted that the Russians were serious in their intention to annex the Pamirs. To safeguard the British position Hunza and Nagir must be brought to heel. They gave orders that 200 Gurkhas were to be sent to Gilgit.

While these decisions were being made in India Macartney was preparing to leave Yarkand and to return to Kashgar. He heard from the Amban before he left that the Chinese authorities were concerned about what appeared to be a British advance towards Hunza. Macartney knew that Petrovsky had tried to counter Younghusband's influence with the Taotai by dwelling on British intentions towards Hunza, and he did not doubt that Petrovsky had also taken care to warn Peking. In a report to the government of India Macartney gave his reasons for believing that the Chinese authorities in Kashgaria regarded Hunza as their dependency. He was sure that trouble with China lay ahead and that not only would the Chinese be defending the Pamirs against the Russians but they might also send troops into Hunza to assert their jurisdiction over that state.

In this report Macartney overestimated the military strength and determination of the Chinese authorities in Kashgaria. The Chinese were past masters at playing a weak hand to the maximum effect. It did not take him long to recognize and discount their propaganda skill which, impressive though it was, could never make up for their lack of well-armed battalions. But he was right in supposing that the British intervention in Hunza would make relations with the Chinese, and in particular his own position, more than ordinarily difficult. It was with some foreboding and a nagging sense of insecurity that he rode back alone to his house in Kashgar.

Settled again at Chini Bagh Macartney had to come to terms with the loneliness of his position. With Younghusband gone and the Russian Consul hostile the situation was very different from the previous winter. Fortunately there was still General Wang, the commandant of the Chinese troops in the Old City. He had shown the two Englishmen the greatest friendliness and hospitality and his attitude had not changed. There was soon to arrive a small group of Swedish missionaries who laboured in the face of much hostility and little success to convert the population. Patient and intelligent, they became an invaluable and neutral part of the tiny European community. But until his marriage seven years after his arrival in Kashgar Macartney was to rely for close companionship on the extraordinary figure of Father Hendricks, a Dutch Roman Catholic priest.

Father Hendricks had originally been sent to the East by a missionary society but he had been dismissed for breaking the society's rules. He had returned to Holland for a short time but then had set out alone again on his travels. He came to know the Far East well and lived for many years in China as well as in Mongolia and Siberia. He had settled in Kashgar a few years before Macartney's arrival. Although no one ever saw his converts he was always cheerful, hopeful, kind-hearted and enthusiastic. He said mass by himself every day on an altar made from a packing case and until Younghusband and Macartney arrived he lived on the few scraps of bread and vegetables that were given to him as charity. When the two Englishmen discovered this they invited him to share all their meals. Shortly after Macartney's return to Kashgar Petrovsky intrigued out of spite to get Father Hendricks turned out of his house in the town, so Macartney invited him to live at Chini Bagh. They were admirably suited as companions. The Dutch priest was a highly intellectual man and a wonderful linguist. He spoke many languages and was an expert in astronomy and geology. It was perhaps for this reason that Petrovsky disliked him and spread malicious gossip about him; the Russian Consul's egotism could not tolerate a rival more accomplished than himself. Father Hendricks proved for Macartney an invaluable collector of news. His chief interest was to scurry about the streets and bazaars of Kashgar in his dirty Chinese coat and dilapidated black clerical hat picking up and distributing what scraps of information he could find. Without him Macartney might have found his first years of inexperience and isolation an intolerable burden. Even with Father Hendricks sharing his house he was still a great deal on his own. He filled his spare time with gardening and reading. Never gifted with small talk, his silence and reticence now became more marked, so that even in later years when he had the company of his wife and children at Chini Bagh he never spoke unless he had something worth saying.

The isolation would have been forbidding enough to a man of mature years and established position, but to a young man of twenty-four, without previous experience of responsibility and no training in diplomacy, the task before him was daunting. His most immediate problem was in staying where he was. He had no status in Kashgar apart from that of guest of the Chinese authorities. Officially he was still a member of the Burma Commission. The Russians were suspicious and would probably try to bring pressure on Peking to remove him from Kashgar, while the Chinese authorities in Sinkiang were not eager to recognize someone who might prove to be another Petrovsky.

In this difficult position Macartney had no one to lean on for support or advice. His most immediate superior was more than 650 miles away in Kashmir and could be reached only by couriers over passes which were sometimes blocked by snow or floods for weeks at a time. In good conditions it took at least five weeks for Macartney to send a letter to Kashmir and to receive an answer. There was no question of the Indian government sending a force to rescue him if things should become difficult. His chance of staying at his post depended on his behaving with a mixture of tact, firmness and caution unusual for one of his years. But it was these qualities that Younghusband had already discovered in him and when he returned to India he acknowledged them to the Foreign Secretary, Sir Mortimer Durand:

> In all he did up there I received very valuable assistance from Macartney, and on one or two occasions I must acknowledge that his more impassive temperament kept me within proper bounds in dealing with the Chinese when their quiet obstructiveness was causing me to lose my self-control. When he has a

little experience of working on his own account I feel sure that you will find him a useful man up there . . .

The precarious nature of Macartney's position was emphasized by his lack of definite instructions from the government of India. The implication was that he would not survive long enough to make it worth sending any. He was left more or less to develop his own policy and to prove his own usefulness. It was only years later that he himself formulated his aims. The policy of the Young-husband Mission which Macartney inherited was to establish friendly relations with the Chinese authorities in Sinkiang and to strengthen and support them against the encroachment of Russia. A secondary aim was to encourage the growth of trade between India and Kashgaria. Thirdly, Macartney carried on as before acting as an advance intelligence officer keeping the government of India informed of any Russian or Chinese moves that affected Indian interests. From the moment of his return to Kashgar in October 1891 he worked towards these ends although the prospects of any real success seemed remote. There could be little hope of challenging the political or commercial domination of Russia.

At first Macartney retained his confidence in the Chinese will to preserve their territories intact. The news he sent from Kashgar on his return was that General Chang with an escort of ten men, accompanied by two officials, had been sent back to Somatash by an order from Urumchi. The Kashgar army officers were talking about 400 or 600 troops going to garrison the Pamirs as soon as the winter was over. There was also a report that the Peking authorities had written to the Governor of Sinkiang asking if it were true that some Russians were on the Pamirs. If so, the Governor was to take proper measures to see that they returned to their own country. The Governor was also to bear in mind that 'not one single inch' of the Chinese empire could be surrendered. The Governor had responded by sending a strong letter, worded in anything but complimentary terms, to the Divisional Commander in Kashgar New City blaming him for simply reporting the arrival of the Russians on the Pamirs instead of sending troops out to oppose them.

If these bellicose noises impressed Macartney they apparently had no effect on the Afghans. News came at the end of October that the Afghans had occupied Somatash and had written to the Chinese saying that until they could look after their frontier posts the Afghans would do it for them.

But the Chinese empire had not entirely lost prestige among its neighbours. Eight men arrived in Kashgar during the second week of November bearing the annual tribute from the Mir of Hunza. Abdur Rahman, Macartney's Persian secretary, who was friendly with the leader of the mission, found out that with the gold was a letter from the Mir asking for Chinese help against foreigners who, he said, 'were going backwards and forwards in his state'. He wanted rifles, gunpowder and thirteen ponies from the Chinese. Abdur Rahman saw the Taotai's reply. The Taotai said there was no precedent for sending ponies but he gave the Mir a gift of money towards a pony for himself. No foreigners, he said, should be allowed into Kanjut without a Chinese passport. But the leader of the delegation told the Taotai at an interview that the British were contemplating invading Kanjut and he asked for instructions. The Taotai replied that there was nothing to fear as he would send an official to Kanjut who would build a house there (Macartney interpreted this as a frontier post) and would proclaim that Hunza was Chinese territory. This would prevent foreigners from trespassing indiscriminately.

The rulers of Hunza and Nagir were to need all their faith in the Chinese empire when they received a letter written on 29 November by Colonel Algernon Durand, the British Agent at Gilgit and brother of Sir Mortimer Durand. On the orders of the government of India he had advanced up the Hunza valley with 1000 men to the fortress of Chalt and from there sent an ultimatum. There were no uncertainties in this composition. In abrupt terms he informed the rulers that their states lay within the boundary of the Indian empire and since the Russians had moved on to the Pamirs and had explored the passes southwards it was necessary for the protection of Kashmir, Hunza and Nagir that British troops should have free access to their country. The Supreme Government had no intention of interfering in the states' internal affairs but they had decided to make a road from Gilgit to Chalt where they would build a fort. From Chalt the road would go on to Hunza and Nagir. Unless the two rulers complied within three days with the demands of the Supreme Government troops would enter their territory. The letter ended with the hope that the rajas would bow to the wishes of the government and so would avoid bringing the calamity of war on their country and people.

The ultimatum met with defiance. Safdar Ali and his chief minister, Wazir Dadu, overcame the doubts of the Nagaris by threatening violence against them, and together the two rulers prepared for war. It was clear from Hunza's reply that they were relying on support from Russia and China. The returning British envoy reported that the tribesmen were confident of holding their fort at Nilt until the spring when they believed they would receive Russian arms and ammunition, and possibly troops. The British reply was to advance into Nagir on 1 December. The next day the British force was before the fortress of Nilt, so formidable that it was proof against any ordinary means of attack. Colonel Durand ordered that it should be stormed, and under direct fire a small band of Gurkhas, led by three British officers, succeeded in blowing up the main gate and entering the fort. Their bravery was to win them two V.C.s. After a brief action the fortress fell.

But the campaign was by no means over. The tribesmen retreated to even stronger positions farther up the valley. Safdar Ali sent another letter of defiance threatening the government of India with the might of China and Russia. For eighteen days the small British force could make no advance beyond Nilt and while they were pinned down by the skill and strength of the enemy two Hunza envoys arrived in Kashgar on 14 December with letters for the Taotai and the Russian Consul. Their arrival signalled the beginning of a crisis for Macartney. Not only was the Hunza affair bringing to a head the conflict of interests between Britain, Russia and China, which could be critical for India's security, but the crisis directly threatened Macartney's own position. It was not to be expected that the Chinese would welcome his prolonged unofficial stay in Kashgar when his government was invading Chinese territory beyond the passes. Petrovsky already referred to him as the English spy.

When the envoys arrived Macartney knew nothing of the start of the Hunza campaign and the crisis opened for him with the appearance at his door on the morning of 15 December of a Badakhshi merchant named Muhammad Azim Boy. He had visited Macartney a short time before and had told him how through a business failure he had become indebted for a large sum of money to an Andijani merchant. As he was unable to pay off his debts he lived in fear of the Russian Consul who could bring pressure on him to repay his creditor. Petrovsky had used this advantage to strike a bargain with him and agreed not to press for the money on condition that the Badakhshi acted for him as an intelligence agent. Both in Kashgar and in Yarkand it was well known that Muhammad Azim Boy was M. Petrovsky's agent and was well disposed towards him. But the Badakhshi told Macartney that despite his plight he was still devoted to the British government, and as proof of this he was prepared to pass on to Macartney whatever information he could gather from the Russian Consulate. Macartney replied in the best diplomatic form that he was sympathetic towards Muhammad Azim Boy's difficulties and as he was a British protected subject, he would always be glad to see him. Clearly the man's protestations could be a clumsy device of Petrovsky's to spy on Chini Bagh.

Macartney had no time to test the man's genuineness before he was faced with a cruel dilemma. Muhammad Azim Boy arrived on 15 December with news. He had just seen the Hunza delegation and had discovered they were seeking Russian and Chinese help against the British. Two hours later the Badakhshi paid another visit to Chini Bagh, this time carrying a packet of letters covered in red linen. He claimed they were written by the Mir of Hunza to M. Petrovsky. His story was that the Hunza envoys had asked him to deliver the letters for them, knowing him to be a Russian agent and fearful of rousing Chinese suspicion by visiting the Consulate in daylight. He had brought them straight round to Chini Bagh. Macartney, in a quandary, turned over the packet of letters. Clearly, if they were genuine, they contained vital information, but the whole thing could be contrived by Petrovsky to produce evidence of Macartney's spying, and so get him· expelled from Kashgar. Macartney hesitated, sorely tempted. But caution won. Although, he wrote in his report, he might possibly have reconciled his opening letters with his sense of honour, he did not think his government would approve, and he suspected a trap. So the letters, unread, went to the Russian Consulate and Macartney preserved his youthful scruples.

His caution was repaid. At seven o'clock that evening Muhammad Azim Boy returned for the third time and reported that the Consul had opened the packet in his presence and found five letters, one addressed to himself, and the other four to Colonel

Gromchevsky, the Governor of Margillan, the Governor-General at Tashkent, and the Tsar. The letter to Petrovsky was in Persian and as the Consul knew very little of the language he asked Muhammad Azim Boy to translate. He now repeated the contents to Macartney. An English army had invaded Hunza and the Mir had been fighting them for three days. The thousand roubles which the Governor-General at Tashkent had sent the Mir that year had done more harm than good and might cost him his throne. The Russians had said they were going to build a fort on the Taghdumbash Pamir, but they had done no such thing. The letter ended with an appeal for help. The Consul did not open the other four letters but sent them to Osh within the hour.

Macartney immediately sent a report of the day's events to Sir Mortimer Durand, the Foreign Secretary of the government of India. He confessed he was in great perplexity whether to believe Muhammad Azim Boy or not, but he was inclined to think that the Badakhshi was betraying the Consul rather than conspiring with him to mislead Macartney. On the following day Muhammad Azim Boy called again with more news about the Hunza envoys. One of them had visited Petrovsky on the night of 15 December and the Consul told him to ask for the immediate help of Chinese troops. If the Chinese hesitated or wished to procrastinate he was to threaten them by saying he would turn to the Russians for help. Petrovsky hoped that the Russians would be able to go to Hunza's aid 'in a couple of months'. All that Macartney knew of the Chinese reaction was that the Taotai had consulted with the Divisional Commander in the New City when he received the Mir's petition and he heard that General Chang was under orders for the Taghdumbash Pamir.

On 18 December the two envoys left Kashgar for Hunza. They took with them a letter from the Taotai to the Mir and a small present. Macartney found out from Muhammad Azim Boy that they also took with them 200 rifle cartridges, a present from Petrovsky. But the Russian was too shrewd to send a letter. He had no intention of providing documentary evidence of his intrigues with Hunza. Macartney felt certain, though, that Muhammad Azim Boy had been giving him truthful and accurate reports of the Consul's intrigues. The envoys had brought with them copies of Colonel Algernon Durand's ultimatum and Macartney noted the terms as he had them from Muhammad Azim Boy so that the

Badakhshi's reports could be assessed at their true value. From all the other information he could gather he felt certain he had not been deceived.

The immediate worry was what the Chinese would do to protect Hunza. Macartney went to see the Taotai's secretary and found that the Kanjutis had asked for General Chang's help. The Taotai had granted the request but General Chang was by no means keen to venture into Hunza. He gave as his excuse his belief that 'once in the country, the Kanjutis would worry him with petitions and probably would not allow him to return until he had satisfied their exactions'. Macartney concluded that the Chinese would do nothing serious to help Hunza. He soon discovered, though, through Muhammad Azim Boy, that Petrovsky was determined to force the Taotai's hand. The Consul let it be known that unless the Chinese kept Hunza the Russians would invade Sarikol. The Taotai's reply, according to the same source, was 'The Russians may go and take Sarikol and shall have it if we cannot prevent them.'

Macartney took care to encourage the Chinese in their defiance by remarking to the Taotai's secretary that between two such friendly powers as England and China Hunza could never become an apple of dissension. He added that it would be easier to reach an understanding if the Chinese remembered that the issue was solely one for the two powers and that the Russian Consul should not be allowed to interfere. The secretary agreed and said he would mention Macartney's remarks to the Taotai. Macartney felt satisfied that Petrovsky's threats would not influence the Chinese. But the Consul's intrigues continued and he ordered Muhammad Azim Boy to bribe Macartney's couriers so that his correspondence with India could be secretly opened and read at the Russian Consulate.

As events turned out there was no chance for either the Russians or the Chinese to go to Hunza's aid. On 20 December a small British force captured what had seemed an impregnable enemy position by a feat of daring which won the third V.C. of the campaign. This success broke the enemy's nerve and the Mir of Hunza, accompanied by a band of followers, gave up the fight and fled up the Hunza valley to seek refuge over the Killik Pass in Chinese territory. The tribesmen surrenderd, and by the end of December the whole of the Hunza valley was in British hands. The

46

two states were temporarily annexed until the government of India had decided on their future.

The British success did not end Macartney's problems. Safdar Ali was a refugee in Chinese territory and there was a danger that Chinese concern for the fate of Hunza would distract them from the Russian threat to the Pamirs. So far, Peking had done little to protect the Chinese position apart from ordering that a new boundary stone should be set up at Somatash to replace that removed by the Russians. To give an air of authenticity the inscription on the stone included the name of a Chinese general who had lived sixty years earlier. The Russians had assured Peking that their recent expedition to the Pamirs had no political significance and they had condemned Colonel Yonoff's action in expelling Younghusband and Davison. Even before the Hunza crisis Macartney was aware that the Chinese were relaxing their attitude to the Russians, and he wrote on 5 December that the general opinion among the Kashgar officials was that they had nothing to fear from the Russians on the Pamirs. He did not share their complacency. He had come to think that the Russians would return to the Pamirs in the spring and that the Chinese would be entirely unable to oppose them. In the face of this threat it would be disastrous if the Chinese became hostile to the British over Hunza.

Macartney's conversation on the subject with the Taotai's secretary apparently had some effect, for when the Taotai wrote to the Viceroy of India on 8 January 1892 asking why British troops were in Hunza, a Chinese dependency, he added that if he received clear information on the subject 'there will continue friendship between the two empires, and there will result peace and quiet on the frontier'. A few days later the Taotai wrote again referring to the presence of Safdar Ali in his territory with 500 followers. He suggested they should be allowed to return and that British troops should be withdrawn. Macartney reported that General Chang, who was going to Sarikol with 160 cavalry, might possibly go on to Hunza to open negotiations with the British agent. But Colonel Durand was under orders to admit no foreign rights on the south side of the Hindu Kush.

One comforting fact for Macartney was that the Chinese did not make Safdar Ali welcome. Parricide was the worst crime in their eyes and the Taoati told Macartney in an interview at the end of January that he had not language strong enough to describe his feelings about the fugitive. He went on to say that he had asked General Chang to make inquiries among the Kanjutis about who should succeed as Mir. It was obvious that he had no intention of abandoning Chinese claims. But the same interview gave Macartney a little more encouragement about the Pamirs. The Taotai revealed that he had strict orders from Urumchi to hold the Pamirs against the Russians, and as a provisional measure he was sending 200 cavalry to Somatash.

Since matters had taken this promising turn Macartney brought another subject to the Taotai's attention. As a result of years of slave raiding by the Hunza tribesmen there were in Kashgaria hundreds of British subjects who had been seized and brought over the passes to be sold into slavery. Macartney was determined to offer them the chance of release and repatriation. He first asked the Taotai for the surrender of seven Gilgitis who were slaves in Sarikol and pointed out that the kidnapping of men into slavery was against Chinese law. The Taotai agreed and was not averse to the repatriation of the men provided the British paid an indemnity to their owners. Macartney was determined not to pay and said that the Sarikolis had abetted a crime in buying the slaves. The Taotai rejoined that there was no proclamation prohibiting their purchase and he proposed a compromise, that he himself, Macartney and the local Amban should between them ransom the slaves. Macartney objected on the grounds that he was not going to pay what was not due from him, and there the interview ended. But Macartney was beginning to feel his way towards greater confidence in his dealings with the Chinese, and he reported his hopes that by 'a little firmness' he would get the Gilgitis released without any ransom from the British.

These hopes of achieving some success in his mission were offset by darkening news of the Russian threat to the Pamirs. The difficulty was in trying to distinguish facts from rumours in the scraps of information that came Macartney's way. Letters from merchants, reports from agents, the observations of travellers, and the gleanings of Muhammad Azim Boy from the Russian Consulate had to be compared and assessed, and still much was left to conjecture. Macartney then knew nothing of the British Ambassador's report from St Petersburg dated 6 January 1892 in which Sir Robert Morier informed Lord Salisbury, 'The scheme accordingly gets clearer and clearer every day; the Khanate of Kanjut, well inside the Hindu Kush, has been designated as the *tête de point* of Russia's Central Asian power.' But reports were coming into Kashgar that troops and stores were being assembled at Osh, that the Russians were making roads on the Alai, and that they were improving a pass on the road between Osh and Kashgar.

On 27 January Muhammad Azim Boy rushed to Chini Bagh in a state of great excitement. He had heard from Petrovsky that the Russians were going to the help of Hunza. Two days later came news that 3000 Cossacks with sixteen guns were at Osh and they were to go with Gromchevsky to Rangkul. More troops were reported at Margillan and rumour destined them for the Alai. Macartney confessed his apprehension to Sir Mortimer Durand. The winter had been exceptionally short and the passes would soon be open to Russian troops. It was possible that the next few weeks would see a Russian attempt to invade Hunza and to seize their '*tête de pont*' beyond the Hindu Kush. Macartney sent off his intelligence reports and waited for the Russians to strike.

FOUR

Assault on the Pamirs

Macartney passed the weeks of February 1892 in some suspense. Contradictory reports and bazaar rumours continued to reach him, but still the Russians made no definite move. Petrovsky spied on all his activities and he was shadowed even when he went out for a walk. The Consul used every means to harm his English rival, and it was at this time that he caused Father Hendricks to be turned out of his house, apparently because of his friendship with Macartney. On 16 February 200 Chinese cavalry left for the Alichur Pamir to build a fort at Somatash, the place from which they had been expelled by the Russians the previous year. But they also had 200 men in Sarikol keeping a watch on Hunza, and General Chang was ordered to defend Chinese territory against both the British and the Russians. To add to the confusion of the political scene news came from an intelligence agent in Sarikol that the Afghans were claiming Somatash as part of their territory of Shignan and they were determined to enforce their demand. The situation was not without its comic element, but it was also full of danger.

In Gilgit Colonel Durand tried to assess the threat to India. It was clear from their road building that the Russians were planning some forward move and there seemed little doubt that they would come into conflict with the Chinese and possibly the Afghans. If they encroached on Afghan territory war with British India might follow. In Durand's opinion the Russians definitely meant to annex the Pamirs that year. Relying on Chinese weakness and the distance of Peking from Kashgar they would no doubt help themselves to as much Chinese territory as they needed. Further, the Russians might consider that the vagueness of their 1873 agreement with Britain over Shignan and Wakhan would allow them to repeat the Panjdeh incident with impunity. If war with India should result Durand was not confident about British strength on the frontier.

By the end of February Macartney, too, felt certain that the Russians were going to annex the Pamirs. Petrovsky had spoken gleefully to a French traveller about the *'tamasha'* he was expecting on the Pamirs that spring and he told Muhammad Azim Boy that Colonel Yonoff was to command the expedition. The Colonel had himself prepared the ground by claiming in a letter to the Taotai that the 1881 Treaty of St Petersburg had given the Alichur Pamir to Russia, and therefore the Chinese had no right to send troops to Somatash. The Taotai had replied asserting his right to do whatever he liked at Somatash, but Macartney sensed from a conversation with his secretary that the Chinese officials were extremely vague about their frontier and that their grasp of the Treaty of St Petersburg was at best uncertain.

It was not long before the Taotai's confidence was shaken by another letter from Petrovsky. In the middle of March the Consul claimed he had received a telegram from Peking saying that the Russian and Chinese governments had agreed that the Kashgar authorities should withdraw their troops from the Pamirs. Petrovsky asked the Toitai to carry out the agreement and to recall his troops, but the Taotai said he would do nothing until he received orders from Urumchi. Macartney thought it quite likely that the Russians had protested to Peking and that the Chinese had agreed to seek a diplomatic solution, a method, he commented, 'which the Chinese are always willing to adopt whenever they find their opponents formidable and really in earnest'. If the news were true there was a chance that the impending collision between Russian and Chinese forces could be averted.

But time was running out. On 21 March Macartney reported that 300 Russians had advanced on the Pamirs as far as the Great Karakul which brought them to within one and a half marches of the Chinese troops at Rangkul. Messages 'at the same time witty and ominous' had been exchanged beween the two camps. The Russian commanding officer had sent to ask if he was to have the pleasure of entertaining the Chinese at Karakul or whether the Chinese expected the Russians to pay them a visit at Rangkul. General Chang replied that he personally would like immensely to visit the Russians, but his duties as commander must unfortunately deprive him of the pleasure. He added that a visit from the Russians to Rangkul had better be deferred, for much as he would like to see them 'yet he was apprehensive lest their appearance at the Chinese camp might not be quite agreeable to certain of his brother officers, who were of a particularly fiery nature, and who might take amiss the delicate attention of the Russians'. The Chinese were watching the Russians keenly. Supplies of ammunition and a further 500 troops were said to be on their way from Urumchi.

The crisis was clearly approaching. Unless an order for the withdrawal of Chinese troops arrived quickly fighting would break out and Macartney could not say who would be the victor. If the Chinese were defeated he thought revolution could follow in Kashgaria. He recalled his conversation with Petrovsky in December 1890 when the Consul had predicted that should the Chinese government suffer any setback the Kirghiz of the surrounding country would seize the opportunity to pillage the towns. Macartney thought he detected signs of discontent in the Turki population; the lower classes were grumbling about taxation while the educated classes were complaining that all the lucrative posts were given to the Chinese. Taken together these facts meant to him that the Russians could foment a revolution in Kashgaria if they wanted to.

An unexpected force, though, was to intervene between the advancing troops. The weather, which had been mild, suddenly changed, and heavy snow blocked the roads between Osh and Kashgar and between Margillan and the Alai. Most of the Russian troops who had been at the Great Karakul withdrew to the Alai and once more the fate of the Pamirs was in suspense.

The temporary withdrawal of the Russians allowed Macartney an interval in which to tackle other urgent problems. In February he had won his first diplomatic success by securing the release without ransom of the seven slaves on whose behalf he had intervened. By March another two had been set at liberty, but Macartney's inquiries revealed that there were at least 500 British subjects enslaved in Kashgaria. Obviously it was going to be no small affair to free them all, and more was needed than Macartney's slender influence with the Chinese authorities. He wrote to Sir Mortimer Durand asking for instructions and suggested that there would be a greater chance of success if the Foreign Secretary personally asked the Taotai for an inquiry and named Macartney as his agent. To Sir Mortimer's brother, Colonel Durand, the

Gilgit Agent, Macartney emphasized the difficulty of his position and his need for official support. Colonel Durand acted promptly. He forwarded Macartney's letter to his brother and he himself wrote to the Taotai suggesting an inquiry into the enslavement of British subjects in which Macartney 'as an officer of the British government' could take part. He told Macartney he was anxious to strengthen his hand in every way, and in a letter to the Resident in Kashmir he expressed his hope that the slavery question would lead to the Chinese giving Macartney official recognition.

Far from there being any hope of this Macartney found himself by the beginning of April in his most difficult situation so far. Peking had telegraphed a strong remonstrance to the British government against the invasion of Hunza and they requested consultations before any change was made in the state. The British authorities had replied that they had never contemplated the annexation of Hunza. The former Wazir was temporarily in charge of the government and a suitable member of the ruling family would be appointed chief. But the Taotai was determined that Chinese prestige should not suffer. China, as the rightful suzerain, should appoint the new Mir, and he wrote to the Indian government asking for the recognition of Muhammad Nazim. In February Macartney had warned Sir Mortimer Durand of the strong feelings of the Chinese on the matter and he had advised a policy of humouring them in the hope that they might in return concede a trade agreement and official representation at Kashgar. The Hunza tribute should be continued and Chinese claims admitted wherever possible. The British authorities were broadly in agreement and on 31 March Colonel Durand wrote to tell Macartney that on the recommendation of his political officer he had recognized Muhammad Nazim as the new ruler of Hunza. He would not go so far, though, as to allow the Mir to answer the Taotai's letter of appointment or to do anything that recognized Chinese rights south of the Hindu Kush.

Before this news could reach Macartney he found that the Hunza affair had caused the Chinese to harden their attitude towards him. The Taotai's secretary told him at the beginning of April that 'as far as Hunza was concerned, the Chinese had nothing to gain by being particularly friendly with Indian officials, for he thought that whether Kanjut would ultimately be given back to the Chinese or not, was a question not to be solved either here or in India, but in Peking'. Macartney was also aware that the Chinese were now disposed to look more favourably on Safdar Ali. He was still in prison and had admitted killing his younger brother, but he claimed that Wazir Dadu was responsible for his father's death. The Chinese were also denying that he had intrigued with the Russians. Their changed attitude after the earlier outburst of indignation was significant. Macartney thought that it suited the Chinese to take a more favourable view of Safdar Ali as it both relieved them of a charge of misgovernment in Hunza and confirmed them 'in the comfortable belief that the English had no plausible reason for interfering in the affairs of that state'. Macartney could not avoid the conclusion that there had been a decided change of feeling towards the British, and as a result the Chinese were disposed to be obstructive and ungracious.

Fortunately for Macartney this state of affairs was not to last long. In April the Taotai was delighted to receive Colonel Durand's letter announcing the appointment of Muhammad Nazim Khan. He triumphantly reported the fact to Petrovsky who had ridiculed the idea that the British would recognize the Chinese nominee. 'Face' had been saved and the Taotai promptly wrote to Nazim telling him not to give trouble to the British but to remain on friendly terms and keep his roads open to them. He also sent Safdar Ali and Wazir Dadu under guard to Hami, the most easterly town in Kashgaria, where they would be out of harm's way.

Macartney could relax. The Hunza affair had been settled to the satisfaction of both powers and it seemed there might be no permanent damage to Anglo-Chinese relations. He took the opportunity to slip off to Yarkand to make further inquiries into the great number of British subjects held there in slavery. When he returned at the beginning of May he found the Taotai ready after a little prodding to concede Colonel Durand's request for an inquiry into slavery, and he felt optimistic that if he pressed hard enough he could get the slaves released without paying any ransom.

The Russians had temporarily withdrawn, and the dispute over Hunza was settled, but it was not long before a threat appeared from a third quarter. In April the Chinese troops at Somatash received a visit from an Afghan officer accompanied by twenty men. The Afghan claimed that Somatash and all the territory along the Murghabi belonged to them and they intended to defend it against the Russians. The Chinese refuted the claim; General Chang reinforced his Somatash garrison, started to build a fort there, and sent for further troops from Kashgar. But the Afghans stayed on and began to threaten violence. When Chang said they should not act without consulting the British government the Afghans furiously protested that they were free and independent. The dispute was settled by an agreement that both forces should leave Somatash. Chang withdrew his troops to Rangkul and apparently left the Afghans in possession of Somatash. A British agent on the Pamirs explained this strange action by the fear in which the Chinese held the Afghans and their suspicion that they were about to join forces with the Russians. They doubted if the British government had any real control over Kabul, a suspicion borne out by the treatment that British travellers received in Afghan Wakhan. Younghusband agreed when he was asked to comment on the situation that the Chinese feared the Afghans far more than their European neighbours because they knew them to be lawless, unpredictable, and not bound by international law and custom.

The Chinese retreat could also be explained by the rumour, which Macartney heard in May, that the Russian and Chinese governments had come to an agreement in Peking to settle the Pamir question by diplomacy. The Taotai told Macartney that he was hopeful there would be no fighting over the question and until it was settled both sides would consider the Pamirs as neutral ground. Clearly General Chang had no wish to fight the Afghans over a place that might be taken from him anyway.

On the other hand there were signs that the Chinese were trying to assert their authority over the Taghdumbash Pamir. The British welcomed this but Colonel Durand thought it would be well to maintain the Hunza claims to tribute over the Taghdumbash, tenuous though they were. Although the British had no wish to expand beyond the Hindu Kush it seemed likely that the Chinese would abandon their claims to the Pamirs and that the Russians would seek to annex the Taghdumbash. If this should happen the Hunza claims might be a useful card to possess.

It was soon obvious that the only claims that mattered on the Pamirs were those of force. At the end of May came the news that a further 200 Afghans had marched from Shignan to reinforce the Afghan garrison at Somatash. At the same time 300 Russians had moved down to the southern shore of the Great Karakul Lake. In Peking the Russians were taking the diplomatic offensive. Talks on the delimitation of the Russo-Chinese frontier broke down when the Chinese refused to surrender their claims to Somatash and the Alichur Pamir. The Russian Minister in Peking informed the Chinese government that since China refused to withdraw from the Alichur Russia would occupy territory along the Murghabi river. The Chinese protested but received no reply. They had previously protested to the British government about the Afghan occupation of Somatash but they now suggested that the Afghans should be left in occupation since if they withdrew the Russians would doubtless occupy the place.

The Russian offensive was about to begin in earnest. At the beginning of June Russian troops had assembled in large numbers close to the Alai, the Pamirs, and the frontier of Shignan. A Russian officer had written to the Governor of Shignan demanding its evacuation by the Afghans on the grounds that it had been for so long a dependency of Kokand. Shignan had replied by sending for Afghan reinforcements. On 13 June Macartney reported Muhammad Azim Boy's news, direct from Petrovsky, that about 2000 Russian troops had arrived in Osh and were laying a telegraph to the Chinese frontier. The Chinese were aware of the Russians' approach but they hoped or pretended that its purpose was not to attack them but to dislodge the Afghans.

The attitude of the Chinese perplexed Macartney. The Taotai had already withdrawn to Sarikol the men he had formerly had at Somatash and Rangkul, and General Chang had returned to Kashgar. It seemed clear to Macartney that the Taotai would give the Russians a clear hand in the whole of the disputed region of the Pamirs, which was all of the country west of a line drawn from the Uzbel Pass to Rangkul and Aktash. If the Russians attempted to invade Sarikol they would meet no serious opposition. It was in sad contrast with the activity that the Chinese had shown in the spring. The only explanation was that the Taotai was acting on orders from Peking.

Macartney did his best to extract information from the Taotai. On 29 June he visited him and asked for his views on the Russian objectives. Had the Russian Consul given any hint of them in his letters to the Taotai? What would be the Chinese reaction if the Russians invaded that part of the Pamirs that the Chinese had always considered theirs? The Taotai replied that he had heard nothing about the Russian expedition from Petrovsky and that as he had been ordered by Urumchi to withdraw Chinese troops from the Pamirs his attitude to any Russian encroachments would be purely passive. Beyond reporting events to the Governor nothing probably would be done. Macartney asked if this also applied to a Russian invasion of Sarikol. The Taotai said no, and when pressed further, added, with some hesitation, that the Chinese would fight the Russians should they occupy Sarikol. Macartney pointed out how few were the Chinese soldiers in Sarikol and received a not very convincing assurance that they would be reinforced if necessary.

It was clear that the Chinese had lost all their will to resist a Russian occupation of the Pamirs and that Macartney could only stand by and watch while the Russians helped themselves to whatever they wanted. It was humiliating to realize that his political hopes were in ruins. But the Chinese element in his character determined on a face-saving gesture to cover the blow to Indian interests. Petrovsky had won, but the inhabitants of Kashgaria should still see that the government of India counted for something with the Chinese authorities. Before leaving the Taotai Macartney invited him to dine at Chini Bagh the following week. He pointed out that he had called on the Taotai many times at his *yamen* without the Taotai once returning the visit as Chinese etiquette demanded. The Taotai replied with frankness. He ceremoniously declined the invitation on the grounds that his visit would give umbrage to the Russian Consul, who, he believed, was jealously watching Macartney and always spied on his visits to the *yamen*. Macartney refused to be put off. He thanked the Taotai for his frankness, but said his behaviour was open to disagreeable misconstructions. He personally did not want to put the Taotai to any inconvenience but as the dignity of his government was involved in his person he 'felt it his duty to require that amount of deference being paid to him as was necessary for him to uphold that dignity'. He failed to see why the Russian Consul should take offence, and in any case the Taotai was master of his own actions and need not consult the inclinations of a Russian official on a purely ceremonial affair. He was sure the Taotai did not intend discourtesy but the impression given to the people of Kashgar was that he had no regard for the honour of an Englishman and was ready to sacrifice it whenever he thought it would please the Russian Consul.

The attack was masterly. Macartney knew by instinct the most sensitive points in the Chinese mentality and his words found their mark. The Taotai interrupted, and professing himself convinced by Macartney's arguments he promised to call when his cold was better. Macartney thereupon complimented him on his resolution and sympathized with his difficulties. But he added by way of a parting shot that he expected the visit some time within the next five or six days. To the European mind the external courtesies were unimportant but Macartney knew when the Taotai called on him on 2 July that he had won a minor victory. Despite the hostility of the Russian Consul the Taotai had acknowledged before the whole of Kashgar that Macartney had some standing in Chinese eyes. By his own efforts Macartney had won some of the status that even his own superiors were reluctant to accord him.

He was to need all the reassurance that the visit gave him. On 2 July he heard from Muhammad Azim Boy that the object of the new Russian expedition according to Petrovsky was the annexation of the Pamirs and Sarikol to put the Russians in a strong position for negotiating with 'everybody'. The Russian Consul had also displayed a letter addressed to him by Safdar Ali's father, the murdered Ghazanfar Khan, in which he acknowledged himself, his family and his descendants as vassals of the Russian government. He claimed Sarikol, Chitral, and in fact the whole of the country in which the Kanjutis used to carry out their raids, as originally Kanjuti territory which had been taken from him by the Chinese after the death of Yakub Beg. When the Russians annexed this territory he hoped the Kanjutis would be entrusted with its administration. The inference that Macartney drew from this news was that the Russians would annex Sarikol on the grounds that it was Kanjuti territory and they might even advance claims on Hunza itself. He reported further news of the Russians massing on the Alai.

The British government was deeply concerned. On 7 July Lord Salisbury sent the Russian Ambassador a Foreign Office memorandum earnestly deprecating the expedition as it involved serious risk of disturbances and would make any final settlement of the border more difficult. The issues should be examined on the spot by a joint survey commission, the principle of which, he understood, had been accepted by the Russian government. The reply from St Petersburg was that Colonel Yonoff was going to the Alichur Pamir with a small detachment of troops to restrain the Afghans from molesting the Kirghiz and to persuade the Chinese to retire from their posts in the disputed territory. Colonel Yonoff was under orders not to attack either the Afghans or the Chinese; he was not to annex territory, and he was forbidden to enter Roshan or Shignan or to approach the passes of the Hindu Kush. At first the Foreign Office was impressed by what it considered to be the friendly assurances of the Russians. But on 16 July Salisbury again urged the Russian Ambassador to telegraph his government before it was too late to prevent the expedition in view of the serious consequences of a collision with the Afghans.

The warning, even if it had been heeded, was already too late. On 5 and 6 July a Russian force of about 1800 men and twelve guns arrived at Rangkul. Two days later 200 of them left for Bozai Gumbaz while the rest marched in the direction of Somatash. On 12 July Colonel Yonoff, with a detachment of eighty men, approached the Afghan post at Somatash, and the first blood was spilt by the Russians on the Pamirs. Both the Russians and the Afghans gave their accounts, the one contradicting the other, of what happened. According to the Kirghiz, perhaps the most neutral observers, Yonoff rode up with his detachment to the Afghan camp which was occupied by a captain and a few men. The Afghan officer immediately sent off two of his men with a message to his superiors in Shignan, and then went out alone and armed to meet the Russians. In reply to Yonoff's question about what he was doing there the officer replied that it was Afghan territory and he did not care for the Russian's orders. Yonoff then struck his face and told him to go. The Afghan fired at him and missed, but the Russian escort's return volley killed the Afghan officer and most of his men. The number killed varied from account to account but when Yonoff sent his version of the clash to the local Afghan commander he said the captain and nine men were killed, two were wounded, and a further seven were taken prisoner.

Was this the beginning of the confrontation that the government of India feared? In its anxiety to restrain the Amir India had sent to Kabul the Russian assurance that they had no hostile intentions towards the Afghans. The irony was that the Amir received this communication at the same time that he was told of the killing of his men at Somatash.

While great issues of peace or war in Central Asia hung in the balance Macartney was on his way from Kashgar to the Pamirs. Before the news of the Russian invasion had reached him the Taotai had asked him to accompany General Chang who was going to Gilgit as the Chinese representative at the installation of the new ruler of Hunza. Macartney had agreed on two conditions: that he could return to Kashgar whenever he liked, and that while he was away the Taotai should keep him informed of developments on the Pamirs. Macartney went to meet Chang at Bulungkul and on 19 July the two men and Chang's suite of sixteen arrived at Tashkurghan in Sarikol. Here they learnt that 500 to 600 Russians had marched to the Chinese post at Aktash and occupied it. Macartney reported that the people of Sarikol were in an unsettled state of mind and many of them seemed favourably disposed towards the Russians. Two of the chief men were acting as Russian agents and there was reason to think that they had been intriguing with some of the Kanjutis. But the majority of the people feared and disliked the Russians and they had fled into the remoter parts of the country so that they could escape if the Russians should invade. They had no confidence in the ability of the Chinese to defend them. There were only about 100 Chinese soldiers in the whole of Sarikol, and their commander told Macartney that he would offer no resistance to the Russians if they came. Macartney decided to stay in Tashkurghan for a few days to watch events while Chang continued his journey to Gilgit.

The situation looked most unpromising for British interests. The Russian government in St Petersburg was merely expressing surprise at the British anxiety and claimed that the whole expedition amounted to no more than 400 soldiers. Even more worrying was the telegram that the government of India received from the Amir of Afghanistan at the end of July. The Amir put forward a theoretical claim to the whole of the Alichur Pamir as far east as Aktash, but as a matter of convenience he now proposed to withdraw not only from this area but also from a great part of Wakhan which he had hitherto occupied continuously and effectively. The announcement came as an unpleasant shock to the government of India. If the Amir acted on his proposals he would uncover some of the Hindu Kush passes which led into Chitral and Hunza and the Russians could command them at will. An Afghan withdrawal from Rangkul and Somatash left a gap of about 100 miles at its widest of unclaimed and unprotected country. Events at Somatash had not changed the Amir's views, but he had written to the government of India asking to be avenged or to allow the Afghans to take their own revenge.

The government of India promised in reply that they would do everything possible to protect the Amir's interests and to secure reasonable terms for him when a frontier settlement was eventually made. But on his part the Amir was expected to follow the advice given him which included withdrawing his troops to the south of the Oxus. If he had followed it there would have been no clash at Somatash. If he followed it now he would refrain from announcing his withdrawal from territory to which he had an undoubted right.

The Russians ranged over the Pamirs unchecked. There was another minor clash with the Afghans and there were reports that they intended to invade Shignan and Badakhshan. The main body of their troops had moved to Murghabi at the junction of the Ak-baital and Aksu rivers, while others were reported at Bozai Gumbaz. Aktash, where they had destroyed the Chinese fort and disarmed the Chinese guard, was the only instance of a direct conflict with the Chinese, but even here the Russians had said that as the two powers were friendly they would pay for the cost of the fort. They had not violated any other Chinese-occupied territory, but they had established themselves in a position to dominate Wakhan, the Taghdumbash Pamir and Sarikol.

Macartney had no time to stay in Sarikol to watch further developments. It must have been with a galling sense of frustration that he turned away from the Pamirs to follow Chang to Hunza. Behind him issues vital to the future of Central Asia were at stake and Britain was only watching at a distance. He had been unable to influence the events that were threatening India's northern security and now he had not even the consolation of reporting them accurately for his government. Instead he was removed from the scene, perhaps by Petrovsky's scheming, merely to bolster the fiction of Chinese power in Hunza. What he had seen of the Chinese authorities in Kashgar and of the Taotai's subservience to Petrovsky must have made him wonder about the usefulness of his own stay there. He could win the friendship of the Chinese and he understood their mentality, but in the real world of power politics the illusions of the Manchu empire were irrelevant.

The journey to Hunza gave Macartney an opportunity to take a detached view of his position and to discuss it with his superiors in Gilgit. He arrived there in August with Chang, but the ceremonial installation of the Mir was postponed to September. Macartney acted as interpreter for Chang and helped to smooth any ruffled feeling the Chinese might still have over Hunza. Chang behaved in a friendly manner but he did not lose any opportunity of asserting Chinese authority and of emphasizing that they had received tribute from Hunza for the last 200 years.

It was Macartney's understanding of the importance that the Chinese attached to externals, coupled perhaps with the comparison that he could now make of his own standard of living with that enjoyed by the officers of Gilgit, that led him to make his first approach to the government of India about his position at Kashgar. He wrote from Gilgit on 16 August to the Secretary of the Foreign Department asking for an increase in his pay and allowances. Neither had risen since he first went to Kashgar although his work and responsibility had greatly increased after Younghusband's departure. The expense of carrying necessary stores to Kashgar from India was twice that of transport to Gilgit and he could not economize by sharing expenses as officers did elsewhere. He stressed that it was politically undesirable for a British officer to show too close attention to economy in Chinese Turkestan. He also brought to the government's notice what he called the 'exceptional hardships' of his lot:

The delicacy and difficulties, the isolation and consequent unpleasantness, of my position in Chinese Turkestan are not perhaps unknown to you; and I venture to hope that government will consider these inconveniences as grounds entitling me to generous treatment, especially as I have already been so long in Kashgar, and there is reason to believe I shall remain there for a further period of indefinite duration.

On 8 September he wrote again asking for more adequate political expenses. His current allowances provided for his rent, the salaries of the hospital assistant, the Indian and Chinese clerks and the expense of couriers, but only 100 rupees were left to pay for political information of the sort supplied by Muhammad Azim Boy. He asked that the allowance be increased to the scale given to Younghusband.

This was not all. When he was at Gilgit Macartney found the opportunity to discuss the anomalies of his position with the acting British Agent, Surgeon-Major Robertson. On 14 September he put his views into an official letter, the substance of which was his request to be transferred from the Burma Commission to the Foreign Department of the government of India. For four years he had been doing the work of a political officer for the Foreign Department and had not set foot in Burma. It seemed reasonable to think that the Foreign Department could employ him officially. The recent Russian advance on the Pamirs would increase the importance of the Kashgar post and the government was apparently anxious to keep him there permanently. In that case he thought it not unreasonable to ask to enter the department he was serving. He added with some asperity, 'My work too, in the event of my request being granted, would considerably increase in interest to me, for I should then feel I was serving my own Department and not one, as at present is the case, which is bound to me merely by its own temporary convenience and interests.'

The new note of self-confidence reflected the maturing experience of Macartney's first year alone in Kashgar. He had learned to rely on himself and had managed to stand his ground in the face of Russian enmity and Chinese evasiveness. It was true that he had failed in the first object of his mission; he had not succeeded in persuading the Chinese to defend their claims on the Pamirs. But he could hardly expect success when the British government could do no better in Peking. He had played a valuable part, though, in reconciling the Chinese to the British invasion of Hunza, both by his advice to his own government and by the relationship he had established with the Taotai. Most convincingly of all he had secured the right of repatriation for those British subjects who were held in slavery in Sinkiang, and so far he had managed to do it without paying any compensation to the Chinese authorities. It was no mean achievement and his superiors

63

in India had to recognize his authority on the subject. Surgeon-Major Robertson paid tribute to his unrivalled knowledge and to his 'dispassionate methods of reasoning, his quiet, careful habits of observation, and his experienced tact in dealings with Chinese officials'.

On 1 September, when he was still at Gilgit, Macartney drew up an official report on the whole question of British slaves in Sinkiang, and he submitted his scheme for securing their release. If the government of India would give him some credentials for conferring on the subject with the authorities in Sinkiang he felt certain the Taotai would concede the British right to demand the release of the slaves. He had already tacitly admitted it by freeing ten slaves. The Taotai would almost certainly demand ransom money from the British as he would be afraid of rousing wide-scale discontent among the deprived owners. Macartney did not intend to concede the Chinese right to ransom, since buying slaves was against their laws, but he would offer one third of the compensation demanded, and the cost of repatriation, as a friendly gesture from the government of India. He felt this bargain was liberal enough. He planned to recover the slaves by suggesting to the Taotai that one of the Begs should work with Macartney's nominee to discover anyone with claims to British nationality. These claims could then be inquired into further by Macartney and the District Magistrate of Kashgar. The freed slaves would be given the choice of repatriation or of staying in Kashgar. The same procedure would be followed in the other towns of Kashgaria. His only doubt was whether he should include Afghan subjects and slaves of mixed parentage among those he sought to release.

The British Agent at Gilgit commended Macartney's scheme, adding only a suggestion that Macartney should get the Chinese to issue an edict that anyone holding British-born subjects in slavery after a certain date would be guilty of a serious crime. The Chinese had long tolerated slave owning among the Muslim population either because they felt unable to cope with it or because they were afraid of exciting discontent in the province. In view of the unsettling effect of the Russian threat to Sinkiang it would be unwise to cause any tension between the ruling authorities and their subjects, particularly if the resulting trouble could be traced to the fact that a British agent had been allowed to stay in Kashgar. It would be better for the government of India to pay full compensation as an act of humanity and kindliness rather than arouse irritation and resentment amongst the Chinese and their subjects.

Macartney had written his report with confidence, but when he had taken part in the installation of the Mir of Hunza and set out on the return journey to Chinese Turkestan he knew that he was entering a world of uncertainties. He could not be sure how he would be received in Kashgar. Petrovsky had enjoyed a clear field during his absence and could have poisoned the Taotai's mind against him. There was no knowing what further inroads had been made by the Russian forces or what their ultimate object was. He was returning as he had first arrived with no better diplomatic credentials than a morning coat and top hat.

He arrived in Tashkurghan in Sarikol on 5 October. It was soon apparent that there was a change of atmosphere. The Pamirs were tranquil and most of the Russian troops had returned beyond the Alai. But there were 200 of them at Murghabi and forty at Rangkul and it was rumoured they were building permanent forts. Many Kirghiz had fled from Aktash to escape the Russian demands for revenue and military service, and Macartney met no fewer than 120 refugee families between Mintaka and Tashkurghan. The Chinese had about 250 troops in Sarikol but in Macartney's opinion they were doing more harm than good. They inspired no confidence in the Sarikolis, but the feeding of so many men was a burden on the country's limited resources and was rousing general discontent. The Chinese were trying to compensate for their loss of prestige by an even closer surveillance of the Begs and headmen. An official had arrived from Urumchi to inquire more thoroughly into the Pamir frontier. Macartney met him at Tashkurghan and learnt that he considered the whole of the Great Pamir, including the Victoria Lake, as Chinese. The Afghans, it was reported, had proposed an alliance with the Chinese against the Russians and they had demanded a satisfactory explanation of the Somatash affair.

For Macartney the most disturbing change was the treatment he received in Sarikol. None of the chief men visited him to pay their respects and he found it very difficult to hire a courier to take his letters to Hunza. He thought that the Chinese official, Tien, who had accompanied Chang to Hunza, was partly responsible for this. He had returned from Gilgit unfavourably disposed towards the British and he had accused the Begs of Tashkurghan of having dealings with the Indian government which he intended to report to the Taotai. But the trouble went further than this. Near Bulungkul Macartney was molested by some Chinese soldiers and it was with some difficulty he avoided what could have been an ugly incident. It was not a good omen for his return to Kashgar.

FIVE

The Pamir Settlement

Macartney rode into Kashgar on 15 October and wasted little time before calling on the Chinese officials. The manner of his reception would show how much useful work he could expect to do. He found he was greeted fairly cordially, and that far from his absence weakening his position he had prodded his government with some success into acting on his behalf. The gain, though, was little enough. The Provincial Governor and the Chinese Minister in London had written commending him to the care of the Taotai but there was no question of official recognition for his position. As before his only strength lay in his own tact and discretion. Officially he could do no business with the Chinese and as he pointed out to his superiors the most he could do for three Hindu traders who had asked him to intercede with the Taotai would be to state their case for them and to remonstrate gently if it were not properly inquired into. Should he try to do more he ran the risk of a rebuff and the questioning of his rights to interfere. The situation was not a comfortable one, and in his first letter after his return he pressed for immediate efforts to improve it. He did not believe that delay would help his cause. While Petrovsky remained as Russian Consul he would continue his intrigues and try to discredit Macartney with the authorities. The Chinese, who above all wanted peace, would therefore be less inclined to add to their problems by giving another European any kind of official status. Immediate action was necessary before Petrovsky's schemes could have their effect.

Macartney had strong evidence to support his views on Petrovsky. The Taotai told him that in his absence the Russian had been as troublesome as ever. When Macartney left Kashgar he happened to engage as a pony driver a man called Kourban whom Petrovsky claimed was a Russian subject. He objected to the man's accompanying Macartney and asked the Chinese to bring him back to Kashgar. The Taotai did not want to offend Macartney and told Petrovsky that if he wanted Kourban back he must find his own means of returning him. The Consul seized the opportunity and sent some Cossacks after the man to escort him to Kashgar. He also wrote to the Provincial Governor complaining of the Taotai's inactivity in the case and of his ignorance of treaty engagements. Macartney surrendered the man to the Cossacks to avoid a row but he told the Taotai he regretted the dangerous precedent of allowing Cossacks to range freely over the country.

He had avoided Petrovsky's bait in this instance, but Macartney knew that it was equally important to assert his dignity in Chinese eyes. He brought up the question of his ill treatment by the Chinese soldiers in Sarikol and received the Taotai's apology for their behaviour. The Taotai also agreed to instruct the Sarikolis to carry Macartney's post and to allow the Kirghiz to sell their sheep to Kanjutis and Gilgitis. But accommodating though the Taotai was Macartney felt he was building with sand. As soon as he had established a principle or made a small gain he had always to be on the watch to maintain it. At the beginning of November he again reminded the Taotai that he had paid him two complimentary visits without receiving one in return. The Taotai assured him that he had intended to call that day and would do so without fail the next.

At least Macartney was to have the satisfaction of knowing that his financial position would be improved. The Resident in Kashmir supported his case for increased pay and allowances on the grounds that in remote districts like Sinkiang an official was usually assessed by the value that his own government appeared to place on his services. There was no doubt also that the heavy cost of carriage to Kashgar put up Macartney's expenses, while his salary should at least be comparable with that of the British Joint-Commissioner of Leh whose work and responsibility was considerably less. He proposed that his pay and allowances should be raised from 600 to 1000 rupees a month, and that his rent and the pay of his office establishment should be covered by separate grants.

Another encouraging development was the Taotai's readiness to cooperate in the release of British subjects from slavery. Macartney believed that if it depended solely on the Taotai the whole question could be settled without much difficulty. The Taotai even implied that he would accept the British demand for the release of their subjects without paying any ransom, and he only questioned the methods Macartney proposed for securing their release. The Taotai wanted to avoid the detailed inquiry suggested by Macartney and proposed that with the Provincial Governor's assent a proclamation freeing British-born slaves should be issued in Yarkand. When Macartney doubted its effectiveness he proposed that the matter should be referred to the government of India for a decision. Macartney agreed and suggested to his government that the best solution would be to combine his own and the Taotai's plans and to issue a proclamation followed by a later detailed inquiry. He added his private doubts about the attitude of the Provincial Governor who might object to Macartney's handling the affair when he had no official standing in the eyes of the Chinese. The Governor might also refuse to act without a reference to Peking in which case a long delay was inevitable. The Indian government's best course was to strengthen Macartney's hand by writing as the Taotai had requested to say which plan they preferred for securing the slaves' release.

Macartney's optimism on this matter was countered by a growing apprehension of further Russian moves on the Pamirs. The Chinese were withdrawing all their troops from Sarikol and there were reports that the Russians were claiming the whole district for themselves. They appeared anxious to protect their forces at Rangkul and Murghabi from any surprise Afghan attacks and the evidence pointed to their preparing a large military expedition to the Pamirs in the spring of the following year. Lord Dunmore, who was travelling with a Russian passport on the Pamirs between September and December, was entertained by the Russian officers at Murghabi. One of them who was closely connected with the Russian survey of the Pamirs helped Dunmore to compile a map of the region and he marked the frontier claimed by Russia. This went far beyond even what she had dictated in the terms of the Treaty of Livadia. She now claimed all the waters which ran into the Oxus. This meant that practically the whole of the Alai, the Alichur, and the Great and Little Pamirs down to the Hindu Kush would fall to Russia, and it disposed of all Afghan and Chinese rights on the Pamirs. Dunmore believed that the Russians were planning a great forward movement in the spring to anticipate the appointment of a boundary commission by the interested powers.

In Kashgar where Dunmore arrived on 1 December he learnt from Petrovsky that Russia claimed as much right as China to

Sarikol. He also heard the Consul's version of his quarrel with Macartney. The two men were by this time not on speaking terms, and Macartney, who was Dunmore's host, asked him to try to bring about a reconciliation. Petrovsky claimed that his Emperor had been insulted when in an exchange of newspapers he had received a copy of *Punch* from Chini Bagh which had contained a caricature of the Tsar kicking the Jews out of Russia. Nothing could persuade him that it was not premeditated. Dunmore's attempts to smooth the quarrel over were in vain. Petrovsky insisted that Macartney had no credentials or official standing and he dismissed the subject by saying, 'I don't know him as a British official; I once knew him as Younghusband's interpreter, and now I only know him as an English spy.'

At the end of the year came the report that more Russian cavalry had arrived at Murghabi, although the numbers were variously put at 300 and 2000. The Chinese had made no military move but this did not mean, as Macartney pointed out, that they would accept whatever situation the Russians forced upon them. He discovered from talking with several Chinese officials that a petition had gone to the Emperor asking for Lew-Ching-Tang, the former Provincial Governor of the New Dominion, to be recalled from retirement because of his special knowledge of Sinkiang and his moral influence over the troops. The Chinese were also preparing their own case on the frontier, and General Chang who had been exploring the Pamirs for this purpose told Macartney in December that in his opinion Chinese territory extended as far west as the Kizil Art Pass which he claimed was identical with that which the Russians called the Uzbel. Macartney knew that there was no chance of the Russians listening to these claims as the Kizil Art was one of the chief passes between the Alai and the Great Karakul. Petrovsky had already sent a strong protest to the Taotai against Chang's so much as going to the Kizil Art without Russian permission. The Taotai rejected the Russian protest but Macartney was sure from studying the map of the Kashgar–Ferghana frontier that Russian and Chinese commissioners had drawn in 1884 that the Russians had right on their side. By January Hai Ta-lao-yieh, the official who had been sent from Urumchi to investigate the frontier, had come to the conclusion that Rangkul was definitely in Chinese territory and that the Russian and Chinese frontiers in fact diverged at the Uzbel Pass. From that point onwards the territory in between was Afghan. With a failure to agree even on general principles there was little chance that the appointment of frontier commissioners would bring a solution any closer.

All the evidence pointed towards a military solution imposed by the Russians which meant their occupying the fertile district of Tagharma, Sarikol, and the Taghdumbash Pamir. Petrovsky had spoken in these terms to more than one person, and there could be little doubt that he was advocating an aggressive policy with his government. Already Russian troops had violated the Taghdumbash in pursuit of a Kirghiz who had run away from Aktash. Colonel Durand at Gilgit took Macartney's warnings seriously and pointed out to his superiors that the Russians could use the resources of Tagharma and Sarikol to provision a cantonment which would completely close the only means of direct and fairly rapid communication between India and Chinese Turkestan. This would mean that Britain would lose her hold on the Hindu Kush passes leading into Hunza, a very serious blow to her prestige and a menace to Gilgit and Kashmir. The alternative was for British forces to occupy Hunza in greater strength and for them to push outposts into the group of passes leading into Sarikol and to improve the communications between Hunza, the Khyber and Misgah. The only hope of forestalling a Russian move in this direction was to raise the rights of Hunza to the Taghdumbash Pamir. Russia of course would deny any further military plans but this would not prevent the Russian commander on the Pamirs from picking a quarrel with the nearest Chinese post. The Russians might hesitate though to infringe British claims. Durand said he was aware that this was only one corner of the board on which the Great Game was being played and he had no wish to exaggerate the importance of the Russian moves on the Pamirs. 'But,' he concluded, 'that they are a serious menace to us there is I presume no doubt, and it seems to me that to lose the opportunity, if we have one, of preventing the move even of a pawn may lead to serious consequences.'

No help could be expected from the Afghans. The Amir sent a map to the Taotai showing the boundary he claimed and it was clear from this that he had abandoned all rights to the Great, Little and Alichur Pamirs. He told the government of India in April 1893 that he had no intention of having any further clashes with the Chinese or Russians on the Pamirs and therefore he had given up a frontier territory 'in which there existed such numerous quarrels'. He emphasized his intentions by pointing out that the government of India had not yet supplied him with the guns it had promised. Without them how could he strengthen his frontier territories? What necessity was there for him to say more?

The Viceroy was able to evade this question when he replied to the Amir later that month. He had heard from the British government that the Russians had given definite assurances that there would be no expedition to the Pamirs that year. The two governments were negotiating for the dispatch of an Anglo–Russian boundary commission to inquire on the spot into the frontiers on the Pamirs. While these negotiations were taking place the British government hoped that the Amir would instruct his frontier guards to avoid giving Russian officers any excuse for aggression.

In Kashgar Macartney felt no such optimism about Russian intentions. He heard through Azim Boy that Petrovsky was exploring every possible claim that the Russians could make to Sarikol. Significantly, after a lapse of several months in which the Russian Consul had not annoyed him Petrovsky had renewed his personal attacks. Macartney was not worried about their effect on the local Chinese officials for they knew the man they were dealing with and paid little attention to Petrovsky's complaints. The danger lay in the use Petrovsky could make of them with his own government. The Russian had fastened upon twelve boxes which Macartney had received from Gilgit. Among the contents were two rifles and two revolvers for Macartney's personal use and two other rifles and two revolvers which were sent as presents to the Chinese envoys who had attended the installation of the Mir of Hunza. Petrovsky heard of their arrival and sent an official letter to the Taotai advising him that Macartney was importing guns and ammunition in considerable quantities into Chinese Turkestan. Instead of the Taotai's rejecting Petrovsky's interference he unwisely allowed himself to be drawn into a discussion in which he claimed that the boxes contained no firearms. The Russian thereupon wrote to the Provincial Governor accusing the Taotai of negligence. It was also more than likely that he had told his own government with suitable embroidery that arms were being sent into the country from Hunza. This was not all, for Petrovsky was doing his best by threats and petty annoyances to stop one of the chief Kashgar merchants from having anything to do with Macartney. This sort of intrigue, if successful, could deprive Macartney of some of his most valuable contacts.

In view of these developments it was no surprise to Macartney when he heard on the very day after he had reported Petrovsky's behaviour that the Consul had announced the reinforcement of Russian troops on the Pamirs and especially at Irkeshtam. The excuse for the Russian action was the Chinese decision to send troops to Sarikol. Azim Boy reported that the Russian expedition would be of not less than 12,000 men. On their side the Chinese were at last showing signs of defending their frontiers. Already they had about 2000 troops in Sarikol and more were on their way. Provisions were going in large quantities from Yarkand to Tashkurghan. It was reported that the Emperor had ordered the governors of Hunan, Hupei and Kansu to move their troops towards the scene of action if there should be any clash between the Chinese and Russian forces.

The tension was obvious in Kashgar. At the best of times there was little harmony between Petrovsky and the Taotai, but they were now on hostile and aggressive terms. They expressed their feelings through attempts to seize each other's couriers. The Titai, the Chinese military commander in Kashgar, who was a coarse, rough-tongued soldier, was so incensed by one message from Petrovsky that he told the Consul's messenger to go back to his master and say that he must cease to be troublesome; if he remained quiet in Kashgar all would be well with him, but if he continued to give trouble he, the Titai, would use his own soldiers to expel him from the city.

If the message reached the Consul it did not alter his behaviour. He began to spread a report that he had received a present and a gold decoration from the Amir of Kabul. Muhammad Azim Boy had seen the decoration but in his opinion it came from the Consul's own government. Nothing was too petty for Petrovsky's use in the propaganda that he directed as much towards his own government as at his opponents. In the middle of May he accused Macartney of abetting his Cossacks in selling property belonging to the Russian government. In his pursuit of the charge, of which Macartney was quite innocent, the Consul not only arrested one of Macartney's servants, but sent a copy of the accusation to the

Provincial Governor at Urumchi. Macartney protested to the Consulate but received no reply. His only consolation was that the Consul was lowering Russian prestige in the eyes of the local Chinese officials by his unreasonableness, petulance and jealousy.

Nevertheless, Petrovsky's letters to Urumchi had the unwelcome effect of bringing Macartney to the notice of the Provincial Governor. The Taotai received a letter asking why Macartney should style himself as 'residing in Kashgar for the transaction of Indian official matters' when he had no power to transact any business. The matter would have to be referred to the Foreign Office in Peking. Macartney had copied the phrase from the designation in his Chinese passport as he wanted to describe his position in a way intelligible to the Chinese and based on documentary evidence which they had seen. But he was aware that it might arouse official reactions and he was anxious not to attract attention to his position. The government of India, with the approval of the Secretary of State, had put his appointment on a more official basis with the cumbrous title of 'Special Assistant to the Resident in Kashmir for Chinese Affairs' but this did not in any way alter the fact that he was unrecognized by the Chinese and Russians, and Petrovsky's intrigues could lead to his expulsion from Kashgar.

Events were moving in the direction Petrovsky wanted. Macartney reported towards the end of June that a Russian officer had been sent from Murghabi to Shignan where the Afghans were reinforcing their troops. Further Russian forces were on their way to the Alai and to Murghabi. On 14 July Macartney sent another report on the movement of Russian troops, but four mounted men, supposedly Russian agents, seized the mailbag containing it at the head of the Mintaka Pass. The immediate Russian moves appeared to be directed against Afghan territory, and far from there being an assault on Chinese Sarikol the news from Peking seemed to indicate a Russian attempt to neutralize China. The Russian Minister had suggested to the Peking government that the two powers should make a joint decision on the Pamir frontier without consulting the British. At the end of July Macartney was reporting his fears that the Russians were prepared if need be to make war on the Afghans.

At the beginning of August 1893 an incident occurred at Kashgar which put to the test Petrovsky's hopes and schemes for

Russian intervention in Sinkiang. Whether it was engineered deliberately or was, as Petrovsky claimed, entirely unprovoked, the incident provided the Russians with an excuse for action, if they had wanted to seize it. Petrovsky's secretary, M. Loetsch, a Cossack officer, and two other Russians were sightseeing in the garden of a shrine 2 miles outside Kashgar when they were assaulted and injured by a Chinese mob. The Chinese commandant of troops had refrained from any action and the Chinese authorities did nothing to discover and punish the ringleaders. It was a golden opportunity for sending Russian troops into Kashgar. That same month the Governor-General of Russian Turkestan moved once more to the Alai, an ominous event in view of what had followed his visit of the previous year. Petrovsky told Azim Boy that the Governor-General would stay on the Alai until the Russians had annexed all the Pamir possessions of the former rulers of Kokand, which included Tagharma and the Taghdumbash. In fact no move was made against Chinese territory.

The reason for the dashing of Petrovsky's hopes lay in events of which Macartney was then ignorant. These had the effect, as he had realized, of moving Russian attention from Chinese to Afghan territory. Macartney had not been wrong about the preparations for another Russian expedition to the Pamirs. One had been on the point of leaving when it was countermanded at the last moment; the Russian and the British governments had agreed to seek a delimitation of the frontier. For some time there was deadlock between them on the line of the boundary as the Russians insisted that the Afghans should abandon trans-Oxus Roshan and Shignan in return for the evacuation of Darwaz. The British wanted to maintain the *status quo* on the upper Oxus and a Pamir boundary line running due east of Lake Victoria. The stalemate continued until the Chinese began sending troops into Sarikol. Fearful of further clashes which might serve as an excuse for Russian aggression Rosebery decided to sacrifice the Amir's trans-Oxus lands for the sake of keeping the Russians away from the Hindu Kush. The difficulty lay in persuading the Amir to accept these terms as relations between the British and the Afghans were at a low ebb. The Viceroy persuaded the Amir to receive a mission led by Sir Mortimer Durand to discuss the whole question of the Afghan boundaries. At the time the Amir was more suspicious of

British advances towards his frontier than he was of the Russians so Durand's task was more than ordinarily difficult.

The Russians could not let well alone. They concluded that the object of the Durand Mission must be to persuade the Amir to hold on to his trans-Oxus territories and they determined on their own solution of the deadlock. While the Durand Mission was on the march to Kabul Captain Vannovsky appeared in Roshan with 100 troops of the Russian Pamir force. He demanded a passage through the district and it was clear that he intended to provoke a fight with the Afghans with the aim of seizing their trans-Oxus territories. The Amir was much disturbed at first and openly regretted his agreeing to receive the Mission but Durand persuaded him to let the Russians pass. Before the Amir's orders could reach his troops in Roshan they had blocked Vannovsky's route by breaking down the cliff gallery on which the road lay. After some days Vannovsky found a line of retreat by a route across the mountains. This was not the end of the affair. Yonoff, the commander of the Pamir force, marched into Roshan with reinforcements and wrote a threatening letter to the Afghan commander. However he did not follow it up, probably on orders from Europe.

The lesson was not lost on the Amir. Durand had no difficulty in making him understand the inconvenience of his position beyond the Oxus where he would always be liable to incidents of this kind. The Amir agreed without much trouble to evacuate trans-Oxus Shignan and Roshan. In return he asked for a written guarantee that the government of India would in future support him against any Russian aggression on his northern frontier. Durand agreed to this and the negotiations continued on the much more difficult subject of control over the independent frontier tribes. At last a settlement was reached, and the Amir was prodded into accepting suzerainty over Wakhan, although he refused to occupy it with troops. The loss of his patrol at Somatash had affected him deeply. Nevertheless his suzerainty over Wakhan meant the Russians could not occupy it without risking direct conflict with Britain. The negotiations were a triumph for Durand and when he and the Amir signed the agreement on 12 November 1893 the way was open for a negotiated settlement with the Russians of the whole Pamir controversy.

Meanwhile life in Kashgar had assumed a more tranquil aspect.

Macartney steadily strengthened his personal standing with the local Chinese officials and on the celebration of the Taotai's birthday on 17 October he found he was received by the Taotai with marked respect and was given the seat of honour at the theatrical performance in the *yamen*. The Chinese were proving very cooperative over the release of slaves and the Provincial Governor had ordered that all those of foreign origin, not only the British-born, should be offered the chance of freedom. Macartney was completely satisfied with the Chinese proposals. They made it possible for him to take up cases of slaves not on the Chinese lists, and none of those liberated would be forced to leave the country against their wish. Pan, the District Magistrate of Yarkand, who had drawn up the scheme, even proposed that the Chinese should pay the full ransom money, although Macartney had previously offered to pay half.

Even Petrovsky could do little to disturb the harmony. With the Russian Foreign Office at least temporarily in control of its army the Consul's scope for intrigue was reduced. The case of the assault on M. Loetsch and the Russian officers dragged on. Petrovsky rejected the Taotai's offer of an apology and complained to Urumchi and Peking. He demanded reparations and the flogging of the culprits. The Chinese claimed that the Russians had started the affray by obstructing a Turki girl. At length the Taotai produced three men but they were not identified by the Russians concerned. Relations between Petrovsky and the Taotai were broken off and the whole case was referred to Peking. After some delay the Taotai received instructions that as the Russian Consul had refused to accept both his apology and the three men he had produced as the culprits he need take no further steps in the matter.

After the retreat of the Vannovsky expedition the Russians lay low on the Pamirs. They destroyed their old fort on the Murghabi river and built a new one on a better strategic site 3 miles farther down the river. It was square and surrounded by a wall about 10 feet high and 4 feet thick. There were about sixty Cossacks quartered there and another thirty at Rangkul but none in the Alai. Some of the troops at Murghabi had been involved in a minor clash with the Afghans and it was reported that the Russians had lost seven men. If the report were true nothing was made of the incident, no doubt because the Russians were preparing for a

Pamir settlement with the British. In return for the concession of the Amir's trans-Oxus territories they offered in December 1893 to accept in principle a frontier line on the Pamirs running east of Lake Victoria and the way was prepared for a settlement.

Macartney used this time of comparative tranquillity to press ahead with the release of the British-born slaves. The task occupied him throughout the first half of 1894 and he spent seven weeks from April to June in Yarkand where most of the slaves were held. By June he had released with the Amban's help 124 slaves. Almost all of them preferred to stay in Sinkiang as free men and Chinese subjects. A further fifty-eight were released in Sarikol. On his return to Kashgar Macartney found the Chinese officials particularly friendly and he reported that the position had never been more stable. The Chinese were still leisurely discussing their Pamir frontier and even Petrovsky started to talk to him again.

The calm, though, was deceptive. The Pamir frontier and the threat from Russia had occupied Kashgar for so long that it was scarcely aware of any threat to China from the east. The vast distances and the desert that separated them even from Peking made the Kashgar officials almost totally ignorant of the rising power of Japan in the east and of her hungry eyes turned towards Korea and Manchuria. The Japanese were bent on carving an empire of their own out of Chinese territory before the Russians could complete their trans-Siberian railway and gain free access to the Pacific. In 1894 they struck, and in a short war of eight months carried all before them. The news of the Chinese defeats filtered through to Kashgar and in October Macartney was told by the Chinese official who had been investigating the Pamir boundary that China was in such danger from the war with Japan that the Pamir question must necessarily sink into insignificance.

For two more months little was heard of the war, but the Chinese ceased to be concerned with the Pamirs. Macartney continued his journeys through the southern oases on behalf of the slaves, and November 1894 found him at Karghalik giving a dinner to all the local Chinese officials who had helped him in the work. However, when he returned to Kashgar in December he found a less happy situation. The Turkis were well aware of the Chinese defeats, though, apart from losing prestige, the Chinese had little to fear from their indolent subjects. But such were the demands of the war that Peking cut its defence subsidy to Sinkiang and the officials whom Macartney spoke to were fearful that the Dungans would seize the opportunity to start a rising.

There were only about 4500 Dungans in the Kashgar district but they formed a majority of the oasis population in the northern part of Sinkiang and in the neighbouring province of Kansu. They were the descendants of Turkish-speaking Muslims who had settled in Kansu in the fourteenth and fifteenth centuries. They made so many converts among the Chinese that the community adopted the Chinese language, dress, and culture while keeping their Islamic religion and the warlike characteristics of the original settlers. In the seventeenth and eighteenth centuries the Manchus had deliberately settled them in the northern part of Sinkiang to maintain Chinese ascendancy over the steppe tribes. Invaluable as soldiers they were nevertheless a difficult people to handle, and under the flag of Islam were as likely to rise against the Chinese as to fight for them.

The Chinese officials were not the only people in Kashgar who were worried. Macartney found when he returned that Petrovsky had altered his attitude towards him, so much so that he paid a social call at Chini Bagh. This sudden affability was a good indication of the changed political situation. The Japanese threatened not only China but most of Russia's ambitions in the country, which depended on the maintenance of the *status quo*. Japanese successes seemed on the point of bringing about China's virtual collapse and the Russians hastened to shore up the moribund empire. If a Dungan rising should cause the administration of Sinkiang to break down the Russians had much to lose. Now that the strategic question of the Pamir frontier was almost settled Russia had no wish to involve herself in a long drawn out conflict in Sinkiang, particularly if it involved fighting the Dungans who had plenty of coreligionists to support them within Russian territory. It suited the Russians much better to stay behind their good natural frontiers and let the Chinese administer the country while they exploited it. They were extending their railway from Samarkand to Andijan and Petrovsky was pressing for a further extension to Osh. The Russian telegraph was coming to Irkeshtam on the Chinese frontier. Improved communications could only increase Russian trade with Sinkiang and tighten her hold on the country. Russia had no wish to see her opportunities wasted by rebellion and civil war. For once Petrovsky's policy coincided with Macartney's although their interests were as far apart as before.

The new accord between the two men was strengthened by the confirmation of the Pamir Agreement in letters exchanged between the Russian and British ministers on 11 March 1895. They agreed to recognize that the Russian frontier ran from the eastern end of Lake Victoria to the Chinese boundary and that the territory between this line and the Hindu Kush should belong to Afghanistan and be respected as a neutral zone. This meant that a buffer state was interposed between Russia and the passes through the Hindu Kush to India. In return the Afghans had to evacuate all their trans-Oxus territories in line with the agreement made between the Amir and Sir Mortimer Durand. The delicate question still to be settled was the 'imperfectly known Chinese frontier', and the two governments agreed to appoint a Boundary Commission to demarcate the whole frontier from Lake Victoria to Chinese territory on which it was hoped they would come to an agreement with the Chinese government. General Sir Montagu Gerard was appointed head of the British Commissioners with Colonel Holditch as surveyor, and they were instructed by the Viceroy to ask for Macartney's help if they felt it necessary. When they set off for the Pamirs in June their baggage train and followers stretched over 14 miles.

The Chinese government was not consulted about the Agreement and paid no attention to it or to the work of the Boundary Commission. Far graver problems absorbed Peking. The Chinese had been defeated ingloriously in only eight months of war against the Japanese and the victors were demanding independence for Korea, the annexation of Formosa and the Pescadores Islands, the payment of 200 million taels, and the cession of the tip of the Liaotung peninsula in Manchuria with Port Arthur. It seemed that the Chinese had no alternative but to accept. The Japanese demands, though, were too much for Russia. With Germany and France she brought pressure on Japan to disgorge some of her gains and forced her to abandon the Liaotung peninsula. Then with the aid of French banks she set about raising the millions that the Chinese needed to pay the Japanese indemnity. Russia, who had been the enemy, was now emerging as the saviour and protector of the Chinese empire.

*   *   *

In Kashgar the rumours circulated. Macartney heard that the Chinese would shortly reimpose customs duties on British trade in order to pay the Japanese indemnity. They had removed the duties the previous year and as a result the trade from India had leapt from forty to sixty lakhs in value. The Russians were exempt from customs dues at least until 1901 so their trade would not be called to bear the same burden. This threat was serious enough, but the news from Kansu was worse. The Tungans had revolted and the trouble had spread to the whole of the Lanchow neighbourhood just beyond the border of Sinkiang. The situation was developing critically and had not been resolved when Macartney left Kashgar on 16 July to join the British members of the Boundary Commission.

China's new troubles and the Pamir Agreement had not removed all friction from the relations between Macartney and Petrovsky. In May 1895 Petrovsky had assumed the added dignity of Consul-General with the same jurisdiction. This mark of his government's confidence increased his zeal and Macartney found that the Russian continued to nurse his suspicions of British designs beyond the Hindu Kush. At the beginning of July he abruptly asked Macartney for a map of Hunza and asked whether the British considered that the Chinese border extended as far south as the Karakoram Pass. Petrovsky clearly suspected them of plans to expand northwards. Macartney found out from the Chinese officials that they considered the Karakoram and Mustagh ranges as the boundary between Sinkiang and India, and if there were an Anglo-Chinese commission they would claim the northern bank of the Wakhan river from its source in the mountains of Hunza to Bozai Gumbaz.

The line of Petrovsky's thought and his own imminent departure to join the Pamir Boundary Commission led Macartney to summarize his views on Anglo-Russian politics in Kashgaria and the usefulness of his own stay there. He had no illusions about the extent of his influence. It was British policy to support Chinese power in Kashgaria against the threat from Russia but a few regiments of Cossacks would be enough to drive the 20,000 Chinese troops out of Sinkiang. There was no active discontent with Chinese rule although the Chinese had done nothing to improve the country. Peace had allowed the people to accumulate wealth and they had no sense of nationalism to unite them against their rulers. If the Russians should invade, the Turkis would submit to their occupation although they would not court it. Macartney discerned in the Chinese a presentiment that their empire was reaching a stage of decline and fall, but they would not learn even from the terrible lesson inflicted on them by the Japanese; they would soon relapse into their previous lethargic state. Civil officials and military officers were alike ignorant, apathetic and corrupt to the core. They had no notion of public duty or patriotism and their sole object was to replenish their purse. Macartney could see no possibility of awakening in the Chinese a sense of the Russian danger or of the necessity for reforms. Even a recognized British agent would be helpless to do more than watch over the merchants and keep his government in touch with the course of events.

His conclusion was that the government of India should prepare itself for Russian annexations in Kashgaria and that its best hope was to negotiate for an intermediate zone between Russian and British territory. Britain could offer not to press Hunza's claims on the Taghdumbash Pamir and on the north side of the Karakoram watershed as long as the territory remained in Chinese occupation. It might even be possible to set up a neutral state including the Taghdumbash Pamir, Raskam and Shahidulla, reaching from Tashkurghan to Polu.

The report was a frank recognition of political realities and of the little that Macartney could expect to achieve at Kashgar. It was typical of him that he should claim nothing for the five years he had spent there and for the relationship that he had established with the Chinese. This quiet and unassuming behaviour was what impressed the British Boundary Commissioners when Macartney joined them at the end of July. General Gerard, the head of the British Commission, had heard with some misgivings from his Russian colleague of the great friction between Macartney and Petrovsky, and he feared that Macartney's arrival might disturb the *entente cordiale* between the Commissioners. It was too late, though, to stop his journey although the Russian pickets made difficulties for him at the Bayik Pass. Macartney had arranged for sheep and baggage ponies to be sent to the Commission from Tashkurghan and in his month's stay with the party he impressed Gerard not only by his practical help in provisioning them but by his general ability. Gerard wrote of him to the government of India:

He is so silent and reticent that he was nearly a month in our camp before I learned that he is a graduate of a French college. You will not easily find another man who knows perfectly Chinese, French, Turki, Persian, Hindustani and English; while his silence and reserve seem to mark him as a very safe Agent indeed in any situation. He is so sober I fancy he drinks about two glasses of wine a week, and he is a perfectly mannered quiet gentleman.

The work of the Boundary Commissioners proceeded harmoniously enough although by September it was obvious to Gerard that the Russians were hoping to get the whole of the Taghdumbash Pamir from the Chinese. They were telling the Kirghiz that the Chinese would hand it over to them after two years. Macartney took Gerard on an 80 mile tour of the Taghdumbash and was able to show that it was effectively occupied and patrolled by the Chinese. Gerard succeeded in getting a declaration from the Russian Commissioner that the Chinese frontier lay on the watershed of the Taghdumbash but he warned the government of India against the Chinese ceding the Pamir to Russia and suggested advancing Hunza's claims to it.

In September Macartney left the Boundary Commissioners and returned to India to see his superiors before going home to England on leave for the first time in five years. His purpose in India was another attempt to improve his status at Kashgar. It was not for him a personal matter but a question of fighting for the official recognition that was essential for his job. Gerard supported him in a letter to the government of India pointing out Petrovsky's increased advantage since he had been given the title of Consul-General. But there was little hope of success. The government of India had acknowledged in July Macartney's excellent service in Kashgar and had improved his pay. They had refused, though, even to put him on the graded list of the Political Department on the grounds that Kashgar was the only post in which his experience and acquirements would be useful. Moreover, there was no officer who could take his place should the appointment be added to those of the Political Department.

After five years Macartney was still a lone agent, an outsider with no recognized status or security in the machine of the government of India. He returned to England outwardly the same reserved, inconspicuous young man who had sailed to India apparently destined for a subordinate role, but at twenty-eight he had achieved an astonishing maturity of character and judgement. For four years he had shown that not only could he live happily in a remote, inaccessible country with no other Englishman to give advice or companionship, but he had proved himself capable of dealing with the unscrupulous schemes of Petrovsky and the deviousness and vacillations of the Chinese. Unsupported by his own government and pitted against opponents who held all the cards in their hands, he had survived to return again to Kashgar for another round.

SIX

The Struggle to Survive

Macartney's first leave from Kashgar was to bring about an important change in his life; he became engaged to a girl of nineteen, Catherine Borland, and they made plans to marry on his next leave. At first sight it seems strange that someone of Macartney's shy and retiring nature should in so short a time have persuaded a young girl to marry him and to spend her life in a remote part of the Chinese empire. But Macartney was no stranger to the Borland family. They had given him a home during his holidays from Dulwich College from the time of his father's return to England. Halliday Macartney and Catherine's father, James Borland, had been friends from their schooldays in Scotland and they had never lost touch with each other. The Borlands' house had given George Macartney his only real experience of family life since he had been parted from his mother and it was natural that he should find in James Borland's second daughter his future wife. Catherine had never travelled abroad before but when Macartney's leave was over she set about preparing herself for her future life in Kashgar with the practical common sense that was to enable her to cope with the many difficulties ahead. Although she was musical and had a fine voice she realized that Kashgar would demand more than drawing-room accomplishments, so she went into the kitchen and learned to cook. For her life in Sinkiang she had one great natural advantage, her personal courage. In crises of acute danger her children never saw her show signs of fear. Like the rest of her family she had a strong Presbyterian faith, and despite the difficulties, she maintained in Kashgar her own outpost of the Church of Scotland in which her children were brought up.

If Macartney had known what was happening in Chinese Turkestan while he was enjoying his first leave he would at times have doubted his return. He had left in charge of his post his able Indian clerk, Munshi Ahmad Din, and it was this man who reported the crisis that threatened to engulf Kashgaria. The Dungans had won the upper hand in Kansu and it appeared they might invade Sinkiang. In October 1895 the Chinese moved eight regiments to Hami to watch the movement of the rebels and they collected vast quantities of grain from Kashgaria to provision their troops. In December came the news of another government defeat at Sining, the capital of Tsinghai province, and of the defection of Chinese troops to the rebels. There was talk in Ili of the Tsar sending 5000 Cossacks to help suppress the rebellion. Massive reinforcements arrived from Peking and soon the rebels were confined to Sining. At the end of January the Tungans were in a parlous state and offered to surrender, but the Chinese general suspected treachery and refused. Sining fell and an inhuman massacre of the Tungans followed. It was a fatal mistake. The massacre provoked a general rising of all the Tungans in Kansu and the revolt spread to Lop Nor at the gates of Kashgaria.

By the end of March 1896 there was general alarm. The food purchases for the troops had started a price inflation and the Chinese doubled their demands for land taxes. Petrovsky claimed that he was unable to feed his Cossacks and he forced the officials to open their wheat stores, which brought about some improvement in the situation. The military position did not improve. In May a Tungan invasion seemed imminent. Peking ordered the Titai to send all the troops from Kashgar, apart from five regiments, to stop the Tungans from breaking through to Ili. Petrovsky protested vehemently and demanded protection for Russian lives and property which he claimed was worth 5 million roubles.

Chinese morale was low. Discipline among the troops was lax and at the beginning of May Munshi Ahmad Din was involved in a serious incident which nearly cost him his life. He was riding in the old city of Kashgar when he was set upon by nine Chinese soldiers who threw him off his horse and beat him senseless. They were caught and confessed their guilt but pleaded drunkenness. They were sentenced to 1000 lashes. The Munshi had experience of these punishments and asked to see the sentence carried out. He reported that it was no more than five strokes on the soldiers' hands with a stick as big as a pen. It was useless to protest against such treatment as the civil power had clearly lost control of the military. The troops had not been paid for several months and were probably responsible for an outbreak of thefts at Kashgar. There was not much hope of bringing them under control until they were properly paid, so Peking's announcement in March that it would end its subsidy to Sinkiang was a cause of further anxiety to the civil authorities. The assault on the Munshi at least had the merit of drawing the Russian and British representatives closer together. Petrovsky asked for an exchange of information between them and offered the Munshi protection in case of a revolt in Kashgar.

The uneasiness, the rumours and the low morale were not solely on account of the Tungan advance and the province's financial state. Petrovsky's talk of a possible revolt in Kashgar and his boast that the Taotai looked to his Cossacks for protection in case of 'complications' was for once not without foundation. The name of the secret society Ko-Lao-Hui, at first whispered, was soon bandied about with sinister implications. The Titai of Kashgar, it was reported, was afraid to march his troops to Aksu to fight against the Tungans because their leader, Mao, was one of the Ko-Lao-Hui. The Taotai's interpreter told Ahmad Din that the Ko-Lao-Hui was about 500 strong in the province and that the Hsietai of Khotan was the suspected head of the Kashgarian branch. The military commander in Artush was a member and he had been given command of the troops sent to Aksu. In May came the report that Mao Ta-jen, an officer of high rank in the military command at Ili had joined with his troops in the Tungan rebellion and had 10,000 men under his orders. It was said that half of the men and officers of the Sinkiang forces sympathized with him or like him were members of the Ko-Lao-Hui. The news was enough to set the Taotai thinking of Russian protection. The Ko-Lao-Hui was not confined to Sinkiang. It was dreaded throughout the Chinese empire as a secret society bent on overthrowing the Manchu dynasty and its regime. The fact that it had apparently joined forces with the Tungans in open rebellion was grave news for the ruling authorities.

The Russian Consul made it known that at the first sign of revolt or invasion troops would be called in from Russian territory. The food situation had not eased and the Chinese officials were divided on whether bread riots or a Russian occupation were the greater danger. In June, though, some of the tension relaxed. News came from Urumchi that the Tungans had been defeated and prevented from entering Sinkiang by the northern road. The only danger now was from the direction of Lop Nor and Charchan on the southern route. Reinforcements of government troops from Ili relieved much of the anxiety.

By the time Macartney returned to his post at the end of September the Tungan rebellion was over. The surviving rebels were sent into the mountains of Tibet and were settled twelve marches beyond the Chinese outposts. Nevertheless, the stability of Chinese rule in Kashgaria had been shaken by the rebellion. The Tungans had been put down but the sinister influence of the Ko-Lao-Hui remained to undermine morale and security. The Taotai was not the man to deal with the situation. Macartney found him unchanged on his return, 'exactly the same superficial, childish, characterless man, his one object to keep up a semblance of friendship with everybody'. He noted with keen satisfaction that absence had not weakened his own position in Kashgar, and it was further improved by Petrovsky's departure on leave on 23 September. The acting Russian Consul, Kolokoloff, was a man of about thirty, guarded, but gentlemanly. Macartney judged him to have good sense but no originality, and thought him not the man to maintain 'the political ascendancy . . . gained by his perverse but brilliant predecessor'.

Without Petrovsky life at Kashgar lost some of its flavour. Impossible though he was, his plots and accusations were more exciting to combat than the devious obstructiveness of the Taotai and his officials. Macartney soon found himself back in the familiar role of shadow boxing with the Chinese. It was a slow, painful business, fought for small gains, but demanding all his resources of patience and perseverance. If he should appear to relax his vigilance or show any sign of weakness, his influence, small though it was, would disappear altogether. He could afford to overlook nothing and yet he had always to tread with the greatest delicacy and caution.

In his first interview with the Taotai after his return Macartney reminded him of the assault on the Munshi. It was a case that vitally affected British prestige as well as the safety of British subjects. Unless the culprits were seen to be punished neither would be respected. He asked for the soldiers in question to be sent to the Foreign Affairs office and there be 'moderately' flogged in his or his representative's presence. The Taotai, aware of his slender hold over the military, refused his request, but under pressure he agreed to Macartney's writing him an official letter on the subject.

The importance of taking a firm line was emphasized when a Hindu trader was assaulted by two Turkis, and a Chinese soldier, entirely unprovoked, gave a sharp cut to Macartney's horse when he was riding in the street. One of the Turkis was acquitted without the case even being heard against him. Macartney protested vigorously to the official responsible, Chang, the manager of the Foreign Affairs Office, and he insisted on the case being tried in his presence. The Turki was sentenced to a flogging. He also pursued his complaint against the soldier. The man's superior officer appealed to Macartney as a friend to drop the case, but Macartney countered with an appeal not to let such an indignity pass without redress. The officer apparently feared his men more than any reprimand from his superiors and he refused to act. Macartney had no other course but to telegraph to Urumchi to request the man's punishment. The reaction of the Kashgar authorities was typical. Macartney allowed himself to be persuaded into sending a representative to see the man punished. He sent two clerks who were first given refreshments and were then taken to see the prisoner. They were told he had been beaten while they were at tea. In answer to Macartney's protest Chang said that the man had been flogged but the clerks had intervened to stop his punishment. He courteously asked Macartney to let the matter drop. There was no other course open to him, but he asked his government to take the matter up with the British Minister at Peking.

The government of India was not unconcerned, and in the following year, 1897, they sent all the correspondence about the assaults on Macartney and the Munshi to the British Minister at Peking and to the Secretary of State for India. They pointed out that the Russian Consul had a large body of Cossacks to guard him and that it seemed only reasonable that Macartney should have similar means of protection. The India Office repeated to the Foreign Office the suggestion they had made in October 1896 that Macartney should be given consular status at Kashgar. But Indian interests were the last concern of the Foreign Office in their dealings with China and again the proposal was put to one side.

More encouraging was the progress Macartney was making in releasing slaves. In January 1897 the authorities in Kashgar issued a proclamation larded with expressions of moral indignation against the keeping of slaves. The practice was made unlawful and the owners were exhorted to release their slaves free of charge. Similar proclamations were made throughout the other oasis towns and wherever Macartney travelled in Kashgaria he received complete cooperation from the Chinese on the matter.

The new harmony in relations with the Russian Consulate was not to continue undisturbed. Plague was reported at Bombay and Karachi and Kolokoloff felt bound to act in the manner of his predecessor. He brought pressure on the Chinese to close the Yarkand–Leh frontier and so exclude Indian trade from Sinkiang, to the advantage of Russia. The British Minister at Peking intervened to prevent this but the Chinese authorities ordered the establishment of a quarantine post on the frontier. Kolokoloff made the most of this and sent a Russian doctor off to Sarikol to supervise the quarantine arrangements. He also circulated rumours that plague had broken out in Sarikol. The Chinese showed their resentment at his interference by preventing people at Tashkurghan from going near the Russian and from selling him supplies.

Despite these activities Kolokoloff was a harmless figure compared with Petrovsky, and Macartney fully understood the feelings of Chang, the head of the Kashgar Foreign Affairs Office, when he called to ask if there was any hope of Kolokoloff replacing Petrovsky in the permanent appointment. The hope was a vain one. In August the return of Petrovsky was announced and it was realized that the comparative tranquillity of the Kolokoloff regime would shortly end. Macartney reported the deep gloom of the Chinese at the prospect.

Kolokoloff could not surrender his charge, however, without some feeling of advantage over his English rival. As though in recompense for the failure of his plague campaign he took pains to point out to Macartney that he would never succeed in gaining his objects in Kashgaria. The rights of Russia in Sinkiang, he said, were of a special character, quite unlike those acquired by her in the Treaty Ports. China had conceded them to Russia alone and all other powers were excluded. Russia would not tolerate any British influence in the area. 'You', he said to Macartney, 'will never have a consulate in Kashgar or even in Yarkand. If the Chinese make you such a concession your Salisbury will hear such a noise at the other end of China that he will soon forget it.' As though to emphasize the seriousness of Russian intentions and as a preparation for the advent of Petrovsky the guard at the Russian Consulate was soon increased from fifty to seventy-five Cossacks.

Macartney's immediate concern before Petrovsky's return to Kashgar was his labyrinthine negotiations with the Chinese. He always held in his hand at any one time the threads of several complaints or proposals which he patiently pursued through a maze of intrigue and politics. Unlike his Russian counterpart he had no direct means of bringing pressure on the Chinese authorities through the British representative at Peking. He had to work through his superiors in the government of India, who, if they felt strongly enough about his cases, would send them on to the India Office in London. It was then up to the India Office to put the case to the Foreign Office, who would get in touch with their Minister in Peking. Sinkiang was usually lowest on the envoy's list of interests and he was seldom prepared to risk objects of greater importance by interfering in the affairs of Kashgaria. The wonder was that Macartney ever received any help from Peking. But the bureaucracy of the empire still functioned and although the lines of communication were slow and cumbrous they were of occasional help.

In September 1897, nine months after Macartney had referred the matter to his superiors, Peking instructed the Taotai to inquire into the three cases of assault on Macartney and the Munshi Ahmad Din. As a result the Taotai apologized to Macartney for the soldier's cut on his horse and he sentenced the man to corporal punishment. The familiar arguments then began about whether this should take place in Macartney's presence, his only guarantee that it would be carried out. The Taotai objected to the presence of any witness but Macartney quietly persisted and on 8 October he saw the man punished. Distasteful though it was Macartney knew the Chinese well enough to realize that his insistence was vital if he were to keep their respect. Without official position or an armed guard he could never risk even the slightest loss of 'face'. His was a struggle to win the respect of his hosts and it had to be unrelenting.

Another negotiation that took months to mature was a suggestion Macartney put to the Taotai in March 1897 of reopening alternative trade routes between Yarkand and Leh. Only one, the Kilian route, was open as the Chinese had closed two others, by Sanju and Kugiar, because of Hunza raids. The Taotai referred

Macartney's proposal to the Governor of the province, but by October he had received no reply. The District Magistrate of Yarkand was interested in the suggestion and in October he gave permission on his own initiative for the opening of the Kugiar route. But at the same time he suggested setting up a military post in the Raskam valley. The proposal put Macartney on his guard. He knew it involved the question which of all others most threatened his relations with the Chinese – namely, the rights of the people of Hunza to graze or cultivate lands beyond the watershed of the Karakoram. It was a subject that aroused all the old Chinese suspicions about British encroachments and it was a worthy *entrée* for the talents of M. Petrovsky who arrived back in Kashgar on 25 October. The renewal of their acquaintance, according to Macartney, was 'marked by every cordiality', but it was not long before the subject of the Raskam valley renewed the duel between them.

Petrovsky had returned in high spirits and bombastic self-confidence. His government, he told Macartney, was bent on increasing the importance of Turkestan and would probably join to it the province of Semiretchia. At a reception he made flowery speeches to the Taotai on the friendship between Russia and China, but while they were being interpreted he spoke to Macartney in French referring to the Taotai as a 'singe'. The Chinese empire, he said, was condemned to a speedy decay; the European powers should partition it, and the policy of Russia could be summed up in two words, '*Nadu Vzait*' (we must take). On Christmas Day, at dinner with Macartney, he was more expansive. The Chinese administration in Kashgaria, he said, was rotten to the core and was detested by the natives. Nothing remained except for Russia to occupy the country. A Kashgarian Beg had only a few weeks ago consulted him about the possibility of the Russians aiding a revolt. Petrovsky had told him that if there was a real chance of success the Russians would give help. Macartney had to make allowances for Petrovsky's boastfulness but he was convinced that in all the Consul's dealings with the Chinese Muhammadan population Petrovsky was preaching sedition. Moreover, the open contempt with which he treated the Chinese officials was gradually undermining their influence in Kashgar.

Despite Petrovsky's talk of Russian annexation he had no intention of allowing Macartney even the slightest diplomatic gain. He bent all his energies to thwarting the Kanjuti interests in Raskam and to stopping the Chinese from reopening the Sanju and Kugiar trade routes. The Kanjutis themselves had brought up the subject of Raskam. Since the British had occupied their country and had finally put a stop to their raiding, the economy of the Hunza valley had gone into a steep decline. There had never been enough cultivable land to feed the population and brigandage had been essential to their livelihood. Now their only hope was to assert the rights they had claimed for generations beyond the Karakoram, particularly in the valley of the Raskam river where there was cultivable land. In November 1897 two Kanjutis arrived in Kashgar with a letter for the Taotai from the Mir of Hunza. The Kanjutis claimed ownership of the valley and a pressing need to cultivate it, as the population of Hunza was increasing. They complained that two of their number who had been farming in Raskam had been imprisoned by the Beg of Kugiar. The Mir of Hunza's son and 300 people intended to settle in the valley.

The Taotai, true to form, was reluctant to take responsibility for a decision. He sent the Kanjutis to explain their case to the Amban of Yarkand. Petrovsky let Macartney know that he was watching the situation closely. He questioned him about the Raskam valley and said that on Russian maps the area was blank, a statement that Macartney knew to be untrue. The Consul then winked to his secretary and said 'the Raskam river will within the near future be the Indian frontier.' Macartney ignored the provocation and said nothing.

The Kanjuti agents returned to Kashgar and reported that the Yarkand Amban had rejected their claim to the valley. Macartney questioned the Taotai who took refuge in referring the case to the Governor of Sinkiang. He told Macartney there was no question of giving the valley to the Kanjutis, but he was inclined to let them cultivate it because of their population problem. In December the Governor telegraphed his consent and shortly afterwards Macartney discovered Petrovsky's intervention in the case. His Chinese clerk saw a letter from the Governor to Petrovsky. It was a reply to one in which Petrovsky had advised the Governor against allowing the Kanjutis to occupy Raskam. He claimed that they would be a disturbing influence on the frontier and that they would consider the country theirs. The Governor replied that the

Kanjutis could settle provided they paid the yearly tax in grain like other Chinese cultivators. It was not the end, though, of the Raskam question. Petrovsky was determined that the Kanjutis should be excluded from the valley, but he was content to await his opportunity.

Meanwhile he had other ways of annoying Macartney and of frustrating British interests. He countered Macartney's request for the reopening of the Kilian, Sanju and Kugiar trade routes by going to the Taotai and demanding as a *quid pro quo* that the Chinese should repair the road to Ladakh so that Russian cloth could be exported to Kashmir. Petrovsky knew perfectly well that the Chinese would not spend money on road repairs and that rather than do so they would refuse Macartney's request. The Taotai would feebly have given in to Russian pressure, but the Amban of Yarkand resisted, no doubt seeing in the new routes a source of increased profits for his own pocket. In March 1898 he issued a proclamation declaring the routes open.

Never at a loss, Petrovsky had started a new intrigue. An English traveller, Ralph Cobbold, had arrived in Kashgar early in 1898 intending to shoot on the Pamirs. Macartney had introduced him to Petrovsky and many pleasant visits to the Russian Consulate had followed. Petrovsky could be a lively and charming host, and Cobbold quickly fell under his spell. He was full of admiration for the breadth of Petrovsky's knowledge and for his critical observations on British rule in India. He delighted in Petrovsky's indiscreet revelations, his boasts of his power over the Taotai, and his scorn of the Chinese empire; it was impossible, the Russian claimed, 'to permit such a nation to continue as a ruling power much longer'. These observations fitted in with Cobbold's own conclusions. Petrovsky, he wrote, 'invested with full authority, enjoying the utmost confidence at the hands of his government, and accorded an entirely free hand, has by generous use of his powers attained such influence in Chinese Turkestan as to practically dominate the very mandarins who nominally govern the province'. The contrast with Macartney's position was galling.

The convivial evenings at the Russian Consulate, though, and the *bonhomie* of the host, were not to last long. As Younghusband and Macartney had found before, Petrovsky's geniality could change inexplicably overnight into hostility and malice. On 27 February Macartney paid a call at the Consulate and was confronted by an irate Petrovsky accusing him of deceit. Cobbold, the Consul claimed, was nothing less than a British secret agent. St Petersburg had telegraphed to him about it and the Russian Foreign Minister had expressed his displeasure at this attempt by Lord Salisbury to impose on the Russian government. He, Petrovsky, was also surprised that a British statesman of such renown should have condescended to an intrigue of this sort.

Macartney was long past feeling any astonishment at such performances. It was pointless to make lengthy denials or to indulge in counter-dramatics. This was Petrovsky's diplomatic style and Macartney coolly wondered what lay behind the latest exhibition. He assumed that it was part of Petrovsky's campaign to prove his vigilance in Kashgar. Later, when Cobbold applied for a passport to shoot in the Russian Pamirs doubts were cast on his succeeding. Macartney heard that the Governor of Ferghana had written that 'before long, further questions connected with the Pamirs might possibly arise between Russia and England'. Macartney could only think that this was connected with the Kanjutis and the Raskam valley. The spy story, it seemed, was part of Petrovsky's way of involving his government in the Raskam affair. For Cobbold the intrigue was not so ridiculous as it appeared. When later he did go to the Russian Pamirs to shoot, he was arrested, almost certainly on Petrovsky's orders, and he spent some uncomfortable days before he was released.

Petrovsky's intrigues were not the only cause of humiliation. In March 1898 Macartney found it necessary to visit Yarkand where the Indian traders had for some time been complaining of conditions. They were finding it almost impossible to recover their trading debts as the official who should have acted on their behalf, the Aksakal, would not bring their complaints before the magistrate. The Aksakal was appointed by the Chinese authorities, and Macartney asked the Amban if the Indians could appoint their own representative in the same way as the Russian merchants. The Amban replied that Indian trade had no official recognition and so the same rules did not apply. Macartney then suggested that he and the Amban together should settle cases that involved British subjects, but his request was turned down. The Amban was clearly hostile to British influence although it was he who had frustrated Petrovsky's attempt to stop the reopening of the Kugiar, Kilian and Sanju trade routes. The reopening of the routes offered financial rewards, but he suspected that the British were behind the Kanjutis' claim to own the Raskam valley. Raskam was part of his jurisdiction and he had no intention of losing it or of allowing British influence to assert itself in any way. As soon as Macartney had left, the Amban took steps to make this clear. He nullified a decision that Macartney had made in a trading dispute between British subjects and he fined others who had presented petitions. He threatened them with flogging and other penalties should they ever present further petitions or entertain an Englishman in the future.

It was a devastating blow. All Macartney's patient work to support British prestige and to protect the interests of Indian traders was undone overnight. The effect was immediate and long lasting. In October 1898 Cobbold told the government of India that reports of the Amban's action had circulated all over the Pamirs. Through Badakhshi and Afghan traders, of whom there were numbers in Yarkand and Kashgar, it had been carried to the Oxus. In July it was still the talk of Sarikol, and the inhabitants expressed their astonishment that the Indian government could put up with such an insult to its representative. Macartney commented in words the more meaningful for their typical restraint: 'In my opinion, this action on the part of the District Magistrate has dealt to our prestige in this country the severest blow which we have ever had.'

It was a depressing situation as there was little hope of retaliation or redress. Macartney could only watch helplessly while Petrovsky made the most of his rival's discomfiture. The next shot was not long in coming, and Macartney had no doubt that Petrovsky was behind it. The Taotai announced that he was considering stopping the cultivation of *charas* (Indian hemp) on the grounds that so many crimes were committed by people under the influence of the drug. The Taotai was not the man to take such a step on his own initiative and Macartney saw it as an attempt to strike at the Indian trade. *Charas* was the chief export from Kashgaria to India and without it the trade would be crippled. The financial consideration eventually proved stronger in the Taotai's mind than fear of Petrovsky and he decided that *charas* could be cultivated in his jurisdiction, apart from Khotan, and that it could be exported to India but not to Russia.

This was a small consolation, but it could not offset the ever-increasing influence of Petrovsky and the dismal prospects for British trade. Discontent was growing among the Kashgarian population as the economic effects of the Japanese war became apparent. The natural outlet for their grievances was the Russian Consulate. In April several wealthy Kashgarians went to see Petrovsky and complained about the oppression of Chinese officials. This had recently taken several new forms. The Chinese were forcing the population to work on the building of the wall round the old part of the city or to supply labour at their own cost. They were also commandeering grain for the army at only one third of the bazaar price and there was a rumour that they would levy a forced loan to pay the Japanese indemnity. This was already being tried in Yarkand where the people had resisted by concealing their money and bringing trade to a standstill. Macartney had no doubt about the rising discontent, especially over grain prices, among the agricultural population.

Petrovsky intervened with the Taotai on the subject, but he had more subtle methods of using Kashgarian discontent to his own advantage. In May Macartney reported that several traders who were Chinese subjects had taken part in the election of the Russian Aksakal at Kashgar and they had bound themselves to pay his fees. This meant in practice that they put themselves in the power of the Russian Consul and escaped from Chinese supervision. They thereby freed themselves from Chinese fiscal demands and gave Petrovsky a greater hold than ever over Kashgarian trade. Chang, the manager of the Foreign Affairs Office at Kashgar, who spoke Russian, was already so much under the influence of the Consul that his fellow officials had nicknamed him 'Petrovsky's son'. This situation and the news that the Russians were thinking of establishing a bank at Kashgar and of linking Kashgar to Andijan by road seemed to presage complete Russian domination of the Kashgarian economy. When Chang and the secretary at the Russian Consulate raided some Chinese houses which they suspected of the prohibited trade in *charas* to Ferghana Macartney commented: 'These incidents, small as they are, have been much commented upon by natives as well as Chinese. The timidity and imbecility of the Taotai stand in painful contrast to the arrogance and prestige of the Russian Consul; and the impression is certainly growing, even amongst the ordinary people, that this country will eventually pass under Russian control.'

The Taotai's failings were sadly obvious over the Raskam affair. The Mir of Hunza had sent an agent, Nazar Ali, to Kashgar with seven Kanjutis, to discuss with the Taotai the partitioning of the Raskam valley. The Taotai's instructions from the Governor of the province were clear: the Kanjutis could cultivate the valley provided they paid taxes to the Chinese. This posed a delicate problem as the Taotai knew that the Kanjutis would oppose the tax on the grounds that Raskam was their territory. Incapable of any firm decision, the Taotai sought to evade the problem by telling the Kanjutis that since they were poor the Chinese would probably not take any tribute from them. When the Kanjutis arrived in the valley they met with obstructiveness from the local officials. Only one small piece of land was given them, and this it was claimed was by order of the Taotai. Macartney discovered later when he questioned the Amban of Yarkand that Petrovsky had threatened the Taotai that if the Kanjutis ever got possession of Raskam the Russians would take 'something' in return.

Something clearly had to be done if British interests were to be maintained at all. The blow to British prestige dealt by the Amban of Yarkand had stirred the government of India to action. The Viceroy telegraphed Sir Claude Macdonald, the British Minister in Peking. Macdonald agreed to bring the Amban's unfriendly conduct to the notice of the Chinese government, but he thought it unwise to press for a joint hearing of cases involving British subjects by Macartney and the local officials. This, he claimed, would involve the recognition of Chinese jurisdiction over British subjects in Kashgar. He would ask, rather, for instructions that the local officials should work in harmony with Macartney.

Meanwhile, the volume of complaints increased from the Indian merchants in Yarkand. The Aksakal whom the Amban had appointed over them, a man called Ahmadyar, continually ill-treated them and refused them justice. He heard their complaints in the bazaar or barber's shop, and would do nothing unless he were bribed. He had persuaded the Amban to appoint him sole *charas* broker which meant that he had a monopoly of all the Indian trade to Yarkand. The Indians were completely at his mercy.

Macartney had passed on all these complaints to the government of India through the regular channels, but since nothing had been done he decided on a final effort. On 31 May he telegraphed directly to Sir Claude Macdonald in Peking. There was no answer for a month, but in July he heard from Macdonald that the Peking authorities would send instructions to the Sinkiang officials to work harmoniously with Macartney in the settlement of cases. Macartney acted immediately. He listed five points that he considered must be conceded if the Indian traders were to have security. The Aksakal Ahmadyar must be dismissed and British subjects must be free to elect their own representative; Macartney should be allowed to settle and revise with the Amban of Yarkand cases still pending or unjustly dealt with; in future all civil suits between British and Chinese subjects should be settled jointly by Macartney and the Amban; British subjects who were parties to a suit should be allowed to petition either Macartney or the Amban.

Macartney put these proposals to the Taotai who characteristically said they must be decided by the Governor of Sinkiang. Peking's instructions had obviously carried weight, for on 12 July Macartney heard that the Governor had sanctioned his terms. But even this authority could not stiffen the Taotai. He returned to Macartney the document specifying the fire articles but there was nothing to show that it had his authority. Macartney knew that this was his way of avoiding any clash with the Amban of Yarkand who had brought pressure on him to refuse recognition of the terms.

The Taotai's spinelessness could only be countered by direct action at Yarkand and on 16 July Macartney left Kashgar for a confrontation with the Amban. Before he left he had the satisfaction of knowing that some Chinese soldiers who had assaulted his servants had been punished by flogging and that the officers were now treating him with obvious courtesy. Sinkiang was not so remote from the centre of affairs that it was unaware that Britain had helped herself in May that year to the port of Wei-Hai-Wei and that she had offered to lend China the vast sum needed to pay the second instalment on the Japanese indemnity. Macartney had called on the Taotai in May to explain the British lease of Wei-Hai-Wei lest the Chinese should have the impression that Britain had joined Russia in the dismembering of China. It was an impression, nevertheless, that was difficult to counter, and Sinkiang realized that it was better not to attract the attention of the British Minister in Peking.

Armed with his new authority Macartney returned to Yarkand to do battle with the Amban who had dealt such a blow to his prestige. He was surprised to find that he was treated with great respect and that the man he had thought such a powerful enemy proved to be, like the Taotai, a weakling in the hands of his underlings. The cause of the trouble at Yarkand was the great jealousy between the Hindu merchants and the Russian-protected Andijani traders who had all the *yamen* interpreters on their side. The Russian Aksakal and the Andijani traders constantly intrigued to avoid discharging their debts to the Hindus and as at Kashgar the Amban was governed by his fear of the Russian Consul. Like the Taotai he sought a compromise. He dismissed the Aksakal Ahmadyar, and flogged him for good measure, but he appointed his own nominee to the post without consulting the Hindus. He agreed to hold a joint court with Macartney and then proceeded to conduct the trials himself with total absence of method. The rules of evidence were unknown to him and he tolerated the most blatant dishonesty from the witnesses. His aim was always to make a settlement between the parties rather than to pass judgement.

For anyone less patient than Macartney it would have been infuriating, but he did succeed in hearing the more difficult cases himself. At least he had made some progress in establishing his position although by the same subtle mixture of pliancy and obtuseness the Chinese had frustrated most of the gains he had made by his telegram to Peking. This was not unexpected, though, and he was prepared to hold his peace and wait. There was nothing more he could do before leaving Kashgar for England on 13 August 1898.

A few days earlier the cumbrous official machinery had delivered a letter from the Secretary of State for India to his colleague at the Foreign Office next door. Enclosed with it were a number of extracts from Macartney's letters, which, said the Secretary of State, illustrated 'the extremely unsatisfactory position of Mr Macartney, and of the disadvantage at which Indian traders are placed by our not having a consul at Kashgar'. Perhaps circumstances would now allow the Foreign Office to press for Macartney's recognition. In India Ralph Cobbold was compiling his own report on Macartney's position in Kashgar which he sent to the government of India. His views were forthright:

If Her Majesty's Government fully realized the intolerable position in which their representative is placed, open as he is, and powerless to defend himself against Russian intrigues, leading to insult from the Chinese (the Munshi attached to the agency in Kashgar was some time ago half murdered by the Chinese soldiery) I cannot help feeling that steps would be taken to alter his status and either give him full Consular powers or oblige the Chinese to accord him official recognition.

After further remarks about the poor impression made by Macartney's top hat and frock coat in the absence of an official uniform, Cobbold concluded: 'Possibly no opportunity may occur better than the present time for improving our agent's position in Chinese Turkestan.' Even the Foreign Office was convinced, but it was soon apparent that it was the Russian rather than the Chinese government they had to persuade.

SEVEN

The Russian Ascendancy

Macartney's second period of leave home was a hurried affair which he snatched from his duties to bring his bride to Kashgar. Macartney bent on marriage was a different man from the quiet, impassive figure who outwardly seemed so lacking in Petrovsky's fire or the verve and glamour of Younghusband. Almost as soon as permission came through for his leave he set out on his journey and was announced in the Borland house when his bride was in the kitchen practising her cookery in the belief that he was still in Kashgar. The astonished Catherine Borland was summoned to the drawing-room and was told by her fiancé they must be married within a week and set off speedily on the return journey to Kashgar. All difficulties or objections were solved or overruled and on 6 October 1898 Macartney and his wife began the long journey through Russia to Kashgar.

For Catherine Macartney it was an awesome change from a sheltered and comfortable home, in which she was one of a large family, to a life in alien and primitive surroundings where she and her husband were the only British people in the province. Years later when she came to write about her experiences she described herself on her marriage as 'the most timid, unenterprising girl in the world. I had hardly been beyond the limits of my own sheltered home, and big family of brothers and sisters, had never had any desire whatever to see the world, and certainly had no qualifications for a pioneer's life, beyond being able to make a cake.' The journey itself was enough to test the endurance of the most hardened travellers and was far from being the ideal beginning to married life. Looking back on it she wrote:

A journey of that sort is a pretty good test to one's temper, for nerves get strained, at times almost to breaking-point. Everything seems to go wrong when one is utterly tired out, and sometimes very hungry.

If two people can go through the test of such a journey without quarrelling seriously, they can get on under any circumstances. We just survived it, and it promised well for the long journey through life.

Macartney's work kept him fully occupied in his office or on his travels, and his wife, who was unable to speak any of the local languages, found the first year or so of marriage a time of deep homesickness. Fortunately, the two wives of the Swedish missionaries spoke English and the three women became firm friends. For Macartney his marriage meant the end of loneliness. When Catherine arrived at Chini Bagh she found a strange collection of wild animals, as well as a family of dogs, which, apart from Father Hendricks, had been Macartney's domestic companions for so long. Now Chini Bagh became a home and he and his family made their roots in Kashgar. His marriage, instead of dividing his loyalties, concentrated them, as the safety and well-being of his wife and children were committed to Sinkiang. The year 1898 was the beginning for the Macartneys of a marriage of mutual support and happiness which lasted for forty-seven years until death ended it, again, strangely, under alien rule.

Macartney found when he returned to Kashgar in November 1898 that affairs had not been going well in his absence. His deputy, Munshi Sayad Bahadur Ali Shah, like his predecessor Munshi Ahmad Din, had been the victim of violence. A Chinese had thrown three bricks at him. The assault was not so serious as in the previous case and the assailant had been arrested and handed over to the manager of the Foreign Affairs Office. The Taotai visited the Munshi in person and apologized for the attack but it was not clear if any punishment would follow. Another British subject, this time an English officer, Captain Deasy, had also experienced trouble in the country. The Amban of Keria had refused to allow him to travel in certain districts named in his passport and had denied him help and supplies. Petrovsky, too, had kept up his campaign to undermine British interests and was again trying to stop the cultivation of *charas* with the object of ruining the Indian trade. There was also a report circulating that the Taotai had ordered the Amban of Tashkurghan to allow Russian subjects to enter Sarikol with Chinese passports and that this was part of Petrovsky's scheme to establish his own officials there.

The most ominous development was over Raskam, a subject that promised to be a running sore in Macartney's relations with the Chinese. The Amban of Yarkand had reportedly given three out of the seven Raskam holdings to the people of Sarikol at the expense of the Kanjutis. The Taotai's only concession to the Provincial Governor's order that Raskam should be handed over to the Kanjutis was to send General Chang to Yarkand on 30 September to supervise the division of the Raskam lands between the Kanjutis and the Sarikolis. The Mir of Hunza's agent, Nazar Ali, was sent backwards and forwards between Chinese officials in his efforts to secure the holdings for his people. It was clear to Macartney that the pitiable vacillations of the Chinese were not the result of hostility to the Kanjutis but were dictated by fear of the Russians. He heard that the Yarkand Amban had even written to the Provincial Governor saying that he wanted the Kanjutis to cultivate the valley as they would act as a British-protected buffer against any Russian encroachments from the direction of Sarikol. According to Macartney's information the Governor had replied that the British could not be relied on as a buffer and he ordered the Amban to make fresh proposals which would satisfy both the British and the Russians.

However favourable were the views of the Amban of Yarkand to the Kanjutis, he, like the Taotai, was governed chiefly by his fear of Petrovsky. This was apparent in his subservience to the Andijani traders. Despite Macartney's success of the previous July when the Amban had agreed to observe the five articles which Macartney had drawn up, he found that during his absence everything had reverted to its former state. Of the fifty-nine cases for the recovery of debts which the Hindu traders had reported in August 1898 only twenty-six had been disposed of by the new year. In November Macartney received a note from the British Joint Commissioner in Ladakh which said that the Indian trade was dwindling to vanishing-point because the traders were unable to collect their debts. The Hindus had over 600 cases to settle in Yarkand for sums totalling one and a half lakhs. The Amban claimed that most of these cases were for the recovery of money lent at interest, a practice prohibited by proclamation, so they could not be dealt with. Macartney felt that the only hope of improving the situation was by gaining powers of direct supervision. He wrote to the Taotai in December asking that where British subjects complained they could not get justice the cases should be transferred to Kashgar and heard jointly by Macartney and the manager of the Foreign Commerce Office. The Taotai made no objections and early in 1899 Macartney took on the heavy task of dealing with the Yarkandi suits.

This solution did not end the troubles at Yarkand. The Hindus began selling their goods for cash only and so their sales decreased. Matters came to a head when the Amban of Yarkand sent a report to the Taotai and to the Provincial Governor objecting to the observance of Macartney's five articles. After some delay the Provincial Governor replied upholding the agreement. But the power of Urumchi, once unquestioned, was being slowly eroded by the personality of Petrovsky and the watchful nearness of Russia. Neither the Taotai nor the Amban would openly disobey the Provincial Governor but they were past masters at delays and subtle modifications. The Amban agreed to the articles as he was directed but he wrote to Macartney in March 1899 asking that when Indian traders sold goods on credit their customers should provide a third party as a surety. He also wanted to prohibit the lending of money at interest by the Hindus. Both conditions were fatal to the prosperity of the Indian trade and it was not difficult to see the influence of the Andijanis behind them.

Macartney refused to agree and went on with the slow and onerous task of dealing with the suits of the Indians that were referred to him. The work was tedious and frustrating. It was becoming more obvious with every month that the discipline within the Chinese civil service was breaking down, a process hastened in Kashgar by the feebleness of the Taotai. His control over his subordinates was so slight that Macartney's complaints to him had little effect. The Taotai would issue orders but his officials ignored them. Nevertheless, Macartney was acutely aware of the difference of treatment between Russian and British subjects, and of his own inability to alter the situation.

If any proof were wanting of the growing power of Russia over the internal politics of Kashgaria it was made explicit in 1899 when the Raskam affair came to a crisis. The year began with an announcement by the Taotai that he had settled the whole question of Raskam. The seven holdings in the Raskam valley were to be given to the Kanjutis in return for the payment of twelve taels of grain tax a year as a token of Chinese authority over the valley. Within a week or two of this announcement 100 Chinese troops left Kashgar for Tagharma in Sarikol as a temporary reinforcement of the Sarikol garrison. Macartney interpreted the move as a precaution against Russian encroachments. The Russian Commanding Officer at Murghabi had reportedly said that if Raskam were made over to the Kanjutis then the Russians would seize Tagharma. Petrovsky, too, had boasted of his government's intention to establish a garrison at Tagharma. The Taotai had reported this to the Provincial Governor who ordered the reinforcement of the Chinese forces there.

In March came news that the Russians were moving up guns and stores to their fort at Irkeshtam on the Chinese frontier. In reply the Provincial Governor sent reinforcements to Kashgar. The Taotai asked him if he should oppose a Russian attempt to occupy Tagharma but he received no clear instructions from Urumchi. However the Governor reduced by two the number of plots in Raskam that he had allocated to the Kanjutis. In April the bold front put up by the Chinese collapsed ignominiously. Peking sent orders that all the land granted to the Kanjutis in Raskam should be withdrawn and the Kanjutis should be sent back to Hunza. The Russian Minister in Peking had threatened that his forces would retaliate for the Raskam settlement by seizing Tagharma and a village near Irkeshtam. He had also asked if it were true that the Chinese had sent 700 troops to Tagharma. In fact there were only sixty there. Macartney thought that Petrovsky was responsible for this exaggeration in his attempt to create friction between the Russians and the Chinese.

It appeared that Petrovsky's lies and machinations were the cause of most of the trouble. When the British government made a protest the Russian Foreign Office disclaimed any responsibility for the Chinese government's withdrawing their Raskam grant. The Foreign Minister denied any threat to occupy Tagharma. This was little comfort, though, to Macartney. If the Russian Foreign Minister were sincere in his protestations then Petrovsky's power was the more to be feared because it was outside diplomatic control. Petrovsky in Kashgar, supported by the Russian War

Office and the Minister at Peking, was capable almost single-handed of achieving a Russian occupation of Sinkiang, whatever might be the policy of the Foreign Minister at St Petersburg.

Petrovsky had no scruples at all about the methods he employed. He matched the magnitude of his lies with a minute attention to detail. No incident was too small for his notice provided it could be used to bully the Chinese or to persuade his own government to tighten the Russian hold on Kashgaria. It was he who was behind the troubles experienced by the British officer, Captain Deasy, who was travelling on the Polu–Aksai Chin route, and who had met constant opposition from the Amban of Keriya, despite Macartney's protests to the Taotai. In June Macartney heard that Deasy was facing further obstacles in his journey, so he went to the Taotai and had what he described as 'an interview, which I think was the most stormy I ever had with any Chinese official in this country'. The Taotai admitted that he had ordered the Amban of Keriya not to allow Deasy to make any road repairs on his route. Petrovsky had told him that the British had designs on the Aksai Chin country and that the Russians would interfere if the Chinese permitted the reopening of the Polu-Aksai Chin route. After making this confession the Taotai agreed under Macartney's pressure to send fresh instructions to Keriya. Knowing his man, and knowing that a stand was essential if Petrovsky was to be restrained at all, Macartney again took the step of telegraphing directly to the Minister in Peking. The move was successful and the Chinese Foreign Office ordered the Amban of Keria not to obstruct Deasy. Nevertheless, a report came in July that the Amban had sent two men to destroy Deasy's track, and that the Russian Aksakal at Keriya was preparing to follow him, on the orders of Petrovsky.

Petrovsky did not restrict his attention to political matters. He regarded anyone in Kashgaria who was not actively pro-Russian as an enemy of his cause and unless it was politically inexpedient he would pursue a personal vendetta against them. These campaigns were remarkable for their persistence and pettiness. Father Hendricks, Macartney's old friend and companion, was a victim of long standing. He had returned to Kashgar from India in June and refused to intrude on the domestic life of the Macartneys at Chini Bagh. Macartney tried to find him a house in Kashgar, but, as had happened before, the task proved strangely difficult. After three months and much pressure the Mayor produced a vacant house. Petrovsky then openly intervened and the offer was withdrawn. But the old Dutch priest was well liked in the town and there were popular demonstrations on his behalf. The Taotai gave in and Father Hendricks made his home in part of the vaccination office, which was little more than a hovel.

It was perhaps some consolation that his tribulations were shared by the Swedish Protestant missionaries who had arrived in Kashgar in 1894. They were on good terms with Macartney and had even asked him to act as their Consul. He had refused, but their request was sufficient to blacken them in the eyes of Petrovsky. In April 1899 a gang attacked the site of their new mission house and destroyed the buildings. The Swedes had quarrelled with their landlord who had stirred up religious feeling against them. The missionaries asked for the help of Macartney and Petrovsky. The Russian at first took a guarded view of the affair but later the missionaries told Macartney that he was using his influence with the Chinese to embarrass the mission rather than to help it. It was not wise to be friendly with Macartney if one wanted a quiet life in Kashgar.

By October 1899 it became apparent that there was more to Petrovsky's behaviour than his customary interference and obstructiveness. His self-confidence had reached such heights that at a dinner he had given in July he had gone out of his way to insult his Chinese guests, the Taotai and the Mayor of Kashgar, and neither had dared show any resentment. Now he seemed to be striving for a break with Macartney. The many provocations of the previous months had not stirred Macartney into any protest or sign of irritation, and Petrovsky was forced to turn to invention for his purposes. A vagrant named Haji Sayad Yusif, who claimed to be a Turkish subject, wandered into Kashgar in September. His was a common enough type; in Macartney's view, a tramp who made his living by passing as a holy man. Petrovsky chose to consider him a suspicious character and had him delivered by the Chinese authorities to the Consulate prison. The Consul then accused Macartney's Munshi of illicit dealings with the man on an occasion when the Munshi was at the Consulate. The implication was that the vagrant was a spy for the British although the accusations and the evidence were deliberately left vague.

Macartney felt deeply insulted but he merely passed on the case to be dealt with by the British Foreign Office. He found, though,

108

when he next called at the Russian Consulate that Petrovsky would not see him. On the first occasion he was said to be in his bath, and on the second, asleep. Shortly afterwards Kolokoloff, who had remained at the Consulate as secretary, and the Taotai's Russian secretary combined to produce a Chinese lithographed newspaper which they circulated free. Its subject matter was chiefly anti-British propaganda and it was full of reports of British reverses in the Transvaal and of plague in India. Petrovsky clearly intended to break off relations with Macartney and from November 1899 until June 1902 the two men did not exchange a single word.

It was obvious that Petrovsky was preparing for a major attack on British interests in Kashgaria, although Macartney could not be certain what form this would take. There were signs that the Chinese in Kashgar were becoming less cooperative and Macartney's protest to the Taotai was unavailing when five people were punished by the local Amban for giving evidence before him in a Hindu trader's suit. In November Macartney was in Yarkand where he was struck by the power and position of the Russian Aksakal. The man not only controlled all affairs connected with Russian subjects but interfered in matters of purely local concern. The Amban clearly lived in fear of him and he had recently given him a handsome present of land to bespeak his good offices with Petrovsky.

While Macartney was at Yarkand the Amban paid him a visit and brought up the subject of Raskam. In August the British Foreign Office had secured an assurance from St Petersburg that the Russians would not oppose the lease of Raskam, and the following month Peking again gave general approval for the grant. But the Amban asked Macartney to advise the Mir of Hunza not to press for the grant of Azghur and Urak, two of the holdings in the Raskam valley, on the grounds that the Provincial Governor did not approve. Macartney knew that the whole of the military party of Kashgar was opposed to the grant, partly on strategic grounds, and partly because a Chinese garrison wanted to cultivate Azghur themselves. The request therefore came as no surprise, regardless of what pressure the Russians had brought to bear on the Amban. Azghur and Urak together formed one third of the cultivable land and it was unlikely that Hunza would renounce them, but Macartney counselled patience. It was best to accept the other holdings first and later to bring pressure on the Chinese for the rest of the land. His advice was accepted, but at the end of December Macartney heard that Peking had again deferred the lease of even the remaining holdings in consequence of hints by Petrovsky that the Russians would expect a *quid pro quo*.

Macartney had not long to wait after this announcement before Petrovsky brought his schemes to fruition. In the first week of 1900 two new Russian officers arrived at the Consulate in Kashgar, and on 10 January Petrovsky told the Taotai that he was sending an officer and five Cossacks to Tashkurghan. The excuse was that they were going to inquire into the stopping of messengers from the Russian Pamirs to Kashgar, but the Taotai and Macartney knew that this would probably be the beginning of a Russian outpost in Sarikol. The Taotai was in a pitiable state when Macartney saw him, fearful and helpless, but ready to accept whatever advice Macartney gave. Macartney went further: he took to the Taotai rough drafts in Chinese of what he felt he should report to Urumchi and what he should say in reply to Petrovsky. He had found by experience that the Taotai's literary gifts were limited and that in the past he had been unable to put Macartney's recommendations in writing without spoiling the effect by faulty expressions. This might be overlooked by Western eyes but to the Chinese the manner of expression was as vital as the substance, and it was essential that Peking should realize the full seriousness of the situation. His draft pointed out the blow that would be suffered by Chinese prestige if the Cossacks entered Sarikol. It was more than probable that they would stay there and build a fort. To Petrovsky he wrote that the Taotai could not allow any kind of Russian jurisdiction over Chinese subjects. The Taotai was convinced that resistance was useless as Petrovsky would get his way by telegraphing his Minister in Peking. But he allowed himself to be persuaded and sent off Macartney's drafts under his own name. Macartney gave what further help he could by telegraphing the British Minister in Peking.

Within a few days orders came from the Provincial Governor forbidding the Russian expedition to Sarikol. Petrovsky was incensed and promptly produced fresh accusations that suspicious characters were entering Chinese territory from Hunza. On 1 February he wrote a letter to the Taotai setting out a list of complaints about the unsupervised state of the Chinese frontiers and the illegal traffic in *charas*. Macartney had no doubts about the meaning of the letter: it was meant to pave the way for a Russian occupation. Petrovsky's policy was:

> to multiply these grievances, to show up to his government the shortcomings of the Chinese administration in their worst light, and thereby to urge upon the Cabinet of St Petersburg the absolute necessity of an intervention in order, forsooth, to put an end to a state of affairs in Kashgaria which for Russia is intolerable. Nor is Mr Petrovsky unassisted in this aim by the Taotai himself whose incapacity to argue a question in a statesmanlike manner is constantly leading him into dangerous concessions.

Macartney telegraphed Sir Claude Macdonald in Peking warning him of Petrovsky's latest move, and he advised the Taotai to write to Peking refuting the complaints. He told him merely to acknowledge Petrovsky's letter and to say nothing more on the grounds that the Russian had no right to intervene in the Indo-Chinese frontier. The Taotai listened but confessed that he hadn't the courage to reply in this way to Petrovsky. Macartney observed in his report that there was no hope of checking Russian influence until the Chinese removed the Taotai and appointed a successor with some experience of international affairs.

Macartney persevered in his attempt to stiffen the Taotai's resistance but with little success. Petrovsky followed up his letter of complaints by intervening in the appointment of one of the native judges in Kashgar. He tried to force his own candidate for the post on the Mayor of Kashgar against the choice of the people. The Mayor found no alternative but to leave the post vacant. Macartney tried to shame the Taotai into action by telling him that he must inform the Governor of India of the situation since the Consul's newly acquired jurisdiction over local affairs was 'of the nature of a political revolution'. The Taotai did nothing. But at the end of February Macartney thought he could detect in him some signs of a serious struggle to free himself from Russian oppression. He feared, though, that he had neither the courage nor intelligence to secure any lasting results.

Meanwhile the British Foreign Office was doing its best to counter Petrovsky's activities by negotiating at St Petersburg. In January 1900 the British Ambassador, Sir Charles Scott, discussed the Raskam affair with Count Mouravieff and stated the British view that Petrovsky's threats were directly responsible for the Chinese withdrawing the lease to the Kanjutis. Scott reminded Mouravieff of their agreement of the previous August in which Russia had withdrawn all opposition to the Raskam settlement. Mouravieff later sent a note saying that Petrovsky had no authority to oppose the lease. Macdonald at Peking informed the Chinese government that the Russian Foreign Minister had disavowed Petrovsky's threat, and he expected the Raskam lease to be given. The Chinese retorted that the Russians had not given any assurances about possible counter-claims and they asked for time to refer to Kashgar.

There was no sign that the disavowals of his Foreign Minister had any restraining effect on Petrovsky. His invention and activity continued unabated. In March, Captin Kornilov, one of the Russian officers who had arrived at the Consulate at the beginning of the year, set out on a mysterious journey to Yarkand, accompanied by two Cossacks. While he was there a series of special messengers from the Russian Pamirs passed through Sarikol to carry dispatches to him, which suggested to Macartney that his mission was of no small importance. Petrovsky continued to invent evidence of British aggressive designs, including a story of the passage of 'suspects' from Hunza to Sarikol, and complaints that the Indian Munshi in Sarikol gave protection to suspicious characters. Macartney interpreted them as a new effort by Petrovsky to justify the stationing of a Russian officer in Sarikol. The Consul also insinuated that the Taotai was receiving bribes from Macartney. These complaints were repeated by the Russian Minister at Peking and involved Macartney in lengthy and detailed denials.

In May Petrovsky had more to say about Sarikol, and Macartney could no longer doubt his intentions. The Consul sent a courier to investigate alleged difficulties in getting post through Sarikol to Kashgar, and he claimed that the man had been treated in an unfriendly manner by the local Amban. He also accused certain Sarikolis of instigating Kirghiz in the Russian Pamirs to flee to Chinese territory. Macartney warned the Taotai of the care he must take in reporting to Peking the story of the Hunza 'suspects' crossing into Sarikol. The Taotai listened to him with close attention and Macartney thought that the warning impressed him so far as his shallow nature allowed. But there was no doubt that Petrovsky was skilfully building up a case to induce his government to intervene in Sarikol.

The Consul did not neglect Russian interests in Kashgar while he was pursuing his expansionist aims. In June he began negotiating with the Taotai for the establishment of a branch of the Russo-Chinese Bank in the town. The Bank had been chartered as part of the price of Russian help at the end of the war with Japan, and its object was the 'peaceful penetration' of north-east Asia. It had wide powers to coin money, collect taxes, secure fresh economic concessions, and even to set up local governments in China. Once established in Kashgar there was no knowing what a stranglehold it would gain over the economy of the province. Macartney advised the Taotai to refer to Peking for instructions. Petrovsky was also pressing for permission to build a cotton weaving factory, and there was a rumour that he would establish a branch of the Russian Post Office. A Russian hospital was already being built.

There seemed no limit to Petrovsky's power and the spread of Russian influence. Macartney needed every encouragement from his government to make his work seem worthwhile, and at last, after ten years, some acknowledgement came. In June he heard he had been made a Companion of the Indian Empire. Better still, in August his pay was increased, 'in consideration of the excellent work' he was performing. He was given the same salary as a political officer of his years' service and for the first time he was brought under the conditions of leave that applied to European service members. It was belated recognition, but was nevertheless welcome.

Within a month of the announcement of his C.I.E. telegrams from Peking brought news of a rebellion which threatened to overturn the whole political fabric of China and to cut short Macartney's career. The Boxers, or Society of Harmonious Fists, was originally one of the many secret societies that flourished in China. It had gained a large following in Shantung province by demanding the expulsion of foreigners who were popularly held responsible for the misery of China. After 1899 the movement spread rapidly in northern China and the Boxers received some support in Peking where they were taken up for her own purposes by the Empress Dowager. In June 1900 the Boxers entered Peking in force and began to attack the foreign quarters. The Empress Dowager threw in her lot with the rebels and regular Chinese troops joined in the attack on the legations. The Peking government ordered all the provincial governors to join in expelling foreigners from the country, but most preferred to watch and wait.

In distant Sinkiang the Governor made no move but vivid rumours circulated in the Kashgar bazaar. On 20 July Macartney reported on a state of alarm and near panic. He had no fears of a rising among the peasants as they were disarmed and leaderless, but he was aware that there were hot-heads among the Chinese who might use the occasion to avenge themselves on Petrovsky. There was a strong rumour that the Titai was preparing to attack the Russian Consulate. Several rifle-shots had been fired within the precincts of the building and the city gates were closed two hours earlier than usual. It was reported that Russian troops were concentrating near the Chinese border and the Taotai was fearful of their intervention. The Tungans in the neighbouring province of Kansu nursed an unquenchable hatred for the Chinese and it was possible that they would join forces with the Russians.

On 18 July it seemed that the crisis had come. The Titai rode into Old Kashgar with over 100 soldiers and the troops stationed near the Russian Consulate were seen sharpening their swords. The Titai returned to the New City the same afternoon, but Petrovsky believed this was a ruse. He and his staff sat up keeping watch throughout the night of the 18th expecting an imminent attack. Clearly, unless something were done Russian troops would be summoned to Kashgar. Macartney immediately went round to see the Taotai and told him the military was acting in a childish way which could prove to be disastrous. The Russians might concentrate their troops on the Kashgar border and alarm would spread to Yarkand and Khotan. People would begin hoarding food and prices would rise steeply. All the riffraff of the population, known as the 'gamblers', who infested the roads of Kashgar, would become a real danger once law and order were in doubt. It was essential to preserve calm and security. Macartney made three proposals which he said should be carried out at once if the crisis were to be averted: there should be no more discussion of the Boxer disturbances in the presence of attendants who would spread rumours about them; the Taotai must countermand his orders for the early closing of the gates; and the Chinese officials

114

must keep up an appearance of friendship with the Russian Consulate.

The Taotai was feeble and anxious but he appeared grateful for Macartney's advice and acted on it. On 24 July Macartney was able to report that the panic had abated considerably because the town gates were closed at the usual time and Petrovsky paid the Taotai a ceremonial visit. Captain Kornilov told the Chinese officials that Russia had made no preparations for war. The crisis did nothing, though, to mend the broken relations between Petrovsky and Macartney. The Russian even went so far as to accuse Macartney's Chinese Munshi of spreading alarmist reports. Nothing further happened to disturb the peace of Kashgar and on 14 August an expeditionary force of Japanese, Russian, British, American and French troops entered Peking and broke the seige of the legations. The Empress Dowager and her court fled to Sian leaving the aged statesman, Li Hung-chang, to negotiate with the foreigners.

The Boxer rebellion was over, but Russia had made use of it to occupy Manchuria which she appeared about to convert into a Russian province. Chinese policy was in the hands of Li Hung-chang who recognized the necessity of dealing with Russia on friendly terms. The only way he could avoid this was by calling on Japanese help, but he feared the Japanese even more than the Russians. In St Petersburg Count Witte's policy of peaceful penetration had given way in face of the Boxer rebellion to the aggressive designs of a more intransigent group, so that in Kashgar Petrovsky was in a stronger position than ever. Macartney could only be relieved when he heard that the Taotai was to leave Kashgar that year on his promotion to the post of Provincial Treasurer. There was some hope that his successor might deal more ably with Petrovsky. The Amban of Yarkand had also received orders to hand over his post to Lew Ta-Lao-yieh, the former Mayor of Kashgar. The Amban, like the Taotai, had been a weakling in Russian hands, so from Macartney's point of view a change could only be for the better.

The Taotai revealed to Macartney during an interview in August 1900 what he had long endured in his feeble struggles against Petrovsky. Macartney had gone to see the Taotai about the archaeologist, Dr Aurel Stein, who had arrived in Kashgar, and wished to travel in the mountains south of Khotan. Macartney asked the Taotai to recommend him to the Ambans of Khotan and Keriya. The Taotai said that Petrovsky raised difficulties about English travellers using the Polu route and accused them of spying. This was the line he had taken over Captain Deasy. He had already made clear his attitude to Stein when he had refused to see him on the pretext of illness. The Taotai said he was afraid to give his permission in direct contravention of Petrovsky's wishes. He then made a remarkable spontaneous confession: 'He knew he might be accused of cowardice; but he was a coward and a fool, and he fully admitted this fact, as well as his fear of Petrovsky.'

There was much that was pathetic in the man's awareness of his own humiliation which also reflected that of his country. It was in sorry contrast with the Taotai's boast to Ralph Cobbold that he pitied Europeans for their 'lack of that lofty dignity of mind inherent in the Celestial race, which rendered it superior to the petty quarrels of nations and enabled them to regard with equanimity the affairs of the outside world without any desire to take a part in it'. Now the merest threat from Petrovsky of Russian intervention was enough to put fear into the Taotai. Macartney could only feel the truth of his confession, but he thought it essential to preserve Chinese dignity. He hastened to assure the Taotai that Stein did not want to see the Polu–Aksai Chin country, and the Taotai felt sufficiently strengthened to make the necessary recommendations.

The Taotai's open admission that he could do nothing without Petrovsky's approval, and Russia's impregnable position after the Boxer rebellion, convinced Macartney that the time had come for a realistic appraisal of British policy towards Kashgaria. In August 1900 he sent to the Political Agent at Gilgit a cool and dispassionate review of British commercial and territorial interests in the area. They were little enough. The commercial interests were no more than ten to fifteen Hindu and five Indian Muslim traders in Yarkand, and about 130 Shikarpuri Hindus who were moneylenders. There were also many Kashmiris who had settled down in the country as landowners and had no intention of returning to India. If there should be more disturbances like the Boxer rising the Hindus would suffer badly, and it was not easy to protect them as they were separated by long distances from each

The market place at Kashgar

Above The Mir of Hunza with his sons

Chu, Taoyin of Kashgar, 1917–1923

other. It would be risky to send troops from Gilgit and in any case military operations were only possible with the assent of the Russians. For the protection of himself and his staff Macartney considered a guard of twenty infantry desirable, but for this he would need the permission of the Chinese government.

Raskam was Britain's only territorial interest in Kashgaria and here, in Macartney's view, there was a real possibility that the Russians would supplant the Chinese. Should this happen the Kanjutis would be deprived of the land they needed and claimed as a right. If Britain failed to protect their claim she would have to make a territorial grant in compensation and her prestige would suffer. It was also strategically inconvenient to have the Russian frontier on the watershed of the Hindu Kush. Macartney thought the best solution was to make Raskam part of a British zone, unde-fended by troops, but at least precluded in peacetime from Russian outposts at the foot of the Killik, Mintaka and Shamshal passes. It was unlikely that Britain could secure this zone by diplomacy with either the Russians or the Chinese, so in Macart-ney's view the only alternative was 'to send a few troops to occupy the country comprised in the zone whenever the occasion is ripe for the measure, and to assert our legal right of first occupant against the Russians. The ripeness of the occasion would depend upon the course of events in Kashgaria and upon the imminence of a Russian occupation.' If the British attitude were to be an active one there ought to be a British officer in Hunza with secret instructions to act immediately the Russians showed signs of advancing.

Macartney's proposals showed how imminent he thought a Russian occupation was, but his conclusions were too radical in the opinions of his superiors. The India Office thought that his recog-nition as Consul and the provision of a guard were desirable and should be arranged with China when a settlement was made, but there was no support for any forward policy beyond the Hindu Kush. In the aftermath of the Boxer rebellion, while there was doubt about the legal government of China, Britain had ceased to press the Raskam question. Within a few months the Chinese had alienated almost all the Raskam lands and they were cultivated by Kirghiz and Sarikolis.

The vulnerable position of British trade was also underlined when Petrovsky forced the Taotai to prohibit the entry of travellers and animals from India on the pretext of plague. Macartney protested to the Taotai that the plague was confined to Bombay and that in a similar situation in 1897 Peking had given orders that travellers should only be quarantined and not refused entry. The Taotai quickly adopted a fresh line and said he would only give general instructions to his officials to look out for plague, and he would not debar a single man or package.

The Taotai had new worries on his mind. Four Chinese soldiers of the Khotan garrison had recently attempted a mutiny in which they threatened to kill the commandant for holding back their pay. Macartney urged the Taotai as a priority to see that the Chinese troops were paid promptly, as once disaffection spread disaster could result. In his opinion the Chinese in Kashgaria had only to maintain a reasonable vigilance and to act promptly against the 'gamblers' at any signs of trouble and they would be able to ride over the crisis created by the Boxer rebellion. The native population as a whole was not ill disposed, and the Taotai doubted if the Tungans would rise. He also thought that the districts south of the Tien Shan could support their own administration if no subsidy were forthcoming. There was, he claimed, a large surplus in the provincial treasury.

Macartney did not feel so optimistic, and within a week he tackled the Taotai again on the subject. Orders had just come through from Urumchi to withhold the soldiers' pay for ten days in every month so that money could be found to maintain the troops round Peking. Macartney again pointed out the danger but the Taotai said there was no cause for anxiety, and there was nothing further that Macartney could do. The Taotai's grasp of fundamentals was always weak, and Macartney found that his warnings and advice seldom had any lasting impression.

The foolhardiness on the part of the Chinese officials was carried one stage further when Lew Ta-lao-yieh, the former Mayor of Kashgar, took over the post of Amban of Yarkand. In Kashgar his regime had been one of extortion amounting almost to open robbery, and he wasted no time in transferring these tactics to Yarkand. He was openly on bad terms with Petrovsky since the Russian was a threat to Lew's system, but he kept up friendly relations with Macartney. This gave little pleasure to Macartney as the activities of Lew in Yarkand could arouse enough popular feeling to overturn the whole Chinese regime in Kashgaria. Lew had assumed office on 1 October and by the 17th there was a riot in Yarkand. Lew's brother held the appointment of customs officer in the city and he had tried to levy a tax on all the domestic animals kept by the people. When they resisted Lew ordered out the troops, but the commandant refused to obey. Lew was then forced to disavow his brother's actions. At least the Indian traders had no trouble from him, and he readily approved their own choice of Aksakal, referring publicly to his friendship with Macartney. By contrast he treated a Russian medical officer who had gone to Yarkand on plague duty with the utmost hauteur. This was little consolation, though, when in February 1901 Macartney heard fresh reports of the Amban's oppression and of his severely flogging people who had dared to petition him against the heavy taxes.

Petrovsky was unusually quiet throughout the last two months of 1900 and Macartney thought that he was treating the Chinese officials with more consideration than usual. It was true that he had been making efforts to win over the headmen of Sarikol and that he had not been unsuccessful. A present of silk had gone from the Consulate to Sarikol and in November one of the headmen received a letter from Petrovsky thanking him for his help. The tactics were different, but the purpose was unchanged, and Macartney felt certain that in the end nothing could hold Petrovsky back.

This conviction made him sit down in the last days of 1900 and put together on paper his thoughts about the whole direction of British policy in Kashgaria and the value of the work he could do there. It was the second report of its kind he had made that year and he had not altered his basic views. He must have known at the time he suggested making Raskam part of a British zone that there was no prospect of his government's agreeing to it, but he thought it should be made to see clearly what the true alternatives were. He began his report by pointing out that he had never received any precise instructions about the nature of his work, but he had always kept four general objects in mind; to establish friendly relations with the local Chinese authorities and to strengthen their rule in Sinkiang wherever possible; to encourage Indo-Turkestan trade; to keep the government of India informed of any Russian and Chinese news that affected British interests; and to oppose through the Chinese authorities the spread of Russian influence in the province.

He had succeeded in his first object in that he had won the friendship of the Chinese and through them had secured the release of British-Indian slaves. The Chinese also favoured leasing Raskam to the Kanjutis and were only stopped by Russian threats. He had gained some improvements in the conditions of British trade: the Chinese had abolished all duties on Indian goods; they had opened the Sanju and Kugiar routes and given some attention to traders' suits for the recovery of debts; they had agreed to appoint an Indian aksakal in Yarkand and had resisted the Russian demand for the closing of the Karakoram route and the prohibition of *charas* growing. But he had won these concessions only after an incessant badgering directed against 'an indolent and ignorant bureaucracy, which certainly had never given, voluntarily at least, the slightest attention to the interests of our merchants'. Looked at coolly, Macartney had only been able to ward off dangers that threatened to extinguish British trade altogether, and he had no hopes of any greater success.

Nor was he optimistic about his task of collecting news. It was almost impossible to obtain political information about Russian Turkestan, and from fear of Petrovsky hardly anyone dared to visit Chini Bagh. The Consul could extinguish a merchant's livelihood overnight by withdrawing permission to trade with Russia. Where Macartney employed an agent of his own, such as the Sarikol newswriter, he and his informants were well known to the Russians who had their own agents watching everything that was going on.

Where Macartney felt that his work failed chiefly was in the most vital sphere of combating Russian influence. He had found it impossible, he said, 'to push the Chinese beyond this passive stage of Russo-phobia into an active spirit of resistance against illegitimate pressure into a sense of their own independence'. The local Chinese officials were entirely governed by acquisitiveness and by their fear of Russia. Petrovsky had more power over them than their own rulers, partly because of his violent personality and partly because of the strong support given to him by his Ministers in Peking.

Russian power in Kashgaria, though, did not rest on personalities; her strength lay in the magnitude of her trade which had come to dominate the economy of the province. No physical obstacle stood in the way of its expansion and already thousands of Chinese subjects were dependent on it for their livelihood. The rouble, not Chinese silver, was the coin of exchange and it was on the way to becoming the ordinary currency of the province. The Russians used their trade as a political lever and their aksakals, customs houses and bank provided both the organization and the pretext for interference. The bank had opened in Kashgar on 19 October 1900 and had an alliance with one of the large Russian transport firms to monopolize the carriage of goods between Kashgar and Russian Turkestan. British trade had no hope of competing on equal terms. The cost of sending goods from Britain to India with the further 5 per cent duty that was added there made prices prohibitive, whereas Russia sent cotton goods to Kashgar for 2·82 roubles a pound, and added a bounty to cover transport costs. If Britain opened a direct trade route from Kashgar to India through Gilgit it might stimulate Russian trade to compete for markets south of the Hindu Kush.

China knew that she had nothing to fear from British power and nothing to gain from British friendship. She had learnt over the Pamirs in 1891 and over the Raskam question that she could do nothing without Russian approval. Now there was a Russian newswriter in Sarikol and trouble seemed to threaten in that quarter. To Macartney the conclusions seemed inescapable: Britain should reconsider her entire policy towards Sinkiang. She should recognize the fact that the local Chinese government in Kashgar had no independent power and should therefore avoid direct political negotiations with China over Russia's head. She should declare to the Russians that Kashgar was outside the British sphere of interest and seriously consider whether the trade in local products between India and Kashgaria was worth preserving. If it were not, then Macartney should be withdrawn. But if it were retained then he should not continue in his unrecognized position, which was a disgrace to the Indian government. He felt that Russia might withdraw her opposition to a British Consul if Britain made it clear that her purpose was commercial and not political. If Russia did occupy the province then Britain could adjust the balance of power by action in Tibet. In any case, said Macartney, the formation of buffer states to the north of the

121

Mustagh and Karakoram was of questionable value. Britain should concentrate on occupying the strategic passes.

Finally, he disposed of two minor questions still outstanding. Over Raskam Britain should wait until the Chinese had reconstituted their government and then resume negotiations, since Russia had already declared that she would not interfere. Secondly Britain should remove a cause of friction with Russia by stopping all open espionage on Chinese territory. It was preferable to obtain news by a reciprocal agreement with Russia to appoint military attachés at Tashkent and Delhi.

On the minor as on the major issues Macartney's grasp of realities and his judgement could not be questioned. He knew from his daily struggles with the Chinese and the Russians the frustration of powerlessness and the little he could hope to accomplish. The government of India did not dispute his conclusions and yet it chose to ignore them. The reason appeared in a letter that the Viceroy wrote to the Secretary of State in June 1901 in which he summarized his views on Kashgaria. 'We regard it as certain,' he said, 'that Kashgar and the New Dominion will sooner or later fall into the hands of Russia. Our influence and our trade in these regions, such as they are, will then disappear, and we must be prepared to see the Russian frontier conterminous with our own.' This development could not be averted but it could be delayed by diplomacy, and Britain would use every opportunity to protest against Russian advances. There was no point in advancing the British frontier beyond the Hindu Kush but the 'temporary intervention of small belts of unoccupied, or semi-occupied, or neutral territory, though not invested with permanent value, undoubtedly tends to keep the Russian and British borders for a while apart, and gives us the means to negotiate and to bargain when the time of trouble arrives'.

Macartney's role was to act as chief agent of this policy. In a sense he had created it. His appointment, at first entirely unofficial and temporary, had been sanctioned by the government of India with little expectation that it would have any value – hence the lack of any official instructions. The most his superiors expected was that he might survive a year or two at Kashgar to give advance warning of any Russian moves against the British frontier. But Macartney had in fact done a great deal more, and although he deprecated his own role there had been occasions when if he had not been there to advise or to restrain the Taotai Petrovsky might long since have engineered the annexation of Kashgaria. For ten years Macartney had helped to ward off this fate and the government of India saw no reason why they should not continue to profit from his services. What perhaps they did not recognize was the possible psychological strain they were imposing on their agent, as alone, and without official credentials, he laboured at a task that in the end he knew to be hopeless. That Macartney showed no obvious signs of this strain in a position that even the India Office recognized as 'very unpleasant' was the true measure of the worth of this most reticent and diffident of men.

EIGHT

The Move into Sarikol

The comparative tranquillity of Kashgar in the last months of 1900 was broken at the end of January in the new year by what had the makings of a dangerous anti-Russian riot. One of the Russian couriers was holding a party in his house to which he had invited three Cossacks and a Russian customs official. They soon felt the need of feminine company and asked some native prostitutes to join them. Kashgar morality was singularly lax but there was a brooding anti-Russian feeling which could be whipped up by the cry of religion in danger. All the Muslim's jealousy for his womenfolk and hostility towards the arrogant foreigners suddenly turned the apathetic Kashgaris into a dangerous mob. The whole street was in uproar and the crowd was about to attack the Russian's house when the *yamen* Begs appeared at the last moment and dispersed the mob. Petrovsky and the Mayor of Kashgar agreed to hold an inquiry into the affair, but 2000 people went to protest outside the Russian Consulate and several blows were exchanged with Cossacks. The entire guard was then called out and drove the crowd off. It was the first real demonstration of Turki feeling against the Russians, but its chief danger was to the Chinese. At all costs Petrovsky had to be denied any excuse for Russian intervention, and danger to Russian life and property was something that his government would not ignore.

On this occasion Petrovsky did not take the matter further, although in March he intervened in the appointment of a new Mayor of Kashgar. Petrovsky would certainly not tolerate another Lew Ta-lao-yieh in this influential post and he rejected the first official appointed in favour of one who was *persona grata* with the Russian Consul at Urumchi. But the reason was not long forthcoming for his unexpected tolerance in face of the riot, and for the recent change in his attitude to the Taotai, which Macartney had noticed. On 4 February a Russian officer, accompanied by four Cossacks and a further four followers, arrived at Tashkurghan in

Sarikol. They had come from Kashgar and the officer handed to the Amban a letter from the Taotai which said that the men were appointed by the Russian government with the permission of the Governor of Sinkiang to supervise the postal services in Sarikol. The rumour was flying round Sarikol that more Russian troops were to follow and the whole district would soon pass from Chinese to Russian hands.

Petrovsky had matured his plans in secret, and the move took Macartney by surprise. The Russian had clearly decided that his object would more easily be gained by applying the diplomatic pressure that the end of the Boxer rebellion had put at his country's disposal. Hence his change of tactics and the effort he had made to conciliate the Sarikol Begs. In this he was not entirely successful. On 8 February a deputation from Sarikol arrived at Yarkand and presented to the Amban three petitions which bore the seals of six headmen and the thumb-marks of about 100 petty Sarikol officials. They protested against the arrival of the Russians and asked to be given land near Yarkand as they were certain that the Russians would molest them. Petrovsky was also soon to complain to the Taotai about the treatment meted out to the Russian officer in Tashkurghan who was refused the supplies of grain allowed to the English newswriter. The Yarkand Amban tried to reassure the Sarikolis by saying that the Russians were only there to supervise the mails and would have no business with the people. The Sarikolis, like Macartney, were not convinced.

Macartney had immediately reported the Russian move to the government of India and suggested a protest to St Petersburg and the dispatch of a British officer to the Taghdumbash from time to time to assert British interests. The Viceroy at once took up the matter with the India Office and expressed his opinion that the Russian move was the first step towards claiming the entire Taghdumbash and Sarikol. He repeated Macartney's request for a strong protest to St Petersburg. Both the India Office and the Foreign Office took a much more cautious view of the affair and denied that Britain had any right to protest against Russian encroachments in Sarikol if they had the sanction of the Chinese government. The British government, they said, had assured both Russia and China in 1899 that Britain did not claim any territorial rights beyond the Hindu Kush. India must trust to the natural mountain barrier to guard her frontier. This was what

Macartney had said in his long report of the previous December, but the logic of this policy, as he himself had stressed, was his withdrawal from Kashgar. Almost without realizing it his government was expecting him to uphold British interests and prestige in Kashgaria without being willing to pay even the smallest price in his support.

By now Macartney had accustomed himself to this situation and he refrained from further suggestions about opposing the Russians in Sarikol. He merely reported the arrival of Captain Kornilov at Tashkurghan on 26 April and pointed out that he was an intelligence officer. According to an informant Kornilov had spent his time at the Kashgar Consulate preparing maps and statistics of the revenue, land cultivation and military strength of each district of Kashgaria. He was also learning Hindustani and read the Indian newspapers. In Tashkurghan he rented the best house in the town and the rumours continued that the Russians would take over Sarikol. In July Kornilov returned to Russia but his place was taken by Captain Tzaichenko.

Before Kornilov left it was reported that he might urge his government to take Safdar Ali Khan, the deposed Mir of Hunza, under its protection as a way of spreading Russian influence in Hunza. The deposed Mir lived in Urumchi where it was known he frequently saw the Russian Consul. The report from Sarikol acquired sinister meaning when the news came in August that Safdar Ali was to leave Urumchi and move to Yarkand where the Hunza *jagir* had been assigned to him. Macartney could not help feeling uneasy. At Urumchi Safdar Ali was a harmless nonentity, but at Yarkand, in contact with the traders from British India and within easy reach of the Hunza border, he could be a dangerous focus for Kanjuti discontent, a discontent only too likely now that the British had destroyed their traditional way of life. The news made it all the more urgent that the Raskam question should be settled in the Kanjutis' favour.

Meanwhile, Petrovsky was taking steps to strengthen further his country's economic stranglehold over Kashgaria. The bazaar value of the Russian rouble in Kashgar was 8·5 tengas although the official rate of exchange was 10 tengas to the rouble, a rate that Petrovsky was determined to uphold. He severely fined an Andijani who sold his roubles at the bazaar rate and got the Taotai to issue a proclamation fixing the rate at 10 tengas. The same proclamation said that shopkeepers must accept roubles in payment for their goods. The Taotai told Macartney that British traders were not bound by the ruling, but this was little consolation in the face of a proclamation that made Russian currency legal tender in Kashgaria.

This move by Petrovsky was soon followed by news that emphasized the strength of Russia's commercial position. The Peking government's subsidy to Sinkiang was to cease and the province had to find 10 million taels in twenty-five instalments to pay the Japanese indemnity. The Provincial Governor was proposing to find the money by blocking all the salaries of higher officials and by reintroducing transit dues. Russian subjects under their treaty rights would be exempt from duties but the British had no such privilege. The Provincial Governor made one concession: for the time being no taxes would be levied on Indian goods imported by British subjects, but this did not cover the greater part of the trade which was imported by Chinese subjects or by Afghans. The only hope of safeguarding Indian interests was through a strong protest at Peking.

Petrovsky was not satisfied with commercial supremacy. After his success in Sarikol he threw restraint aside and with the new power that the outcome of the Boxer rebellion had given him he brought pressure on Urumchi. His object was complete control over the officials of Kashgaria. One by one his enemies were removed. The first to go was the Amban of Yarkand, his old adversary, Lew, under whom the Hindu traders had flourished. He was replaced in August. Then began the bigger campaign to remove Chang Titai, the man whose manœuvres outside the Russian Consulate at the height of the Boxer rebellion had caused Petrovsky to lose a night's sleep. In October he threatened the Taotai that unless Chang was removed from his post he would increase the number of Russian troops in Kashgar. The Taotai was too feeble to resist although he feared Chang almost as much as Petrovsky. He suggested a replacement, but Petrovsky insisted that only the Titai of Kan Chow would be acceptable to the Consulate. Caught between two fires, the Russians and his own Commander-in-Chief, the Taotai collapsed under the strain and finally solved his problems by dying. His funeral took place on 12 October and Petrovsky attended at the Chinese cemetery with the full dignity of his Cossack guard. Macartney saw him there, but apart from raising their hats to each other the two men did not exchange any greeting.

Macartney had long wished for Huang Taotai's removal in the hope that a successor would take a stronger line with Petrovsky. But Huang had become a familiar part of his life in Kashgar and despite his pathetic inadequacy he had always shown friendliness to Macartney and had been willing at least to listen to his advice. His failings were familiar whereas his successor's were unknown. It was possible that the new Taotai would give up even Huang's shreds of independence and be ruled entirely from the Russian Consulate.

Huang had died before anything was settled about the fate of Chang Titai and scarcely was the funeral over before Chang took the offensive. He started a campaign for the posthumous degradation of Huang on the grounds that he had betrayed Chinese interests by his weakness towards the Russian Consul. Macartney noticed that Chang had stiffened the attitude of the Chinese officials, and that their bearing towards the Russians, although correct, was now much more dignified. Despite Chang's local support he could not command the wider influence of Petrovsky, and the Russian was bent on his destruction. The Provincial Governor rejected the petition for Huang's degradation on the grounds that the late Taotai had been well intentioned and his failings were the result of ill health. Petrovsky then telegraphed the Governor asking for the fulfilment of his promise that Chang should be removed. The new Taotai was apparently commissioned by the Governor to reconcile Petrovsky and Chang, but, perhaps wisely, he refrained from the attempt. Then in March 1902 the order came from Peking that Chang should revert to his previous subordinate post as Chantai of Aksu. Petrovsky's nominee, Tsiao, was appointed to succeed him at Kashgar.

Petrovsky had boasted of Chang's removal three weeks before the order came through and everyone in Sarikol had known of the affair before Chang was officially informed. The result was striking. Macartney commented: 'The moral effect of Petrovsky's, or more correctly, of the Russian Minister's victory, has been splendid for Russian prestige, which now, in Kashgar and in Sarikol, simply carries everything before it.' It was not a good portent for the reign of Chu Ta-jen, the new Taotai, who had taken up his duties in Kashgar on 13 January. With a Commander-in-Chief who was Petrovsky's nominee and with his superiors in Urumchi and Peking subject to Russian pressure there was little hope of Chinese independence in Kashgar.

The Russians were using every means to increase their influence in Sarikol. The Russian officer in Tashkurghan asked for more men to be stationed on the passes on the grounds that the British had appointed two men to watch the Mintaka and Dafdar passes. Two Sarikoli Begs were active in spreading false reports about the British government, and Cossacks several times obstructed the servant of the British-paid Sarikol newswriter. In January the rumour spread that the Russian guard at Tashkurghan would be increased to fifty.

But Petrovsky was not entirely in control of his country's policy in Kashgaria. The wheels moved slowly at the highest levels of diplomacy but the promise the British government had extracted from St Petersburg that the Russians would not oppose the Raskam grant at last began to bear fruit. The first hint came in January 1902 when Petrovsky instructed his Chinese secretary to investigate which holdings in Raskam were sought by the Kanjutis. Later Macartney learnt that the Peking government had arranged with the British and Russian Ministers to lease five holdings in Raskam to the Kanjutis provided the Russians did not object to the sites chosen. Petrovsky was appointed to inspect them. The Consul's tactics, as could be anticipated, were prevarication and delay. He announced he could do nothing without referring to higher authority. Macartney's comment on the situation was: 'It looks as if the battledore and shuttlecock game between Petrovsky and his superiors is to be resumed.'

Throughout February 1902 the Consul continued to assert the same reasons for his failure to inspect the Raskam holdings. Then at the end of the month Macartney reported seeing the son of Safdar Ali at the Mayor of Kashgar's *yamen*. It immediately occurred to him that Petrovsky might be planning to use the Raskam concession to his own advantage. When the lease was made the Chinese would need a Beg to administer the area for them, and if Safdar Ali or his son Muzaffar Khan could obtain the post with Russian backing they would become a direct rallying point for Kanjuti discontent. Macartney saw the same motive behind Petrovsky's request to the Provincial Governor that Safdar Ali's arrival at Yarkand should be delayed lest it should complicate the Raskam question. In Macartney's view Petrovsky had every intention of making Raskam into a source of trouble for the British but he was subtle enough to see that 'the appointment of a keeper, before the beast has been properly brought into existence' might alarm his opponents prematurely.

In Sarikol Petrovsky's policy of penetration and absorption was succeeding with few complications or opposition. The Russian officer at Tashkurghan gave a dinner to seven of the local Begs in the course of which, according to information received at Kashgar, they invited him to send for the Russian troops at Murghabi and to occupy Tagharma during the absence of the Amban of Sarikol. The Taotai immediately ordered the Amban back to his post but it was obvious to observers that the Sarikolis were becoming nervous and were inclining towards the Russians. In May there was a legal case in Tashkurghan involving a Russian soldier and the pro-British Karim Beg. From it three results emerged, all favourable to Russian interests; the case established that the Amban could not hear alone suits involving Russian subjects; the threat to Karim Beg led the Sarikolis to conclude that for their own protection they should support the Russian cause; thirdly, the obvious weakness of the Amban gave the impression that the Chinese were afraid of the Russians. By June, predictably enough, it could be said that all the families, apart from two in the Taghdumbash, had been brought under Russian control, and there were signs now of their obstructing everyone who was not pro-Russian. Macartney was actively made aware of this when a band of Sarikolis waylaid the Hunza couriers on their way from Tashkurghan and forced them back. In Macartney's view the Amban of Sarikol was not ill disposed to the British but to make him actively friendly it was necessary to show that Britain had the power to remove him by bringing pressure to bear in Peking. If this could not be done then the Russians would be left in the ascendancy in Sarikol.

This was Macartney's last report on Sarikol before he left Kashgar for his third period of leave in England. But before Captain Miles, who was appointed to act in his absence, took over his duties, Macartney left on record another serious warning about the undermining of British interests in Kashgaria. In March Macartney had heard from the Kashgar officials that the province was in financial trouble because of the demand made by Peking for 400,000 taels a year towards the Japanese indemnity. It seemed that there were only two ways of meeting it; either customs duties would be reimposed on foreign trade, or the Russo-Chinese Bank would come to the 'assistance' of the province in return for rich concessions. The Bank was already spreading its tentacles over the economy of Kashgaria, and in the same month Petrovsky proposed to the Taotai that Russian silver should be regularly accepted by the Chinese mint, which Macartney saw as the Bank's first measure to control the mint.

The local officials were at first opposed to the reimposition of customs duties on the grounds that it would injure home trade, but in June, only a few days before he left Kashgar, Macartney saw the new tariff regulations which re-established in its entirety the customs system as it had been before 1893. Indian trade, whether carried on by British or Chinese subjects, would have export or import duties to pay at Kilian, and further transit duties would be imposed at interior barriers in towns such as Maralbashi and Aksu. Russian subjects, of course, were exempt from the duties and so would become once more a highly privileged class. Macartney recognized that a protest would be useless as the Russians had acquiesced in the system.

This blow to British trade, added to all the evidence of growing Russian dominance and of the success of Russian designs in Sarikol, was not a comforting reflection for Macartney as he prepared for his leave in England. Again he must have wondered if there would still be a post for him in Kashgar when his leave was over. The day before he left he resolved to break the long silence in his relations with Petrovsky and he called at the Russian Consulate.

After a period of two and a half years of living in the same small town while completely ignoring his fellow European's existence, the Russian Consul, unpredictable as always, gave Macartney the warmest of welcomes. Petrovsky, when he chose to be, was irresistible, and Macartney might have left Kashgar in an atmosphere of eternal Russo-British friendship. But he was experienced enough in the ways of the Consul to realize that Petrovsky was at his friendliest when he had least regard for his opponent's power. Petrovsky showing warm feelings and cordiality meant that he considered British influence almost extinct in Kashgaria, and inwardly Macartney could not help but agree with him. It had been an unequal contest from the beginning between the two men. Petrovsky had every advantage on his side; Macartney had none. Now the Consul, too, was thinking of a long leave, but in this last interview with Macartney he was sure that his work had triumphed. He could afford to be generous to the man who had so little to show for his twelve years in Kashgar. On 23 June Macartney and his wife left. It was to be almost two years before they returned.

Captain Miles took up Macartney's duties in the warm sun of Petrovsky's cordiality and his first reports described further Russian gains. They were establishing their own post office at Kashgar and were proposing to extend their telegraph line from Osh to Irkeshtam, and possibly to Kashgar. Furthermore, they were planning a permanent building to house their troops at Tashkurghan. For his part Miles found that the reimposition of customs duties by the Chinese was beginning to have an effect and he brought up the need to register British subjects to stop merchants from changing their nationality to suit their convenience. It was not only the customs dues that were threatening British trade; *charas*, which was one of the main exports, was proving unprofitable in India, so the traders were finding it difficult to remit their money. When the Russo-Chinese Bank started importing silver, which it sold at a profit to the Kashgar mint, Miles asked the Taotai if Indian silver would be accepted as the current rates of exchange offered Indian merchants a profit of 30 per cent. Permission was refused and the Russo-Chinese Bank continued to strengthen its hold on the currency. Before long it was proposing to do business in Chinese coins as well as in roubles as part of the Russian strategy to control the economy of the province.

The Chinese on their side were using every means to extract more money from the population to pay the instalment on the Japanese indemnity. Double the usual revenue was collected from the landowners in the Kashgar district and there were signs of active discontent among the people. The local temper was not improved by a series of earthquake tremors in the summer of 1902, a summer of extreme heat. One tremor destroyed the large village of Artush, causing the death of about 700 people and injuring another 1000. Financial stringency spurred the Chinese to attempt some economic enterprise. The Russians were employing their own

Above The Macartney
family in 1913 with
Macartney's brother Donald
at the back of the group

Macartney with
his son Eric in 1913

The British Consulate-General in Kashgar after it was rebuilt in 1913

geologists in the region, and rather belatedly some Chinese mining engineers began to examine the gold deposits near Khotan. A new Taotai, Yuen Wung-fu, who took office in February 1903, brought money in from Shanghai to develop the gold mining industry in Keriya, but he succeeded only in losing most of his capital. A more profitable speculation were the Chinese government lotteries which began in the province, trading on the fever for gambling in the country. These promised to make a profit of 25 per cent for the government.

Over one of their economic measures the Chinese had second thoughts. Shortly after the new customs regulations had come into force the Taotai announced that British-Indian subjects and their goods would be treated in the same way as the Russians and that this privilege would be extended to Afghans and to Indians domiciled in Kashgaria. This was a relief to traders but it immediately exacerbated the nationality problem. Miles received numerous petitions for certificates of British nationality. He refused to grant any until he had received instructions from India about who could rightly claim them. His only guidelines were proposals that Macartney had sent to the Resident in Kashmir in June 1901. He had suggested that Hindus should always enjoy British protection, irrespective of their domicile, but that any Indian or Kashmiri Muslims who had not visited British India for five years or more should be classed as immigrants and as Chinese subjects. Macartney had stressed that Britain was only concerned to protect her traders and was not interested in giving British nationality to large numbers of people who only sought it for motives of personal gain. He thought that the Chinese would agree to his proposals. But the government of India was averse to laying down any rules and told Miles to treat each case on its individual merits. They deprecated any special activity over the nationality question, presumably to avoid rousing Chinese hostility, and rejected the suggestion Miles had made that Afghans should be able to claim 'most favoured nation' treatment through him.

The concession the Chinese had given to British trading interests was more than matched by Russian gains in Sarikol. For some time since Macartney's departure Petrovsky had been pressing the Taotai to allow the Russians to build their own quarters at Tashkurghan. The Taotai had referred the request to the Provincial Governor who had refused. The most he would allow was that the Chinese should put up a building which the Russians could rent from them. Petrovsky was not prepared to accept this decision and he asked his Minister at Peking to intervene. Within a month or two it was reported that the Russians had begun building their own quarters. From the foundations they were laying it appeared to the Sarikol newswriter that the building was to be a military fort. By August 1903 it was housing nineteen Russian soldiers as opposed to the five who had originally manned the post. A cart track was also opened between Murghabi and Tashkurghan. Clearly the Russians had more in mind than the supervision of postal services.

The other Russian triumph in Sarikol was the appointment of a new Amban in place of the one who, though weak, had not shown himself entirely ready to fall in with Russian demands. The new official was a civilian, the secretary of the Foreign Commerce Office, who spoke Russian, and in Miles's opinion was no more than a Russian official. The English newswriter was soon reporting that the new Amban received him with scant attention whereas the Russian commandant was accorded a full ceremonial reception.

It was at this high-water mark of Russian prestige and influence that Petrovsky chose in August 1903 to slip quietly out of Kashgar to begin his leave in St Petersburg. Those who saw him go reported that he seemed frail and in bad health. In fact he was not to return. His secretary, a young man called de Lavroff, took over his duties. Petrovsky left Kashgar in the belief that some of his most cherished plans were coming to fruition: Russian power was firmly established in Sarikol, poised when the opportunity offered, for another leap forward; the local Chinese officials were subservient to his will and Peking bowed before the wishes of the Russian Minister; Russian traders and the powerful organization of the Russo-Chinese Bank had the economy of Kashgaria in their grip, and Petrovsky had succeeded in blocking the chief aims of British policy in the area. He could take his leave in the conviction that Kashgaria was Russia's to do with what she wanted.

Britain, though, was not so defeatist about her position in Kashgaria as at first sight appeared. At the very time that Petrovsky was packing for his leave the government of India was again pressing on London the necessity for Macartney's official recognition as

Consul in Kashgar. In their view the Chinese had never disputed the principle of appointing a British representative; it was only a question of bargaining over the terms. For once they received some support from the British Minister in Peking, Sir Ernest Satow. He suggested that the Foreign Office should appoint Macartney as Consul without first asking the Chinese government, a proposal for which there were two precedents. Macartney was consulted about this plan in England, and agreed to it although he warned that only the strongest pressure would make the Chinese consent and that opposition must be expected from Russia.

Macartney can have had little hope that an official announcement from London would make any difference to his status in Kashgar. But he was not to know when he was preparing for his return to Sinkiang at the beginning of 1904 that international affairs were moving towards an unexpected adjustment of the balance of power in Asia. In January 1902 Britain had agreed with Japan on a formal treaty of alliance. From the British point of view it secured Japanese recognition of British interests in China and was a powerful means of diminishing the Russian menace in Asia. Tokyo considered that the treaty gave her British recognition as a world power and acknowledged her aspirations in Korea. In Japanese eyes it also protected her from outside interference in a possible war against Russia. Japan immediately set out to secure from Russia acknowledgement of her 'unique status' in Korea in return for recognizing Russian gains in Manchuria. When Russia showed herself unwilling to concede all these demands the Japanese government severed diplomatic relations and immediately blockaded the Russian base at Port Arthur, attacked Russian ships at sea, and landed a military expedition in Korea. Before war was formally declared on 10 February 1904 Japan had control of the sea. There followed a series of naval and military disasters for Russia in which her losses were staggering and outnumbered Japanese casualties by more than three to one.

The effect on Russian prestige throughout Asia was immediate. As early as the end of February 1904 news of Russian defeats was circulating round Kashgar although the Consulate preserved silence on the progress of the war. It was not only Russian prestige that was involved. The Japanese victories were the first of an Asiatic people over a European power since the Opium War had

135

first exposed China's weakness to the outside world. Now Japan had proved that the Europeans were not invincible and throughout China revolutionary thought and action, although still insignificant, began slowly to grow in strength, fed by rising nationalism. It was to this China that Macartney now returned.

NINE

Diplomatic Adjustments

Macartney and his wife had intended to spend only one year in England on leave but their first child, Eric, was born in September 1903 just before they were due to return to Kashgar. Macartney was granted a further extension of leave and the next few months were spent in preparing Eric for the rigours of the journey through Central Asia. The baby was taken out in the coldest weather and was given only cold milk to drink. In February 1904 the five month old traveller set out with his parents to cross Russia and the cruel passes of Turkestan. It says much for Catherine Macartney's spirit that she was determined that nothing should divide her family. No matter how arduous the conditions or how remote from European schools or medicine she was resolved that she and her husband and children should not be separated. Her courage was matched by that of the nurse she took back to Kashgar with her. Miss Fanny Heath was no longer young and had been with Catherine's family since her childhood, but so great was her sense of family loyalty that even the unknown terrors of barbarous lands could not separate her from her charge. Macartney himself, whose reports usually excluded any reference to his personal affairs, could not help but express his pride in his son by announcing that he arrived on 8 April in Kashgar, 'with my family'.

His appointment by the British government as their official Consul in Kashgar had already been gazetted in London, a fact that could not escape either the Chinese or the Russians, but there was complete silence on the question in Kashgar. The Taotai had received a telegram from the Provincial Governor saying that the Chinese Minister in London wanted every attention shown to Macartney on his arrival, and both the Chinese and the Russians met him with evident courtesy and help. It was some compensation for his lack of recognition, although this caused him no great surprise. He knew that an announcement in London would not greatly affect the issue in China so he contented himself with

137

asking the British Minister in Peking for instructions on his status. The reply came that he was to wait, and in July the Chinese government instructed the Taotai that they had refused to agree to the establishment of a British Consulate in Kashgar.

Nothing appeared to have changed, except that Macartney heard from de Lavroff, the acting Russian Consul, that Petrovsky had definitely retired from public service, and his successor was to be Kolokoloff, his former secretary. At least Macartney could expect less consistent hostility from the Russian Consulate, and in Kolokoloff a pale imitation, rather than the lion himself.

The first reports of Russian activities, though, were not reassuring. In Baku Macartney himself had learnt that 80,000 Russian troops were being sent either to the Persian or the Afghan border, and he had found the station at Krasnovodsk full of officers and troops who were said to be moving up to Afghanistan. Reports reached India that the army of Turkestan was fully mobilized and the Cossacks at the Kashgar Consulate were boasting of its numbers and of the reinforcements that could shortly be poured in when the Orenburg–Tashkent railway was completed. The Consulate guard itself was to be doubled from fifty to a hundred men.

The government of India and the Foreign Office in London were concerned at these developments while at a loss to explain them satisfactorily. The British Ambassador in St Petersburg thought that the Russians were deliberately trying to create a scare in India to stop the British from interfering in the peace negotiations with Japan. An intelligence report sent to the Foreign Office suggested three other explanations: the Russian troop movements might be aimed at compelling China to remain neutral by threatening Sinkiang; Russia might be merely strengthening her frontier against a possible combination of the Afghans with the Muslim tribes of Central Asia; or it might be a Russian move against Kashgar in reply to the British action in Tibet.

The government of India had sent troops into Tibet in December 1903 in a determined attempt to exclude Russian influence and to stop the Tibetans' violation of the Sikkim frontier. The expedition fought its way to Lhasa at the beginning of August 1904. The Dalai Lama had fled with his Russian adviser and in September the British signed a peace treaty which gave them what they wanted, including an indemnity and the provision of three centres for their trade. The Russians had every reason to retaliate but it was difficult to see what they could gain by advancing on Kashgar as their hands were already full with the war against Japan. As the magnitude of Russia's defeat became apparent any possible threat in Central Asia diminished and the reports of troop movements, which had been exaggerated in the first place, gradually died away. By August it was reported that Russian Turkestan was only garrisoned by second-class reservists of advanced age.

Macartney's personal relations with the staff of the Russian Consulate remained friendly, although there had been an incident in which the Cossacks had diverted all the water supply from Chini Bagh. This had been sorted out satisfactorily with apologies. The Russians could not conceal their anxiety about the Japanese war and were aware of their loss of prestige in Kashgaria. The old aggressive policy of Petrovsky was scarcely possible or appropriate, but the Russians did not intend to let the Chinese make capital out of their defeat. A joint Russo-Chinese commission had been appointed to settle all outstanding civil and criminal cases between the two nationalities, and the commissioners were due to arrive in Kashgar in August 1904. The Chinese had been making great preparations for their reception since their chief commissioner was a Manchu nobleman, imperially appointed. The Russians, however, did everything to belittle the status of their commissioner to show that a man of the lowest Russian rank was good enough as a colleague for the Chinese commissioner. Their representative was only the head clerk in the office of the Governor of Semiretchia, and not one Russian turned out to greet him when he arrived in Kashgar. The commission had to deal with 1700 Chinese complaints against Russians and 2800 Russian complaints against Chinese. Many of the cases were ten years old.

Macartney, too, was swamped by traders' suits which, without Chinese cooperation, were proving difficult to deal with. The District Magistrate of Kashgar, the Taotai's deputy, paid no attention to them. He was the son of the general who had reconquered Chinese Turkestan in 1877, and was very young for one of the most lucrative posts in the province. He was renowned for his laziness and luxuriousness, and Macartney's efforts to secure his cooperation were fruitless. The customs levied on non-British subjects continued to make the nationality problem troublesome, and Macartney received a deputation of Baltis from Yarkand who asked to be enrolled as British subjects and to be relieved from customs dues. When he visited Yarkand in the autumn Macartney was petitioned by the Afghans for British protection and he foresaw a growing problem from the Shikarpuri moneylenders who were flocking into Yarkand in ever-growing numbers and whose trade was bringing the name of the government of India into disrepute.

The Chinese naturally resented the increasing numbers of those who sought to evade taxation by claiming foreign nationality. In Yarkand this resentment showed itself in September 1904 when the Amban flogged eighteen men and paraded them through the streets with boards round their necks while they were made to cry out 'This is the punishment for those who petition to the Farangis.' Prince Louis d'Orléans had passed through Yarkand on a tour through Kashgaria and the prisoners had petitioned him for exemption from customs duties. Macartney took up the case because, as he told the Amban, everyone understood 'Farangi' to mean the British. The Amban agreed to punish the orderlies who were responsible for the parade and British prestige rose accordingly. Macartney also told the Amban that he felt himself bound to protect the interests of the Afghans, although he was aware that in this he was going beyond his official instructions.

The point did not escape the government of India who ordered him only to use his good offices in an informal way on the Afghans' behalf. Macartney defended himself by pointing out that there were between 300 and 400 Afghans in Kashgaria and theirs was a waiting game, always ready to play off the Chinese against the British and vice versa. It was important to pre-empt their interest for Britain and to make sure that the Chinese understood this. These views, though, evoked little enthusiasm in higher quarters and Macartney had to drop his scheme for taking the Afghans under his protection.

At much the same time Macartney was putting forward fresh ideas on the Hunza problem in answer to the Resident in Kashmir's request for his views on Hunza's rights over the Taghdumbash Pamir. Before and since 1891 the Kanjutis had levied taxes in kind from the Wakhanis on the Taghdumbash Pamir south of Dafdar, but the Chinese claimed for themselves two valleys which the government of India wanted within its own frontier. In

140

Macartney's opinion the Chinese would never allow the Kanjutis to claim territorial jurisdiction over the area and would turn them out by force if they tried. If Britain claimed Darwaz, which was within the actual territorial limits of the Mir of Hunza, Russia would almost certainly seek a new adjustment of her frontier with Kashgaria. Since the Raskam question showed little signs of solution and the Mir of Hunza appeared to be losing interest, as he realized that any Kanjutis who went to Raskam would more or less become Chinese subjects, Macartney recommended a complete change of policy. He advised the government of India to barter Hunza's claims to Raskam for its release from Chinese suzerainty, and then to bring up the question of Hunza's frontiers. They could either claim the Taghdumbash area in virtue of Hunza's rights and as a recompense for the presence of Russian troops in Sarikol, or they could leave the country under Chinese control if the Chinese renounced their rights to cede it to a third power or to station European troops there.

For once Macartney's views were eagerly adopted by the government of India and they urged the Secretary of State to follow a policy which in return for abandoning all Hunza's claims to Raskam and the Taghdumbash provided for the severance of Hunza's relations with China, the inclusion within the British frontier of the small projection beyond the watershed near the Shimshal Pass and Darwaz, and the recognition of Macartney as Consul in Kashgar. But again the Foreign Office had other priorities, and Lord Lansdowne, the Foreign Secretary, refused to press these terms until he had secured China's adhesion to the Lhasa Convention which was designed to settle the problem of Tibet. On Christmas Eve 1904 Macartney received a telegram from the British Minister in Peking telling him not to assume the title of Consul at least until the negotiations over Tibet were settled. Once again he could only wait patiently.

In October 1904 Kolokoloff had returned to Kashgar as Petrovsky's successor, and he and Macartney were soon on friendly terms. It was obvious that the new Consul had no intention of imitating either Petrovsky's policy or his methods. He had returned from a stay at Port Arthur with what Macartney described as 'revolutionary ideas of the most pronounced order'. He spoke strongly in condemnation of the Russo-Japanese war and of

Russian policy generally in the Far East and even went so far as to say that Russia should have a constitutional government. He confided to Macartney his fear of Colonel Lastochkin, the Russian intelligence officer at Kashgar, whom he described as a dangerous, ambitious man, hostile to Kolokoloff. In the Consul's view Lastochkin wanted to stir up trouble between Britain and Russia and he sent sensational reports to Tashkent, including one that the British were preparing to occupy Sarikol in the spring.

Kolokoloff's confidences even extended to his showing Macartney the instructions he had received from his government about not recognizing Macartney as Consul. The Russian warned Macartney that the British government would have a hard struggle to secure his recognition, but that now was the best time to press his claims as the war party in Russia was discredited and the moderate counsels of the Foreign Ministry might prevail. He promised Macartney friendly personal cooperation in the settlement of cases, but officially he could have no dealings with him, either direct or indirect. Kolokoloff continued to express himself as full of good intentions, but twelve months later Macartney commented ruefully that he was still waiting to see the proof of them in results, which were then conspicuous by their absence.

Russian influence in Sarikol had waned, and instead of bullying the people the Russians were going out of their way to conciliate them with presents. But apart from this, and despite Kolokoloff's protestations, little had changed outwardly in Russian policy. At the beginning of 1905, de Lavroff, who remained as secretary at the Consulate, left for a tour of the southern oases, on what Macartney called a 'filibustering mission' to revive Russian prestige. He spent part of his time preparing lists of the Andijani inhabitants and Macartney thought that the Russians might be planning additional consular representation beyond the provisions of the Treaty of St Petersburg.

In April Kolokoloff put two proposals to the Taotai. One was harmless enough – that Kashgar should have electric lighting –. but the other had more sinister implications: that the Kashgar–Naryn trade route should be made fit for wheeled traffic. Macartney warned the Taotai of the military significance of this road to Russia and told him that if he agreed to Kolokoloff's proposals he was preparing an invasion route for Russian use. The Taotai was fully aware of the road's military possibilities and he refused his consent although he agreed that Kashgar should have electric lighting.

Later that year Macartney went on a short reconnaissance towards the Russo-Chinese border by way of the Kashgar–Naryn route to see if there were any truth in the vague rumours that the Russians were preparing a move into Kashgaria. There was no evidence to be seen of any preparations, but in the last few months the Russians had built a cart road from the crest of the Turgat Pass to At Bashi near Naryn. The new road was 27 feet wide and the Russians had also carried a section down the Chinese side of the pass about half a mile long. Macartney found that the road between the Turgat Pass and Kashgar could easily be made fit for wheeled vehicles, which would give good communications with the Russian military depot at Almati. This, if any, would be the likely route for an invasion.

If the Russians should move the Chinese could do little about it as the whole country was quite ungarrisoned by Chinese troops. Only a short time before, the Kashgar officials had dissuaded the Provincial Governor from visiting Kashgar and inspecting the frontier. In Macartney's view they had bribed him not to make the inspection because they did not wish him to see the shortage of troops and their administrative malpractices. They had resisted his orders to raise native troops on the grounds that they could not be trusted and there was no free land available for them to cultivate. Macartney's comment on Chinese defences was: 'The tomfoolery that passed for soldiering years ago is still what is practised, and the whole situation is conspicuous by its utter absence of military regeneration.' He advised his government to press for permission to mend the trade route on the Chinese side of the Karakoram Pass as this might stiffen the Chinese to resist further Russian demands.

The Russians, though, were not to be resisted. In October Kolokoloff visited the Taotai accompanied by a Russian official who had made the cart road from At Bashi to the Turgat Pass. Together they pressed the Taotai for an extension of the road to Kashgar on the grounds that it would cut by half the cost of transporting goods from At Bashi. The Taotai refused to agree saying he had no funds for the purpose and he could not use the Kirghiz for forced labour. Kolokoloff then claimed that the English were employing two American travellers, Barrett and Huntingdon, to repair roads for them near Keriya and Polu, and if the Taotai allowed this he could also let the Russians build roads. The most they could get from the Taotai, though, was that he would have to refer the matter to Peking.

Kolokoloff's reaction showed that he had learned his profession under Petrovsky. He summoned the leading traders of Kashgar and told them he was thinking of refusing them Russian visas and of stopping the export of their goods. His excuse was the large number of unsettled debts owed to Russian subjects. One merchant had the temerity to say that Russia gained by the Chinese trade, a remark that infuriated the Consul. The traders were unaware of the accumulation of debts to which the Consul referred and they saw as the real cause of his threats the Taotai's refusal to build the cart road from the Turgat Pass to Kashgar. The Taotai did not weaken under pressure but the Provincial Governor, instead of supporting his stand, merely referred the responsibility for a decision back to him. The Taotai again told Kolokoloff that he had no funds to build the road and for the time being the matter rested there.

Events in Russia in the autumn of 1905 did not encourage the Russians to continue their threatening attitude. Towards the end of December reports came through to Kashgar of trouble in Tashkent. The railway stopped running and Kolokoloff told Macartney that because of strikes he had received no letters or telegrams from Russia for a fortnight. This was the first that Macartney heard of the attempted revolution of 1905 which had begun in January with Bloody Sunday in St Petersburg. Industrial strikes, demonstrations and mutinies had been followed by violent peasant risings. At the end of August Russia had concluded her disastrous war with Japan by ceding the southern Manchurian peninsula with the ice-free Port Arthur and the southern half of the island of Sakhalin and she had recognized Korea as a Japanese sphere of influence. The war had started the ferment in Russia but the peace did not end it. Throughout the countryside the peasants rose and seized the private estates. The revolution reached its climax in October in a nationwide strike which brought the country almost to a standstill. Count Witte defeated the revolution and temporarily saved the monarchy by forcing the Tsar to agree to the popular election of a *duma* which drew moderate opinion to the government's side. It was not until December, though, that the government was strong enough to strike at the St Petersburg soviet, and with the suppression of a rising in Moscow, was able to begin the task of restoring law and order by repressive measures throughout the empire.

Had the government of India realized the full extent of Russia's internal dislocation throughout most of 1905 it would not have worried about rumours of a move into Kashgaria. But as it was, Russia's worst troubles were over by the time Macartney and the Chinese authorities in Kashgar realized that their overbearing neighbour had been temporarily crippled. The Russian government's recovery of its power and nerve did not make Macartney's relations with Kolokoloff any easier. By March 1906 he was complaining that Kolokoloff's expressions of friendship did not help to settle his trading cases. The following month was spent by Macartney in Yarkand where he received unprecedented attention from the Chinese officials. When he returned to Kashgar the Russian Consul immediately engaged him in a hot discussion over commercial contracts between Russian and British subjects. Kolokoloff said these were not valid unless they were attested by the Russian Consul or by a Kazi (judge). When Macartney said he would warn British traders of this Kolokoloff told him that if he did so he would prohibit Andijanis from trading with British subjects. He said Macartney was not to send over any more petitions from British traders and added, 'The fact was . . . there was a Russian Consul here and no British one.'

Macartney was not provoked by this childish outburst and changed the subject without further comment. He was convinced that the reason for it was his own friendly reception at Yarkand and Kolokoloff's recent lack of success in dealing with the Chinese. Macartney's discretion, though, did not appease Kolokoloff and for the second time in his career at Kashgar Macartney found himself ignored by the Russian Consul. This time the breach lasted for a year.

The difference between the two men, which Kolokoloff never openly explained, led both sides to use the Chinese as intermediaries in settling cases between Russian and British subjects. This measure was both undignified and unproductive and led Macartney to comment: 'That two European officers cannot treat face to face, but must dodge each other around the Chinese is a spectacle which must give infinite amusement to the latter, but at the expense of the former.' The sooner that a British Consulate was established, he said, the more dignified it would be. There were hopes at last of some move in this direction. In June the Resident in Kashmir wrote to the government of India that since China had agreed to Britain's treaty with Tibet the time had now come to press for Macartney's recognition. 'Mr Macartney,' the Resident wrote, 'has in my opinion only been able to cope with the existing situation by his great ability and *personal* influence.' The government of India said it had no objection to the Foreign Office raising the matter in Peking at once, so again Macartney had cause to hope for the long-awaited recognition.

Nineteen hundred and six was proving to be a year of changes for him. In the spring his daughter Sylvia was born and in August he heard that his father, Sir Halliday Macartney, had died. When the news was announced all the Chinese officials in Kashgar called in a body to offer their condolences. The death of a father was always an awesome event to the Chinese but in the death of Halliday Macartney even the officials at Kashgar realized that China had lost a faithful servant. Another personal loss to Macartney was the death in June of his old friend Father Hendricks whose generous nature and intellectual gifts Macartney alone had valued at their true worth. The old priest had suffered in his last few months from cancer of the throat and despite the Macartneys' pleas that he should be nursed at Chini Bagh he preferred to die in the sordid hovel that had been his home for the last few years in Kashgar. Since relations had been severed with the Russian Consulate Macartney had now only his family and the Swedish missionaries to provide sympathetic companionship.

Apart from these personal changes there was little alteration in the problems Macartney had to deal with. The Hunza question still dragged on intermittently as neither the Russians nor the Chinese had any real interest in its solution. Since the government of India had ceased to press for the Raskam leases Safdar Ali had disappeared into the background. He had bought a house and land at Kucha and reports spoke of his fast becoming a drunkard. Then in May 1905 the deposed Mir's son, a young man of about twenty called Muzaffar Khan, paid a visit to Macartney in Kashgar and explained his wish to obtain a post under the government of India. He had, reported Macartney, 'a noble and prepossessing appearance', and had no wish to return to Hunza. Macartney was in favour of showing sympathy to the family to stop them from becoming the tools of Russia, and he argued the case for giving the son employment in India where he would always be under the government's eye.

At the beginning of 1906 Safdar Ali sent a further petition to Macartney in which he asked for asylum and a pension for himself and his sons in Kashmir. It was soon followed by a report from Sarikol that Karim Beg was planning to marry Safdar Ali's youngest daughter. In Macartney's view this could result in Karim Beg's house in Tashkurghan becoming an agency for spreading the influence of Safdar Ali's son into Hunza and for passing on Hunza news to the Russians at Tashkurghan. In these circumstances Macartney urged the government of India to give Safdar Ali what he asked for and to allow him to live in Kashmir with a pension where he would be under full British control. Reluctant to commit itself to any definite policy over Hunza, the government of India replied that it did not propose to take any action for the time being. Macartney must have wondered privately whether it was worth thinking about Hunza at all as his superiors seemed so reluctant to act on his advice.

Hunza was not the only familiar problem. Despite the severe setbacks of the Russo-Japanese war and the 1905 revolution, which still lingered on in strikes and demonstrations in Tashkent, the Russian Consulate in Kashgar was quick to reassert itself. In September 1906 the Taotai at last gave in to Russian pressure and agreed to build the road from the Turgat Pass to Kashgar on condition that he received a loan for the purpose from the Russo-Chinese Bank. A loan of 20,000 roubles was negotiated which was to be recouped by tolls on the road. Construction was begun immediately under the supervision of the Amban of Sarikol. At the same time Macartney received reports that the Russians were making the Andijan–Naryn road fit for wheeled traffic which meant that they would have a cart road from the railway at Andijan right through to Kashgar. It was a strategic triumph achieved at minimal cost, and was completed by the contract that Kolokoloff negotiated with the Chinese in December. This gave the Russo-Chinese Bank the monopoly of all the transport of goods, mail and passengers between Kashgar and Andijan in return for an annual payment to the Russian and Chinese governments. The

Bank planned to provide its own carts and to give loans to its customers for transport at lower interest. It was an economic as well as a strategic gain for Russia.

Macartney had no gains of his own to offset the Russian success. Instead his troubles appeared to increase. He came into conflict with the Taotai over an attempt by the new owners of the Hindu traders' quarters to force them out by hanging fresh sheep and cowskins on the veranda. The Taotai refused to act in the matter and Macartney was made aware that there was a trial of strength between them. He could not understand the Taotai's attitude although he knew he was ill thought of by the Provincial Governor. In Macartney's opinion the Taotai did little beyond playing cards with his subordinates, and he had acquired a reputation for 'jobbery and graspingness, rare even amongst Chinese officials'. How much the Russian success over the Turgat road was due to the Taotai's propensities was a matter of speculation, but there was much cause for suspicion.

Yarkand provided more worries. The Amban was uncooperative in settling traders' suits, but this was nothing to the trouble that was brewing there between the British-Hindu traders and the local Muslim population. For some time Macartney had warned his superiors of its likelihood as the number of Shikarpuri moneylenders arriving in the country grew year by year. At the end of 1905 there were 400 in Kashgaria and the following year a further fifty arrived. Such was the local taste for gambling that their services were much sought after, and at interest rates of 10 per cent per month the profits made the risks worth while. Macartney had always refused to take up moneylending cases as he knew he would be flooded by hundreds of applications, and he let the Shikarpuris see plainly that he had no sympathy with their trade. When he toured the southern oases he was besieged by hundreds of their destitute victims and he warned his superiors of the discredit that the moneylenders were bringing on the Indian government. The evil was not one sided. From his investigations Macartney concluded that the Shikarpuris kept their books honestly and although they bullied their debtors where they could the borrower's attitude was careless and happy-go-lucky and he generally sought to repudiate his debts. The tensions and hatreds, though, continued to grow.

This was the background to an incident in Yarkand in March

1907 which had the makings of an ugly situation threatening the whole British position in Kashgaria. It began when a group of Muslims accused a Hindu of taking a Muslim woman to live with him. A crowd of 400 or 500 men soon gathered eager to create a disturbance and the Muslims went on to accuse the Hindus of insulting their mosques. The Amban tried somewhat weakly to work for a compromise, and as soon as he heard of the situation Macartney set off for Yarkand. He was met at the gates by a mob of 5000 to 6000 people who jostled him and shouted accusations against the Hindus. Feelings were running at a high pitch and the Muslims were bent on forcing the Hindus into an abject surrender. The Andijanis were conspicuous as the leading agitators and the situation had become dangerous in the extreme. The Amban handed over all responsibility for a settlement to Macartney who realized that bloodshed was very near.

The affair had gone beyond negotiation and immediate action was necessary. Macartney got up and spoke to the mob in Persian. He ordered some of the obstinate Hindus who had prevented an amicable settlement to be beaten and the rest he sent to give a sum of money to the mosque and to salaam before it. In return he told the Yarkandi Muslims to respect the settlement and not to kill cows or to sell beef near the Hindu quarters. The crowd was satisfied and dispersed. Macartney recognized that the Hindus had the worst of it, but he called his settlement 'submission to *force majeure* in order to save Hindu lives, to allay an incipient revolt – to avert a possible Russian intervention'.

Younghusband told the government of India that Macartney's tact and ability had saved a very awkward situation and that his success was remarkable considering that the Chinese had withdrawn from responsibility and that the Russians were ready to take advantage of any mistake. He suggested that in future Macartney should be given an escort of Indian troops for his protection. The government agreed that Macartney had acted promptly and with admirable discretion but said that an escort must depend on his having consular status. This seemed no nearer realization although the Yarkand incident must have made it obvious to the Chinese that the British subjects needed someone to govern as well as to represent them.

There was one satisfactory development, though: relations were restored with the Russian Consulate. Without any explanations on either side Macartney found when he called at the Consulate at the beginning of May that Kolokoloff treated him with the old friendliness and for the first time transferred to him debt cases between British and Russian subjects. It seems likely though that it was not the Yarkand incident that impressed the Russians so much as the changing climate of Anglo-Russian relations in the international sphere. At the end of July Russia signed a convention with Japan in which both parties pledged themselves to respect the territorial and treaty right of the other and which guaranteed the integrity of China. This was followed a month later by a convention with Japan's ally, Britain, which closed the long period of mutual suspicion and hostility between the two powers in Asia. The agreement was concerned principally to settle spheres of influence in Persia but Russia also renounced direct contact with Afghanistan and agreed to regard Tibet as a neutral buffer state. The convention formed part of the general settlement of disputes which created the Triple Entente of France, Russia and Britain. Kashgaria, of course, was of no concern to the authors of the agreement, a fact which Macartney pointed out jokingly when Kolokoloff translated its terms to him, but Kolokoloff seemed to take it for granted that Macartney's official appointment as Consul would soon be announced.

Kolokoloff was in a despondent mood about Russia's future. He saw ahead only gloom and anarchy. The country was in a critical financial position, he told Macartney, and the government would spend nothing on the Kashgar Consulate. The Anglo-Russian convention, he claimed, was not made with a responsible Russian government because there was no government then in the proper sense of the word. Later he told Macartney that since the Japanese war the Russian legation in Peking had given up the game of bluff against the Chinese; pacific penetration, not filibustering, was the new policy.

The outlook seemed drab indeed after the excitements of the Petrovsky era. It was not only in Russia that things were awry: both Kolokoloff and Macartney sensed a change in the atmosphere of Kashgar. The Chinese were proving distinctly less cooperative in settling traders' cases, and were showing signs of haughtiness to the foreigners. Talk of reform was in the air and there was growing agitation among the local population.

When Macartney went on leave in the summer of 1908 he

sensed that an era had come to an end in Kashgaria although he was unaware at the time of its significance for him personally. On 30 June he left Kashgar for the last time as the unofficial representative of the government of India. In August Captain Shuttleworth who was acting in his place was told by telegram from Peking that the Taotai had been instructed to recognize him as His Britannic Majesty's Consul in Kashgar. After eighteen years of painstaking labours it was typical of George Macartney's career and personality that the event that should have been a peculiarly personal triumph was left to another to celebrate in Kashgar in his absence. Macartney being the man he was probably felt no bitterness at the chance malice of events. He was aware that it was the shifts of high diplomacy that had brought him the long sought for recognition: Russia had dropped her opposition after the signing of the Anglo-Russian convention and so Peking was brought without any difficulty to agree.

Macartney's personal satisfaction needed no outward celebration. He had achieved nothing spectacular in his eighteen years either in the political or economic field, but despite all the forces ranged against him, both Russian and Chinese, he had hung on and survived. It was a personal triumph which only those closest to him, and who knew something of the man behind the reserve, could fully understand. For most of his life he had lived in something of a no-man's-land, psychologically if not physically; half Chinese and half British; employed by the government of India but of doubtful status under it; acting in an official position in Kashgar but unrecognized by the Chinese government; offered friendship by the Russian Consulate and then repudiated and ignored. Only a man of exceptional balance and integrity could have resolved these conflicts. This Macartney had done with conspicuous success, and his official recognition as British Consul, though important to his work, came after eighteen years as only an outward expression of a status he had already achieved.

TEN

Recognition and Reforms

Macartney had much to occupy his mind on the long journey across Russia to England. Captain Shuttleworth's arrival at the end of June 1908 was unexpected and had posed a difficult problem for their journey. At this season the rivers on their usual route to Osh were in full flood but waiting for better conditions meant losing time which could have been spent on leave. Macartney decided to go on the northerly route by Naryn where there was only one river crossing to make. It was a journey of 800 miles to the railway at Aris accomplished at times under terrible conditions. They had a month of anguish at Chimkent where the children, then aged five and two and a half, went down with dysentery. For three weeks it was a fight to save Eric's life and Sylvia too was desperately ill. Their parents nursed them without a single night's rest, cooped up in two small rooms. They experienced great kindness from the Russians, many of them complete strangers, who did everything they could to help. When they set off again Eric was too weak to stand but they eventually arrived in England safely in September.

When his mind was not occupied by the anxieties of the journey Macartney could let his thoughts run on the changes he had seen coming in the last year or two in Sinkiang. In a report he had sent to Younghusband in March 1908 he had told him that the spirit of renewal that was active throughout China was becoming apparent in the New Dominion. As early as January 1907 the Reverend George Hunter of the China Inland Mission, who was stationed in Urumchi, reported that the Chinese were attempting military reforms in the north of the province and had opened a school to teach their officers the Russian and English languages and European drill.

Economically, real efforts were being made to develop the province's resources. New mining regulations were issued to encourage Chinese enterprise and to restrain foreign activities.

The Taotai of Kashgar advised the local merchants to organize themselves into companies so that they could compete more effectively with the foreigners. He was also showing some interest in the coal and iron mines near Yangi Hissar and in the petroleum grounds near Kanjugan which he encouraged the Kashgaris to exploit. In August 1907 he formed a joint stock company of the leading Kashgari traders to improve and exploit the gold mines near Khotan. The capital subscribed was 12,000 taels and the government, which had a monopoly of all the gold produced, was pledged to pay dividends to the shareholders on the annual output. A Russian expert, though, had to be brought in to supervise the mine's operations.

This burst of interest in the economy of Kashgaria was not due to any conversion of the Taotai from the old ways of laxity and corruption. There was no sudden zeal for improvement on the part of the local officials, but even Kashgaria, remote as it was, could not completely ignore the edicts for reform that had begun to issue from Peking. In 1898 the Empress Dowager Tsu Hsi had imprisoned her nephew, the Emperor Kuang Hsu, because of his radical attempts at political reform, but after the failure of the anti-foreigner cause in the Boxer rising, she became convinced that only new policies could save the Manchu dynasty. The Empress was never converted to the principle of reform but from 1902 until her death in 1908 she did her best to satisfy both the progressive party and the conservatives in an effort to maintain the power of the imperial family. Politically this meant a policy of centralizing power in Peking by attempting to break down the autonomy of the provinces, and at the same time encouragement for popular participation in government under the supremacy of the Emperor. The inspiration behind this policy was Japan whose military successes were ascribed to the adoption of Western political institutions without sacrificing the power of the dynasty.

In the central government new ministries were organized but care was taken to see that Manchu rather than Chinese officials held all the higher posts. Peking also created financial supervisors who were intended to control the provinces by taking over responsibility for the provincial taxes. In August 1908 four or five secret officials from Peking appeared in Kashgaria and began to probe into the administration of the Ambans. They wanted to know how the people were taxed and what happened to the money. As a result of their activities the Ambans of Lop Nor, Goma, Karghalik and Yangi Hissar were summarily denounced and dismissed without the opportunity to defend themselves. The attempt at military reforms in the northern part of the province was also due to Peking's efforts to centralize the training of army officers. In June 1908 Kashgar learnt that its familiar garrison of gardening soldiers was to be disbanded along with the garrison at Aksu and that they would be replaced by 5000 foreign-trained troops. These would not be permitted to stay long in one place in order to avoid their forming local loyalties.

The dynasty's efforts to introduce an element of popular government began in July 1908 when Peking ordered provincial assemblies to meet within the year. The electorate was small and the powers of the assemblies limited, but the government proposed a nine-year programme of constitutional reform which would culminate in the establishment of a parliament in 1917 elected by all literate male Chinese subjects. Its role, though, was to be little more than advisory and it was obvious that the dynasty had no intention of divesting itself of power. At the local level the officials were ordered to introduce consultative councils. In April 1908 the Taotai of Kashgar called a meeting of the local notables and told them that every district was to have a council of eight men. They would be responsible for keeping the officials informed of local conditions and could also bring complaints to the Taotai. In Kashgar the council was to have twenty elected members with powers to raise local taxes for the repair of roads and bridges. It was obvious, though, that the *yamen* had no enthusiasm for the experiment and would do everything to restrict the council's power. The Taotai's first step in this direction was to appoint a Chinese official to preside over the council's deliberations.

Peking was not content with a framework for political reform. The government realized that it was essential to modernize and greatly extend the educational system if any real progress was to be made. In 1901 they ordered the building of schools throughout China and introduced a curriculum on Western lines alongside the Confucian system. In 1905 the old civil service examinations were abolished which removed the chief obstacle to educational advance. In Kashgar, where education meant that Muslim boys went to the *mullas* to be instructed in the Koran, it was 1908 before the idea of a school was mooted. The notables agreed with some reluctance to raise funds for one by a tax on landed property.

The first efforts were also made at this time to apply Western ideas of taxation by imitating the Russian trade licence system in which traders had to buy a licence every six months to carry on their business. But the innovation that caused most local resentment was when Chinese officials took over the collection of customs dues from the local traders who had previously acted as contractors for the government. Nothing was done, though, to improve the debased state of the Kashgar coinage and it was the eve of the revolution before the imperial government tried, too late, to tackle the whole problem of China's chaotic currency.

Macartney watched the fumbling attempts of the Chinese officials in Kashgaria to obey the edicts from Peking and he was quick to notice effects that the reformers had not intended. At the end of 1907 he reported that the Chinese were beginning to curry favour with the Turkis and that there was a subdued atmosphere of discontent in both communities. Among the Chinese the imperial prohibition against opium growing and the restriction put upon its sale were highly unpopular. Opium smokers had to register themselves and this particularly offended the military among whom the drug was ubiquitously used. More seriously, the activities of the secret emissaries from Peking, who were themselves far from being uncorrupt, had the effect of lowering the authority of the Taotai and the Ambans without any attempt being made at constructive and systematic reform. At the beginning of 1908 it was becoming a common occurrence for the local populace to march to Kashgar and to petition against their taxes. The Kashgaris themselves presented a memorial to one of the secret officials for transmission to Peking in which they protested against their bad government and asked for the Muslim voice to be heard in local affairs. They wanted to see the Taotai's post abolished and replaced by a council of ten on which the Turkis would be represented with the Chinese.

Otherwise the Kashgari reaction to the programme of reform was one of indifference when it was not hostility and rejection. The Taotai's proposals for the Kashgar council or *'duma'* as it was called locally, met with determined opposition. The traders took the line that if they were no longer fit to collect their customs dues they were not fit to serve on the *duma*, and in any case there was no point in such an institution if a Chinese official was to preside over it. Shortly afterwards the Chinese increased the customs dues to $6\frac{1}{2}$ per cent and the opposition grew stiffer. The merchants said they would do nothing about the *duma* until the heavy customs dues were revised, and they announced they would not pay the new rates. There the matter rested for the time being since the Taotai could not even force self-government on his unwilling subjects until his foreign-trained troops arrived from Urumchi.

The much talked of military reforms proved as disappointing as the attempts to introduce self-government. The old garrisons remained unrelieved at Kashgar and in the other southern towns, and no new regiments appeared to take their place. In the north of the province there was some reorganization but it showed itself principally in new uniforms for the troops modelled on the Japanese style. Mr Hunter of the China Inland Mission thought there was much to be desired in the discipline of the new regiments and in his opinion the officers were a very poor lot. Over China as a whole the reforms failed to achieve their first object which was the unifying of the country's armed forces. The military remained under the control of the provinces and not of the centre. Where the provincial armies were modernized they became personal weapons in the hands of the powerful governors.

The Taotai's attempts to inspire economic enterprise in Kashgaria met with an equal lack of success. The joint stock company he organized for the Kashgari traders aroused no enthusiasm and little was done to exploit the mineral wealth of the area. The merchants, though, were showing keen resentment at the trading privileges of the Russians and there were signs of their organizing themselves into companies to fight against foreign domination. In Artush, where they had an able and wealthy leader, a trading company started business, but although a trade guild was formed in Kashgar it made little progress. The merchants collected a large sum of money for its capital but appeared incapable of investing it. They had no real understanding of what a company was or how to run it and constant intrigues among themselves made any permanent cooperation impossible. Kashgar and Artush were supposed to combine their operations but the long-standing rivalry between them soon caused the two sections to be at loggerheads. The Taotai's proposals for a bank run by the rich traders aroused no keener response. It was doubtful whether any of their number was sufficiently educated to run a bank and to keep its books.

There was one conspicuous exception to the lethargy and conservatism of the local community. Hosein Bai Batcha was a millionaire merchant of Artush who had read widely and travelled extensively in Europe. On his own initiative he had founded a charitable organization in Artush to build schools and libraries for the education of both girls and boys. He had personally paid for young men to study abroad and was responsible for organizing the Artush trading company. Macartney went to see him just before going on leave in June 1908 and found him a quiet, unassuming man but a shrewd observer. He knew all about the Chinese attempt to boycott Japanese goods and was capable, thought Macartney, of turning the boycott machinery against Russian or British trade. He was the natural leader of the Kashgar and Artush merchants both on account of his wealth and his ability and he was proposed by them as president of the abortive *duma*. The inspiration behind the millionaire's activities, though, was not Peking but Constantinople, and his interest lay with the liberal pan-Islamic movement rather than with the regeneration of the Manchu empire.

Both Macartney and Kolokoloff were agreed that although the Turkis were coming to realize that they could agitate successfully against extortion and corrupt government there was no real nationalistic or religious movement among them. Captain Shuttleworth reported trouble from crowds of local children who were encouraged by their parents to follow foreigners about calling out 'Kaffir' and other insults, but the Chinese soon put a stop to this. European and pan-Islamic influence was gradually making the Turkis aware of their civic rights but there was no widespread discontent among them. They accepted the fact that they must be ruled by the Chinese or the Russians and opinion seemed unanimous in preferring the Chinese ways they were accustomed to.

On the part of the Chinese there was evident an increased assertiveness towards foreigners. Japan's defeat of Russia had destroyed the myth of the invincible European and throughout China hopes began to rise of ridding the country of foreign domination. In Kashgaria this showed itself in the jealous eye the Chinese now turned on the foreigners' trading privileges and acquisitions of land. Kolokoloff suspected that China was trying to circumvent or revise the provisions of the Treaty of St Petersburg and in December 1908 orders were issued forbidding Chinese subjects to mortgage or sell land to either Russian or British subjects.

But along with this jealousy of foreign privileges there was a growing conviction among the Chinese that China could only reassert herself by copying foreign ways. This extended even to dress. Gradually the imposing Chinese costumes were put aside to be replaced by what they imagined were European fashions. In Catherine Macartney's words the effect was 'undignified and utterly ridiculous'. By 1915 even the highest officials had adopted this mode of dress and the Titai turned up at the Macartneys' new year dinner wearing 'a black frock coat, flowered waistcoat, tight black silk trousers evidently made by a Chinese tailor, a bowler hat, and to give the finishing touch to his toilet, his bright green tie was tied round the top of his collar. It was more pathetic than comical to see men who would have been imposing and dignified in their beautiful silks and amber beads making themselves look like scarecrows.'

Abortive though most of the attempted reforms were Macartney sensed as he left Kashgar that the old era was passing away. Within a few months of his departure events confirmed his views. Captain Shuttleworth was recognized as British Consul first by the Chinese and then on 5 September 1908 by the Russian Consul on instructions from St Petersburg. The effect on British prestige was immediate. Within a few months Kolokoloff was complaining that he had not so much standing with the Chinese as the British Consul and according to Shuttleworth he was going out of his way to show that he was friendly with the British. Plans were laid for the building of a new British Consulate, designed by one of the Swedish missionaries, and the Taotai promised all possible help for the project. In a country without doctors the new Consulate gained added prestige when the government of India allowed it to import sufficient medicines to treat the Chinese officials as well as British subjects.

British trade with Sinkiang was flourishing and in the space of two years between 1906 and 1908 Indian imports into Kashgaria doubled. Only the difficulties of transport prevented further expansion. Progress was also made in dealing with the Shikarpuris whose activities had threatened to damage Anglo-Chinese relations. The initiative came from the Chinese, which from the first had been Macartney's wish. The Taotai issued orders prohibiting moneylending among Chinese subjects and the Shikarpuris were told that they could only stay on to collect their old debts. Captain Shuttleworth found out from one of them that about 60 per cent of them were not moneylenders in their own right but were employed as servants to collect bad debts. They had been lured to Kashgaria by promises of sudden wealth, but found when they got there that they were treated little better than slaves. Most of them wanted to go back to India. Shuttleworth inquired into these cases and ordered that the men should be paid enough to cover the cost of their return journey. He reported that the Chinese officials were helping to collect the Shikarpuris' debts and to settle their affairs. By 1909 he was able to say that half the Shikarpuris were returning to India that season. There was no further trouble in Yarkand and when Shuttleworth went there in August 1909 the Chinese officials arranged a great feast for him to which they invited all British subjects. This was entirely without precedent.

There were changes, too, at the Russian Consulate. In October 1908 Kolokoloff went on leave and it was soon announced that he would not be returning. He had seen the opening of the Kashgar–Naryn road to traffic but his cherished project quickly proved a disappointment. The Chinese levied exorbitant tolls so that the road was little used and there was only a trickle of trade between Kashgar and Naryn. The road would have no practical value until the Russian railway reached Naryn which was expected to be a long time ahead. By then the road would be out of repair and practically useless. The acting Russian Consul hinted to Shuttleworth that Kolokoloff had constructed the road more for his own glory than for any useful purpose.

In St Petersburg Kolokoloff became a member of the commission appointed to consider the revision of the 1881 treaty between Russia and China. The treaty was the foundation of Russian power in Sinkiang and one of its provisions was that Chinese goods could enter Russia free of duty in return for trade privileges in China. In April 1909 it was reported that Russia was about to violate these conditions by levying customs on certain Chinese goods imported by her. They were to come into force in January 1910. The Chinese retaliated by proclaiming a boycott of Russian cloth and when the time came for the Russians to levy the customs they postponed them for another year. Nevertheless, talk of revising the treaty was very much in the air and the Chinese were hinting at a more aggressive line. When Dr Morrison, *The Times* correspondent in Peking, visited Kashgar he reported that the Provincial Governor wanted to press for the removal of the Russian Consul's guard. As if to emphasize that an era was over the news came in February 1909 of Petrovsky's death.

One other death marked the changing times. On successive days in November 1908 the deaths were announced of the Emperor Kuang Hsu and of the Empress Dowager, Tsu Hsi. The passing of the Emperor had no significance for apart from his abortive 'Hundred Days' of reform he had been a prisoner or a puppet in the hands of his formidable aunt. But Tsu Hsi had ruled China for over forty years, for twenty-seven of them as sole regent. She had first entered the imperial palace as a concubine and her chief concern in ruling China was to consolidate her own power and wealth and to support the Manchu dynasty against its political opponents. Remarkable though she was much of China's weakness during her regime could be ascribed to her follies, superstition and reactionary policies, culminating in her support for the Boxer rebellion. Just before her death she nominated a two-year-old child, P'u Yi, as successor to the throne under the regency of the late Emperor's brother. But with the guiding hand removed from the central government no one could be sure how long the dynasty could keep the reins of power. In Kashgar, at any rate, the Empress Dowager's death was received with indifference, arousing neither hopes nor fears. Provided they were left alone the native Kashgaris were content, and neither revolutionary plans nor the government's reforms inspired enthusiasm.

The new government continued the policy of reform started by Tsu Hsi and in April 1909 the Peking investigators turned their attention to the Kashgar Taotaiship. Soon the rumours went round that the Taotai would be dismissed for his part in debasing the coinage. Instead of being pure silver it now had a 20 per cent mixture of alloys. The military Ambans were also threatened with dismissal for drawing pay for non-existent soldiers. The following month the Taotai left for Urumchi to answer the charges which had been brought against him. In Shuttleworth's as in Macartney's opinion he was steeped in every villainy but by July it was rumoured that he had succeeded in bribing the Provincial Governor and was returning to Kashgar. In August he did return and although officials arrived from Urumchi the following year to report on his administration the Taotai remained in office.

Corruption was accepted as part of normal life in Kashgar but when its exposure undermined the Taotai's prestige without reforming the system that perpetuated it there was danger for Chinese rule. Macartney had commented on the growth in the numbers of loafers, gamblers and thieves who swarmed in the streets of Kashgar and its suburbs. On one occasion when a prominent gambler and trouble-maker was arrested there were rumours that his fellows were planning to attack the District Magistrate and the Taotai. It was these people who had been behind a lot of the trouble in Yarkand and they could be relied upon to make the most of administrative difficulties. The year 1909 saw a partial failure of the crops and food prices quickly reached famine rates. The government sold grain from its stocks at low prices for the poor but it was bought up by the rich who then sold it at a high profit. Shuttleworth and the acting Russian Consul agreed to intervene to save the situation. Shuttleworth drew up a plan based on the Indian famine schemes in which people were employed on public works in return for food. The Chinese officials took up many of his suggestions but within a month or two the natural fertility of the countryside overcame the problem and food prices returned to normal.

When Macartney returned to Kashgar on 1 November 1909 there was little sign on the surface of the changes that had taken place during his absence, apart from the obvious growth of British prestige and the increased respect shown to him as British Consul. His return was followed a month later by the arrival of M. Sokov, the new Russian Consul, who was accompanied by his daughter. Macartney's first impressions of the man were not favourable. He was about forty-five, a short man with bulging eyes who spoke French fluently, and English fairly well. He had cultured manners and appeared to be well informed about Russian–Chinese affairs. A few months later, after a better acquaintance, Macartney commented, 'Mr Sokov is gentlemanly and smooth-tongued. But he does not strike me as taking much interest in things beyond the routine of his office. Ordinarily he has but little news to give.'

Otherwise the chief actors on the Kashgar scene remained much as before although the hand of Peking now lay much heavier on the *yamen*. The newly created ministries of the central government were constantly issuing orders, calling for reports, or asking awkward questions. Despite the Taotai's success in avoiding dismissal he found it necessary within a few months to borrow large sums of money to make up the deficits in the treasury.

No number of orders or inquiries from Peking could awaken the Kashgarians to the need for self-government and enlightenment. The Chinese started a census of Sarikol and ordered the Kashgar *mullas* to keep a register of births, deaths and changes of tenancy. They also started numbering the houses in the European fashion and had another attempt at establishing the *duma*. Since the leading merchants showed the same reluctance to elect representatives the Taotai nominated six Kashgar elders to serve and chose another fourteen from among the influential men of the district. He could do nothing, though, about the still-born trading company and in December 1909 it was formally dissolved and the money returned to its members.

The Chinese had gone ahead with their school building programme and in providing free education both for Chinese and Muslim children. Nearly every village now had a school, and attendance was made compulsory. The children were taught Chinese, physical drill, and the Koran, but Muslim resistance to state education continued unabated and disturbances were reported. Hosein Bai Batcha made known his view that the new educational policy was making boys disrespectful to their elders; they were losing their faith and were joining the ranks of the gamblers. Several people had even migrated to Russian Turkestan to escape sending their boys to school. Macartney reported a great deal of unrest over the schools throughout the whole of southern Turkestan, both on religious grounds and because of the taxes levied to build them. The Chinese officials in Kashgar were uneasy about the situation but the Hsietai (garrison commander) at Urumchi was known to make money out of collecting the taxes and building the schools.

The new educational policy and the census were the only signs of progress that Captain Oliver, a British army officer, could report when he travelled from Gilgit to Yarkand and Kashgar in August 1910. In his view Chinese rule was still carried on by bluff and had no strength behind it. The garrisons were ill armed or non-existent, and he was struck by the absence of a police force, sanitation or public works. Despite the attempts at political reform the open sale of government posts continued. Macartney, he thought, should have a consular guard so that he need not depend on the cooperation of the Chinese authorities. As it was he had to put his strong box in the Taotai's charge when he was away from Kashgar, and in his judicial work he had to use Chinese soldiers as escorts for prisoners.

As the summer of 1910 wore on events in the northern part of the province suggested that a consular guard might have other uses in Kashgar. In July there were serious riots among the opium cultivators at a small town near Urumchi. As part of the campaign to control the use of the drug they had been ordered to dig up their crops. Twelve of the ringleaders were beheaded but the people seized a government official and held him as hostage. A punitive expedition was sent from Urumchi but the government wisely adopted more conciliatory measures and in August the affair was settled. The opium growers handed over their hostage and received in return free cattle and seeds to replace their crops.

The same month, though, saw a much more threatening outbreak of violence in Urumchi, this time among the new corps of foreign-drilled troops. Their commandant had beheaded one of the soldiers for an offence and a mutiny broke out in which 100 shops and houses in the capital were set on fire. Property worth 3 million dollars was destroyed. Sixteen of the incendiaries were caught and five were beheaded on the spot. Peking summoned the Provincial Governor to explain the violence and to answer charges against his administration. Clearly all was not well in the army, and as Macartney had warned the Taotai some years before, once disaffection spread among the soldiers, Chinese rule in Sinkiang was a fragile thing.

A new crisis was also brewing in Russo-Chinese relations. In January 1910 Sokov had protested to the Taotai about the orders that had come from the Provincial Governor prohibiting Chinese subjects from selling land or houses and from marrying their women to Russians. The Consul claimed that these orders were a violation of the Treaty of St Petersburg and that the Chinese were enforcing them by threatening punishment for any of their subjects who disregarded them. The Taotai's attitude to the Consul was stiff and formal and by the end of the year Sokov was complaining bitterly to Macartney that he could get no cooperation from the *yamen*. His letters were unanswered and there were more than 100 suits involving Russian subjects which the Taotai left unnoticed and unsettled. Sokov poured out his complaints to the Russian Minister at Peking and he urged his government to uphold what he claimed were Russian rights under the Treaty of St Petersburg.

Russian prestige had declined in Sinkiang and the Kashgar officials were taking full advantage of the fact. But the orders forbidding the sale of landed property and marriage to Russians were not mere provocative gestures on the part of the Chinese. Since the Russians had announced their intention of taxing Chinese imports into Russian Turkestan the Chinese had grown more militant in their attitude to the Treaty of St. Petersburg. In Kashgaria there was increasing bitterness about Russian privileges which enabled them to undersell the local traders and to escape all forms of taxation. In Russia on the other hand Chinese traders were subjected to full Russian taxes. Russian claims to tax exemption particularly affected the sale of land and houses in Sinkiang. The Chinese levied a 13 per cent *ad valorem* tax on sales and a $6\frac{1}{2}$ per cent tax on mortgages of property. If a Russian subject were involved in one of these transactions no tax was levied at all. It was therefore of advantage for Chinese subjects to give preference to sales with Russians and to claim Russian nationality wherever possible, a course that received every encouragement from the Russian Consulate.

It was not difficult to claim Russian nationality since the children of a mixed marriage always assumed the father's nationality up to the third generation. In a country where a man was allowed four wives at a time and where marriage and divorce was so common that it was not unknown for a man to have fifty wives in his lifetime it did not take long for Sinkiang to swarm with Russian subjects. Chinese concern at this state of affairs lay behind the Provincial Governor's prohibition of mixed marriages although there was a conspicuous lack of success in enforcing it.

Both the Russians and the Chinese had every intention of improving their position when negotiations began at the end of the year for the renewal of the Treaty of St Petersburg. Apart from Sokov's insistence that Russian subjects should have the right to marry freely and to buy and sell land and houses in Sinkiang

Macartney did not know what terms each side would make. He felt certain, though, that the Chinese wanted to tax Russian trade to improve their revenues. If new terms were negotiated it was possible that Russia would use the opportunity to strengthen her position at the expense of British interests in Sinkiang. Macartney had mentioned this possibility to the Resident in Kashmir as early as February 1910 and in August he submitted a lengthy memorandum for the Indian government's consideration. He acknowledged that since the Russians had recognized the British Consulate much of the bitterness had gone out of Anglo-Russian rivalry in Sinkiang but there remained none the less several areas of possible conflict in which Britain must see that her interests were protected.

In Macartney's view the best solution was an Anglo–Chinese convention over Sinkiang. A frank exchange of views between Russia and Britain over their respective frontiers in Sarikol might solve that particular problem, but Britain needed a final settlement of the Hunza question with China. Nothing had been decided about Raskam and the disputes continued over the Mir's collection of grazing dues from the Kirghiz on the Taghdumbash Pamir. China's prestige was high in Hunza since she had reasserted her authority over Tibet and there were factions in Hunza ready to ally themselves with the Safdar Ali party and to intrigue with the Chinese. Also Macartney thought it essential to settle once and for all with the Chinese whether Britain was entitled to 'the most favoured nation' treatment in Sinkiang or whether this was merely a courtesy that could be withdrawn at will.

He suggested a convention with China which would protect Britain's essential interests by renouncing Hunza's grazing and cultivation rights on the Taghdumbash and in Raskam in return for Hunza's release from Chinese suzerainty. In addition Britain could press for a delimitation of the Indian–Chinese boundary and for an undertaking that Safdar Ali should be kept under detention at Kucha. Britain could offer to admit Chinese goods into India free of duty, apart from opium and *charas*, in return for the free importation of British goods into Sinkiang. Both powers should agree to ban all trade in firearms and to grant each other extradition rights. Macartney also thought that Britain should press for the appointment of consuls in all the towns of Sinkiang where there were other foreign consuls in exchange for reciprocal rights in India.

This attempt by Macartney to stimulate his government into a constructive policy towards Kashgaria met the fate of its predecessors. While the government of India was not obliged to notice Sinkiang it was only too pleased to do nothing and let events take their course. In February 1911 its reply to Macartney's proposals summed up the general attitude which he had to contend with: 'The government of India sees no advantage in raising these questions at the present moment and does not propose to take any action in the matter until necessity arises.'

Macartney had more success in influencing the Chinese. Towards the end of 1910 the Peking government instructed the Taotai to cease pressing the new educational system in Kashgaria and Macartney discovered that this was the result of his report to the British Minister at Peking which had been passed on to the Chinese government. Macartney felt some embarrassment at his own success and explained to the Taotai that it was his duty to report any unrest that might have political consequences. He had no wish, he said, to interfere in local affairs. The Taotai thanked him for his action and said that he had complained many times to Urumchi about the new system and the unrest it was causing but his protests had been ignored.

The government's concessions over the schools eased some of the tension in Kashgaria but in other ways Peking's efforts to introduce reforms were producing administrative chaos in the province. Lien, the Provincial Governor, who had been summoned to Peking after the mutiny of the new corps of troops, was dismissed from his office. It was not so much this event that brought about his downfall as the activities of an official who had been sent to spy on the Urumchi authorities by the governor of Kansu. He had denounced Lien and the Provincial Treasurer, Wang, for auctioning government posts, and twelve lesser officials were accused of bribing the Treasurer. Among them were the Ambans of Keriya, Khotan, Goma, Karghalik, Yarkand and Kashgar New City. A Peking official was on his way to investigate the charges. Government posts had always been bought and sold and it was doubtful if a single official in the province would escape denunciation should the scope of the inquisition be widened. Feelings of apprehension and insecurity began to spread among the ranks of the Chinese bureaucracy.

Administrative scandals continued to be the chief topic of

conversation throughout the winter of 1910–11 but the officials had more than their personal careers to worry about. The provincial deficit was running at more than a million taels a year as Peking was unable to increase the amount of its subsidy. Urumchi's answer to the problem was to manufacture a million taels in paper money and so inflation was added to the province's problems. Paper currency superseded silver in most transactions in the towns. The exchange value of the tael against the rouble had already fallen from 0·6025 to 0·875 in the years 1906–8, and from 0·39 to 0·56 against the rupee. Clearly the province could not go on manufacturing money to cover the deficit in its revenues but no one appeared capable of tackling the problem. The fall in the value of the tael cut British imports into Kashgaria by a third during the year ending March 1910 and the Provincial Government's efforts to increase its revenues by levying heavier customs dues threatened hopes of recovery.

This was the uneasy condition of the province when on 16 February 1911 the Russians tried to harry the Chinese into negotiating the Treaty of St Petersburg on their own terms by delivering an ultimatum in Peking. It was Russia's reply to the operations of the American and European consortium which, in return for lending 50 million dollars to the Chinese government, had taken over the control of certain state revenues to guarantee repayment. Secure in the agreement they had made the previous year with Japan the Russians threatened that if they received no satisfactory reply from Peking there would be a demonstration of force on the Mongolian frontier. News of the ultimatum did not reach Kashgar until 12 March although six days earlier Sokov had called on the Taotai, and according to reports 'high words were exchanged'. The Russian demanded the immediate settlement of trading cases and complete satisfaction on the questions of buying land and houses and marrying local women. The Taotai shuffled for some time but finally gave in although he maintained that the Russians could only buy land in towns and not in the countryside. Despite these concessions, by 10 March the rumours were flying round the bazaar that the Russians intended to occupy Ili. Three days later the Hsietai of Kashgar reported to Macartney his conversation with Sokov in which the Consul talked of Russian cavalry massing on the Sinkiang border.

On 16 March the tension mounted further when the sixty-five Cossacks of the consular guard rode in formation through the streets of Kashgar and scattered the crowd in the market place. Parties of Cossacks also took to patrolling the town at night and to minor demonstrations of force over cultivated fields. Macartney did not discuss the ultimatum with Sokov and apart from advising the Chinese to be conciliatory and to be punctilious in their observance of treaty rights he stood aside watching events. In the middle of the crisis, on 15 March, he received the King's commission appointing him Consul-General at Kashgar, a promotion that was intended to give him the same diplomatic standing as Sokov. He was careful, though, to write to Sokov immediately addressing him as 'M. le Doyen', so that the Russian should know he considered him as senior Consul. For once he was not entirely without sympathy for the Russian demonstration in Kashgar, and considered that if its object was only to frighten the Chinese British interests might benefit. The Taotai had irritated both consuls by his neglect of their trading cases and his attitude to Macartney had not been above reproach. Nevertheless, it was conceivable that this was the beginning of a revived Petrovsky era and that he would soon have to cope with Russian aggression in Sarikol and a more dictatorial attitude generally in Sinkiang.

In the face of Russian provocation and reports of additional troops arriving at Osh, Irkeshtam and Naryn, the Chinese in Kashgar showed calmness and a readiness to be conciliatory. They made no military preparations, due less to diplomatic restraint than to a serious lack of cartridges. The Taotai began disposing of Sokov's trade cases and was most helpful to Macartney in his purchase of the Chini Bagh site for the new British Consulate building. But throughout April and May relations between Sokov and the Taotai remained strained and the Russians continued to act in a nervous and provocative manner.

At the beginning of June a new element appeared in the situation. Edward Behrens arrived in Kashgar to take up his post as secretary at the Russian Consulate. A Baltic Jew, like so many in the Russian diplomatic service, he had acted as Russian Consul-General at Shanghai and Mukden and he struck Macartney at once as having 'a good deal of push'. It must also have occurred to him that the appointment of a man of such experience and obvious ability to the comparatively humble post of secretary at the Kashgar Consulate was an unusual, if not significant, event, but he contented himself with reporting that if Behrens and Sokov worked harmoniously together Russian strength in Kashgar would be greatly increased. Behrens made his attitude clear in a talk he had with Macartney soon after his arrival. He berated the Taotai and his officials for their utter laziness and incompetence and went on to discuss the possibility of Russia's occupying Sinkiang. The regime in Kashgar, he said, was 'effete and rotten; his personal view was that the Chinese should be swept out of the place; and as Sinkiang was not worth Russia's taking – for the revenue would never cover the expense – it should be made into a Muhammadan State, in which case it would still be a buffer between Russia and India'. Behrens's arrival noticeably stiffened the attitude of the Russian Consulate. Although Macartney heard that Sino–Russian relations had improved since the February ultimatum the Russians in Kashgar had become even more harsh and overbearing and they were threatening the use of Cossacks on every occasion.

In Sarikol the tension seemed about to erupt into a dangerous crisis. For some time there had been antagonism between the officer in charge of the Russian post and the local officials over the question of firewood. This was extremely scarce and difficult to find in Sarikol. The Russian officer was demanding that the Chinese should supply him with fuel whereas his predecessor had made his own arrangements with a local contractor. When the Chinese officials refused to agree the Russian, Captain Kolbine, sent his men to cut down trees belonging to a Sarikoli. The local Amban kept out of the Russians' way and was hardly ever in Tashkurghan, but in July the Captain sent his men for the third time to cut down trees, this time the property of Karim Beg. Macartney warned both the Taotai and the Titai not to give the Russians any pretext for urging their government to send troops to Kashgar and he privately urged the British authorities to press the Chinese government to make concessions. He suggested that Peking should send special legal commissioners to dispose of the outstanding trading cases which the local officials were incompetent to deal with. He also thought that the Chinese should show a willingness to discuss the land transfer tax with the Russians, over which there were still disputes, and that the Russians should

169

be told to renew their previous private arrangements over fuel in Sarikol.

Before anything could be done at government level eleven Cossacks went on 5 August to the Amban's headquarters in Tash-kurghan and demanded immediate supplies of fuel. The Amban's secretary explained his inability to do anything in his master's absence whereupon the Cossacks seized him by the ear and took him to the Russian fort. Kolbine threatened that unless he supplied 100 ponyloads of firewood he would take over the administration of Sarikol. The secretary gave in and was then entertained to tea and the Russian's gramophone.

This, though, was not the end of the Sarikol affair. On 13 August 1911 Macartney sent an urgent telegram to his Minister in Peking saying that a virtual Russian dictatorship had been established in Sarikol. He heard from Behrens that a Russian subject had lodged a complaint against a beggar and Sokov had asked the Taotai to send the man for trial to Kashgar. The Taotai refused and Sokov retorted that if the Taotai had not the necessary leisure to attend to his judicial duties then he would lend him some friendly assistance. The result was that extra Cossacks were brought into Sarikol to 'assist the Chinese administration' and Russian commands assumed the force of law. The Russian Pamir garrison was also reinforced by 200 men.

Macartney was preparing for a major confrontation on the Hunza border when the crisis fizzled out as quickly as it had erupted. The Peking government gave in to pressure and in September sent an envoy to St. Petersburg to reopen negotiations over the Treaty. The Russian customs officer in Kashgar started work again on the basis of the *status quo* and Behrens left on a tour of the Tarim Basin to settle outstanding cases involving Russian subjects. Freed from his disturbing presence normal relations were resumed between the *yamen* and the Russian Consulate. Sokov called on the Taotai in September for the first time since they had exchanged 'high words' in March and in the middle of the month all the Chinese officials dined at the Consulate. The extra troops were withdrawn. But there was no doubt that what Macartney called the Russians' 'filibustering' had won them important gains. Their prestige had risen in the province and the Chinese had been made to feel that the Russians would dispense with their cooperation if necessary. The Russians had their way in all the points at dispute and Behrens had started an indefatigable campaign for the mass registration of Russian subjects.

In Macartney's view the *status quo* could only be preserved by the Chinese taking steps to conciliate their subjects who had shown a noticeable lack of sympathy for their rulers in that summer's crisis. They must abandon their educational scheme, which had done more than anything to alienate local opinion, and they must either get foreigners to accept equal taxation with Chinese subjects or stop levying customs dues altogether. The customs contributed a relatively small amount to the provincial exchequer but the abuses they gave rise to encouraged registration as Russian subjects. Some check must be placed on the methods the Russians used in their registrations and on undue claims of extraterritorial rights. Finally, to stop the Russians making use of further grievances Macartney recommended the appointment to Kashgar of a Chinese judge with sufficient foreign experience to deal with the complexities of cases between mixed nationalities.

Behrens's tour of the southern oases was causing Macartney anxiety. Wherever the secretary went he succeeded in stirring up trouble and not only was his registration of Russian subjects promiscuous but he was bringing pressure to bear on people whose parents had come from Baltistan, Chitral and Gilgit, to declare themselves of Russian origin. Macartney had no wish to claim them as British subjects since they were born in Yarkand but he had no intention of seeing them swell the ranks of Russian retainers. Behrens's intrigues at Yarkand led to bad feeling between the Andijanis and the British subjects, and in Karghalik he encouraged the Andijanis in insulting and aggressive behaviour towards the Chinese. In these circumstances Macartney thought it politic to show the British presence in the southern towns and he set off on tour in Behrens's wake. As a result of Behrens's activities he found himself urged by the Chinese officials at Karghalik to register British subjects and so to put an end to the disputes over customs exemptions.

The ill effects of Behrens's tour were not confined to his indiscriminate registrations. When he and Macartney met in Karghalik he claimed Sarikol as a dependency of Kokand and questioned the British right to enjoy in Kashgaria privileges that belonged only to Russian subjects. Macartney found when he arrived in Yarkand that the Chinese customs official had been instructed by

Behrens on these lines and was now questioning the claims of British subjects to enjoy exemption from customs dues. Macartney told him sharply not to meddle in high politics since the instructions from the late Governor of Sinkiang about treating Indians in the same way as Andijanis should be sufficient authority for anyone.

Macartney's parting with Behrens at the beginning of November had been cordial enough but as the Russian rode off to Khotan to continue his tour he must have wondered how this provocative policy would end. He was not to know as he returned to Kashgar that in the previous month revolution had broken out among Chinese troops at Wuhan in the Yangtse valley and that it was then spreading among the garrisons of other towns to the northwest to the province of Shensi.

ELEVEN

Revolution in Kashgar

The revolution that the dynasty had tried to avert by its belated reforms was begun by an accidental explosion in a house in Hankow. Investigators found a collection of arms and a list of men who were planning a rising the following week. Some of them were officers of the local garrison who promptly mutinied to avoid arrest. In the face of remarkably little opposition they seized Wuhan, Hankow and Hanyang, and soon city after city in southern and central China had joined the rebellion. The risings, spontaneous and uncoordinated, were chiefly led by soldiers, but they had behind them the sympathy and support of the educated class who were disgusted with the corruption of the Manchu regime. They saw the only hope for China in the destruction of the dynasty and political reform. Beyond that the revolutionaries had no common objective and each provincial group acted independently until Sun Yat-sen accepted the presidency of a provisional government which revolutionary representatives set up in Nanking.

Sun accepted the post on 29 December 1911. Four days earlier the revolution had reached Sinkiang, encouraged by secret emissaries of the insurgents and members of the secret society, the Ko-Lao-Hui. The first outbreak was at Ili where on Christmas Day 1911 an ambitious young Brigadier called Yang Tsuan-hsu mutinied with his men and stormed the fortified Chinese town of Kora near Kuldja. This was the headquarters of a military dignitary known as the 'Tartar General' who ruled the frontier districts jointly with the Governor at Urumchi. The rebels looted the treasury of 200,000 taels, killed the Tartar General and raised the standard of the Republic. As a figurehead for the movement they produced a frightened old former Tartar General called Kwan and made him their commander-in-chief. Within three weeks they had overrun the whole of Ili, and held strategic points on the road to Manass and Urumchi.

Meanwhile, in the same week as the Ili rising, Urumchi had a narrow escape. On 28 December a mob of about 100 rowdies led by four Honanese members of the Ko-Lao-Hui made a determined attack on the citadel of the Chinese town and tried to rush the armoury, the Governor's *yamen* and the police headquarters. The 'old style' troops were staunch and the rebel mob was repulsed at the cost of an artillery officer killed and the chief of police seriously wounded. The four Ko-Lao-Hui leaders were captured and beheaded immediately; other members of the secret society who were arrested later were put to death by slow torture.

At this juncture Governor Yuan Ta-hua turned to his Chief Justice Yang Tseng-hsin for help. Urumchi was safe for the time being, but the threat from Ili remained. Yang's name first appears in the Kashgar reports as 'Director of Foreign Intercourse' on the Governor's staff, in which capacity he telegraphed to the Taotai of Kashgar giving details of the Ili revolt and instructing him to request foreign consuls 'not to be influenced by false reports and not to accord the rebels a hasty recognition'. The Taotai duly read this telegram to Macartney and his Russian colleague.

Early in the crisis, on 30 November 1911, Macartney had reported that though there was considerable unrest along the North Road among disaffected Chinese who included some 'very bad elements' he was convinced from his knowledge of the Turkis of the south that they would not rise in sympathy. On 15 January Sokov consulted Macartney about the alarming news of the revolt in Ili and the attempted *coup d'état* at Urumchi. The two consuls-general agreed that Sokov should apply to St Petersburg for seventy more Cossacks to reinforce his escort and Macartney to the government of India for an armed guard of thirty Gilgit Scouts under a British officer. A month later Macartney repeated his request on the grounds that though there was nothing to fear from the Turkis, there was danger in the southern towns from the Chinese underworld of gamblers, opium smokers, tramps and, worst of all, soldiers disbanded because there was no money to pay them. The safety of the Swedish missionaries was at stake and, among the British Indians, of the Shikarpuri moneylenders who were unpopular and vulnerable.

Macartney's requests for an armed guard were reluctantly refused by the government of India, chiefly for logistic reasons; the General Staff jibbed at the expense and difficulty of maintaining a military force, however small, at so remote and inaccessible a post. Though not surprised Macartney was disappointed, less because of the perils of his own position than because all at Chini Bagh disliked intensely the idea of being dependent on the Russians for their protection.

Towards the end of February 1912 news came that the Manchu Prince Regent, Prince Ch'ing, had abdicated and that Yuan Shih-k'ai, the strong man of the northern provinces, had been appointed by imperial decree to negotiate a 'Provisional Republic' with Sun Yat-sen's revolutionary party at Canton. This was the parting of the ways for the Chinese at Kashgar; many of the officials were loyal to the regime, but others were excited at the prospect of throwing off the Manchu yoke, an act symbolized by cutting off that badge of servitude, the queue, or pigtail. But the remnants of the old provincial army were known to be antagonistic to the revolution, and no one knew which bandwagon was the less dangerous to climb on. As March passed more and more of the Chinese removed their queues and adopted the solar calendar of the Republic, but all were puzzled by the absence of any orders on the subject from Governor Yuan at Urumchi who refused, even when asked by telegram, to inform the Taotai officially of the abdication. Why was he so obstinately pro-Manchu? His life was said to be in danger because he had repressed the abortive *coup* of 28 December with needless barbarity. He was also blamed by both sides for the loss of 2000 lives in his unsuccessful attempt to recover Ili from the republican insurgents. The general opinion was that it was now too late for him to change his coat and declare for the Republic.

Again, it seems, it was the Chief Justice, Yang, who came to the Governor's help. Yang had served for several years with distinction in Kansu where he had won a reputation for integrity and for skill in managing Tungans. In April Macartney reported that 2000 troops had arrived in Urumchi from Kansu and that 'a judge', almost certainly Yang, had gone from Urumchi to negotiate with the Ili revolutionaries in the hope of ending the deadlock that had resulted from the inconclusive fighting in February. He was apparently successful for there was no further mention of serious clashes.

In April things also began to happen south of the Tien Shan. At Aksu on the 13th a mob, presumed at Kashgar to be revolutionaries, stormed the *yamens* of the Taotai and another high official and killed them both. Three days later Macartney was shown by the Taotai a telegram from two Chinese officials at Aksu informing him of the *coup*, and the message was significant in view of what happened later at Kashgar:

> The mob swarmed into the *yamens* like bees, all we could do was to parley with them. They agreed to refrain from further violence on condition that no enquiry should be made. They insisted that we, Cha Ch'en-tai and P'eng Chih-fu, should carry on as Taotai and Prefect respectively. We consented and hoisted the flag of the Republic.

The effect of this news from Aksu, only twenty-four marches away, on the official world at Kashgar was electric. The Taotai cut his pigtail off at once and advised everybody else to do the same. The District Magistrate of the Old City, Chang, and other officials followed suit. Only the Titai, Chiao, refused at first to take the Taotai's advice without orders from Urumchi; he feared the 'old-style troops' under his command who professed loyalty to the empire. He agreed, though, to fly the republican flag at his *yamen* in the New City.

In the last week of April news of the slaying of officials at two more towns on the southern road, Kucha and Karashahr, renewed the panic at Kashgar. The Titai lost his nerve and decided after all to dispense with his queue; this did not please the soldiery who criticized their officers for having 'become foreigners'. But the commander-in-chief refrained from issuing any orders on the subject to his troops, and a rise in pay soothed their feelings for the time being. In a dispatch dated 29 April Macartney feared a 'scramble for power among vagabond Chinese, especially in the New City where three or four hundred of them openly talked sedition'. On 4 May he again asked urgently for a small armed escort, more to deter Russian intervention than a mob attack on the British Consulate.

In May 1912 the Macartneys' eldest son Eric was eight and a half, Sylvia five and a half, and their youngest child, Robin, had been born only six months earlier. The children had an English governess, Miss Cresswell, and staying in the house at the time were Macartney's brother Donald and the missionary from Urumchi, the Reverend George Hunter. In the compound lived

176

the two Indian and the Chinese Munshis with their families. The numerous domestic staff and three orderlies were housed just outside the walls.

At five o'clock in the morning of 7 May the Macartneys were awakened by a servant who told them that one of the Cossacks of the Russian consular escort had brought a message from Sokov asking Macartney to come and see him at once. Hurriedly dressing and telling his wife to rouse the household he went to the Russian Consulate-General along a road patrolled by Cossacks. There an agitated Sokov told him that at about 4 a.m. one of the gates of the city had been opened for a minute and a Russian Muslim agent had slipped out with the news that the Taotai's *yamen* was being attacked by a Chinese mob with murderous intent. He, Sokov, relying on his strong Cossack guard, was preparing for possible attacks on 'foreign devils'. After discussing the possibilities and agreeing to pool information Macartney hurried back to Chini Bagh.

At seven he and his wife were sitting down to breakfast when one of the orderlies who had been patrolling the grounds came in with strange news. The high wall of the Old City was visible from a corner of the compound and his eye had been caught by signalling from the top of it. He made his way to the foot of the wall and recognized a Turki Beg on the staff of the Hsietai (garrison commander). The Beg threw down his master's red paper visiting card and shouted a message: the Taotai and the City Magistrate had been killed by assassins, but the British and Russian consuls-general need have no anxiety; no foreign nationals would be attacked nor would their property be touched. It would be better, though, if they stayed at home for a few days until the excitement subsided.

At 9 a.m. the west gate of the city was opened and the news was confirmed. The Hsietai was said to be negotiating with the gang of toughs, mostly disbanded soldiers, who were responsible for the murders. During the rest of the day one refugee official after another came to the British Consulate-General with their families hidden in the carts of Turki helpers and begged for sanctuary. The Macartneys took in as many families as they could find tents or huts for, eighteen in all, and advised others to go to the Russian Consulate-General. One of the first refugees, the wife of the City Magistrate, had seen her husband literally hacked to death in

177

bed. The assailants had seized her small son too and were about to kill him but she threw herself upon them imploring them to spare him and they, having bigger game to hunt, let him go. She kept wailing, 'I saw it all, the picture will always be before me.' That evening Macartney heard the whole story from a Chinese he knew as the Telegraph Superintendent, Chow, who came to see him and announced that he had been appointed City Magistrate in place of the murdered Chang. Macartney was careful not to acknowledge his newly acquired rank but he listened to him and reported his story in a long dispatch to the Resident in Kashmir.

It seemed that on the evening of 6 May placards had been put up in the New City violently attacking the Taotai and demanding his execution for corruption and treachery to the regime. During the night fifty desperadoes collected at the shop of an Old City pork butcher called Pien Yung-fu and at 3 a.m. forced their way simultaneously in two parties into the private quarters of the Taotai and the City Magistrate. The Taotai and his wife were in bed, apparently unguarded; they were hacked to pieces where they lay. One of the assassins told Chow that he had struck at the Taotai's wife in the dark thinking she was her husband, and he sincerely regretted his mistake. The rest of the gang overpowered the City Magistrate's bodyguard of ten without difficulty and dispatched him with a few sword cuts, but spared his wife and child. The assassins then ransacked the *yamens* and tore down all the Republican flags and notices which had been put up at the order of the murdered men.

The drama then took a surprising and peculiarly Chinese turn. Pork butcher Pien, the leader of the gang, and his second in command, a pawnbroker called Wei, did not follow up their success, as might have been expected, by massacring a few more officials, looting the treasury and seizing power for themselves; instead they waited to see what Authority would do. In due course the commandant of the Old City garrison, Yang Hsietai, arrived with a few of his 'old style' soldiers and faced the assassins. He greeted them reproachfully but with respect, even humility. Would they kindly explain why they had killed the Taotai? Because, they said, he was corrupt and had made a large fortune out of his job; because he had cut off his pigtail and had made other officials do the same; worst of all, because he had intrigued to succeed

Governor Yuan at Urumchi, though he was seventy-two and far too old for the post.

The Hsietai then parleyed with the gang. They refused to disperse saying that most of them were disbanded soldiers who could not get back to their homes because they had no money. Could they not be enlisted again? The Hsietai agreed and it was decided that they should form the nucleus of a 'New Regiment' to be recruited and armed as soon as possible. They clamoured for arms at once and the Hsietai had to issue them with sixty rifles and some ammunition from the arsenal. They then insisted on 'electing' successors, not only to the men they had murdered but to the retiring Governor at Urumchi. As Taotai they chose the chief magistrate of the New City, Wang, and for the post of Old City Magistrate, the Telegraph Superintendent, Chow. The gang promised, in return for an amnesty from the government and the appointment of their nominees to the Kashgar posts, to commit no more murders and also (the Hsietai was very definite about this) to leave all foreigners and their property strictly alone. On no account was the Russian Consul-General to be given an opportunity to intervene.

It was probably at this stage that the Hsietai sent one of his men to signal to the British Consulate-General from the top of the city wall. But the day was still young. At about eight o'clock he went over to the New City to report to the Titai and inform the magistrate, Wang, of the dangerous promotion that had been thrust upon him. Doubtless a telegram was also sent to the Governor informing him of the promotion proposed by the assassins for the Titai; needless to say nothing came of it. In the afternoon the Hsietai came back with Wang and Chow and presented them to the gang who mounted a guard of honour for them with blood-bespattered swords. The seals of the Taotai and the City Magistrate and the keys of their treasuries were formally handed over to the new incumbents; not one copper 'cash' in either of them had been touched. The four gates of the town were then opened and a few of the braver shopkeepers took down their shutters. The new Taotai, Wang, put placards up announcing the 'rightful elimination' of his deceased predecessor and his own interim appointment.

Tension relaxed at Chini Bagh and among the Swedish missionaries with whom the Macartneys kept in close touch. But

Macartney knew well how dangerous the situation still was with eighteen Chinese refugee officials in the compound and outside it the 'New Regiment' of murderers, armed and hourly increasing in strength.

Next morning Yang Hsietai himself came to see Macartney and was in the middle of a long account of the part he had played in the events of the day before when the interview was cut short dramatically. A soldier burst in with the news that the New City was in revolt, shops were being looted, Chinese officials had been killed. The Hsietai hurriedly took his leave and rushed off. Early in the afternoon a message came from the Russian Consulate-General that troops from the New City were marching on Kashgar to fight the men who had killed the Taotai; they were out to loot and burn and no foreigner would be safe. Panic swept the town, Cossacks picketed the Russian quarter and Macartney, as he put it in his report 'took what precautions he could against surprise'. In his wife's words:

> Rolls of bandages were prepared and I packed up the children's clothes and the baby's food into bags in case we found it necessary to run and hide in a place we had already decided on. . . . My husband and his brother even arranged between them how we women and children were to be dispatched if the mob was too strong for us, though this I did not know till long after-wards. . . . Our servants armed themselves with any kind of weapon they could find . . . knives, sticks, old swords, etc. . . . and even our governess, Miss Cresswell, took the big carving knife and steel to bed with her. . . . Having made all preparations possible, we lay down fully dressed, while Donald and Mr Hunter took it in turns to do sentry duty round the house and garden.

Nothing happened until midnight when three cannon shots boomed out from the walled town, shaking the house. The Macartneys leapt from their bed and everyone in the house came running thinking that the attack had begun. But silence descended again upon the town until dawn brought relief and some sleep to the weary inhabitants of Chini Bagh.

It turned out that the rumour of a rebel march on Kashgar was a false alarm. A mob of mutineers and disbanded soldiers in the

New City had indeed run amok and killed a colonel and a high civil official, but they were now under some sort of control and had come to the Old City merely to join the New Regiment. How the Hsietai did it Macartney does not report; he probably took pork butcher Pien and his fellow assassins along with him to the New City and acted as peacemaker between the two factions. That night, at any rate, the strength of the New Regiment was announced to be 400; the night before it had been ninety, so it appears that the 300 or 400 'vagabonds' in the New City whom Macartney had mentioned in a dispatch of 29 April were accepted as recruits for the New Regiment on the same terms as the murderers of the Taotai. The three cannon shots at midnight which had alarmed the household at Chini Bagh were the salute fired at the funeral of the Taotai.

Once more tension relaxed slightly at Chini Bagh. George Macartney and his brother Donald rode daily through the city unattended to show that they trusted the Hsietai's word that no one would harm them. Catherine Macartney was even braver; she let her brother-in-law take Eric riding with him one day. The little boy on his pony was mobbed, but by admiring townsmen bringing cakes and sweets. One of them offered Eric a bag of sweets in one hand while he held in the other the bleeding head of a victim. The Macartneys needed all their courage, for the situation remained dangerous and, to Macartney, extremely puzzling. Who had engineered the murders and for what political purpose? If revolutionary partisans, why had they torn down the insignia of the Republic and why were they persecuting officials who had cut off their queues? The refugees sheltering in the two consulates-general were still in terror of their lives; some of the richer ones were offering large ransoms to pork butcher Pien and his second in command, Wei the pawnbroker. If, on the other hand, the assassins had been hired by a reactionary junta of army officers why did they nominate civil officials to fill positions of power and hand over the contents of the treasury to them? The Hsietai was no would-be dictator, he was a well known and respected senior officer, the last person to be privy to the murder of two colleagues.

As the days passed it became clear that the New Regiment of illiterate loafers and disbanded soldiers with grievances had no political views at all and were out for nothing but money and, in many cases, revenge on a hated official class. They soon became

N   181

known in the bazaars of Kashgaria simply as 'the gamblers' because they spent most of their time and the money they squeezed out of their victims in gambling dens and brothels. The regular or 'old style' soldiers of the garrison were evidently in league with the gang; as for the officers who had been spared, they had probably been popular with the troops but not necessarily in the conspiracy.

What impressed and greatly relieved Macartney was that not one of the merchants, moneylenders and other comparatively well-to-do members of the Russian and British-Indian communities was interfered with by the gamblers. The same applied to the other towns of the southern oases with the exception of one small township in the Keria district, Chira. Everywhere the struggle, whether violent or not, was between Chinese, and foreign nationals were not involved. The reports of the British Aksakals along the Keriya road indicated that there had been revolts of self-styled 'New Regiment' riffraff, all Chinese or half-breed Turkis, at the larger centres, but only at Yangi Hissar, the nearest town to Kashgar, had they taken over complete control. There the commandant of the regular garrison had run away and his son had taken the family fortune to the Russian Aksakal for safe custody. The Amban had also disappeared and the New Regiment had 'requested' the Taotai to appoint another official from Kashgar in his place, one Tsou.

Elsewhere the officials had either come to terms with the rebels by enlisting them as 'bodyguards' or by paying over large sums to them, or, with the help of loyal regulars, they had defied them. Only at Keriya, the last stronghold on the ancient Silk Route, 400 miles from Kashgar, had there been serious fighting with loss of life, but it had resulted in victory for the District Magistrate and his soldiers. Among all the reports there was no mention of any harm or even threat to foreign nationals or their property.

However obscure might be the allegiance of the gamblers there was no secret about the reason for their scrupulous restraint where foreign subjects were concerned. Fear of the Russians had long been endemic in the bazaars and *yamens* of Sinkiang. The Hsietai was frank about it at a meeting with the two consuls on 12 May. He told Sokov that he had persuaded the gang to desist from further violence by telling them that it would result in Russian intervention. 'I borrowed your prestige' was how he put it. Sokov made no comment but asked the Hsietai if he had heard the rumours that the New Regiment might attack the Russian Consulate? Did he think it would help to keep the country quiet if his Cossack escort were strengthened? Yang assured him that the rumour was absolutely unfounded and that no reinforcements were needed. Sokov explained that he himself had not asked for more troops, but the situation was still very serious and he had told his government so.

Macartney feared the worst. To him a Russian military occupation was an even less acceptable contingency than a complete breakdown of the administrative machine. The possibility that Russia would make use of Chinese weakness during the transition period between the imperial and republican regimes had from the first been a major anxiety. It was surely more than a coincidence that the first outbreak of the revolution in Sinkiang had been in Ili, the stategically important north-western district which the Russians had taken over forty years before in the Yakub Beg rebellion. If they now occupied the southern oases they would command the strategic Pamir plateau and the routes to India through Hunza and Ladakh. Even if the occupation were not permanent it would be a powerful lever to secure revision in Russia's favour of the 1881 Treaty of St Petersburg; the economic hold this might give Russia would be a death blow to the British-Indian trade.

Apart from Sokov's prevarications there had already been an ominous sign of possible Russian intervention. The Consul's secretary Behrens had ridden off with six Cossacks down the Khotan road a few days after the murders to see what was happening in the southern oases. He was sending back alarmist reports of danger to Russian interests which were not confirmed by Macartney's agents, the Aksakals of the local Indian communities. It turned out afterwards that what he had really gone to do was to collect as many signatures as possible on a monster petition to the Taotai of Kashgar asking him to arrange for the protection of all foreign nationals by the Russian army. At Yarkand he annoyed the British Aksakal very much by exhorting a crowd of Indians and Afghans to join the Andijanis in the petition. Macartney foresaw in Behrens's activities the creation and exaggeration of 'incidents' which would justify Russian intervention.

*　　　*　　　*

On 29 May the blow fell. Sokov came to see Macartney and told him in confidence that about 750 Cossacks, half cavalry and half infantry, with two machine-guns, were expected at Kashgar from Andijan in a week's time. They were summoned to protect British as well as Russian lives and property and he hoped this would be appreciated. Next day Macartney was present when his Russian colleague received the new Taotai, Wang, whose appointment had just been confirmed by a telegram from the provincial government. Wang's consternation when Sokov told him of the approaching Cossacks was very evident, and it increased when the Consul-General mentioned casually that some of the troops might be sent to other towns such as Yarkand and Khotan for the protection of Russian subjects. All the astonished Taotai could say was that so large a force would cause a scare everywhere. After he had left, Macartney did his best to impress on his Russian colleague that the gamblers had done no violence to anyone but their own countrymen and that foreign interests were not affected except by the loss of trade. He deprecated in particular Secretary Behrens's tour to Yarkand at such a time; it was bound to encourage the trouble-makers. When Wang and the Hsietai consulted him later he earnestly advised them and the gamblers to accept the inevitable and make the best of the Russian intervention by treating the troops as guests when they came.

Three weeks later, on 22 June 1912, the first European-trained fighting troops ever seen in southern Sinkiang halted on the Ferghana road within sight of the long brown walls of Old Kashgar. Half of them were Cossacks under Colonel Bobrov, half infantry under Lieutenant-Colonel Petrov, with a total strength of twenty-eight officers and 700 other ranks. Colonel Bobrov was in command of the whole column. They had marched from the railhead at Osh in seventeen days, crossing the 12,000 foot Terek Pass and entering Chinese territory at Irkeshtam. To the disappointment of the battle-hungry Cossacks they were received not with artillery and machine-gun fire but with welcoming arches and roadside tea drinking by Consul-General Sokov in uniform and by Macartney in his morning coat and topee. The Chinese were represented by Yang Hsietai on behalf of the Titai and by the Taotai's Secretary for Foreign Affairs. Four days later Sokov and the officers of the detachment escorted by 200 Cossacks called on the Taotai, the

Titai, the Swedish missionaries and the British Consul-General.
Next day the Chinese officials returned the calls with Russian
troops lining the streets. The troops were accommodated in several
caravanserais and a large schoolhouse in the neighbourhood of
the Russian Consulate.

When Macartney returned Bobrov's call on 28 June the Colonel
seemed disgusted with his mission. 'The gamblers exist only in the
air,' he said. 'Why has my force been sent here when the Consul-
General's escort is amply sufficient to deal with the situation?'
The gamblers, however, still existed in the flesh but they were
discreetly quartered in houses to the south of the town and forbidden to use the North Gate. In a dispatch which he sent just
before the detachment arrived Macartney noted with surprise
that they were becoming quite respectable. Pork butcher Pien and
pawnbroker Wei were actually cooperating with Wang Taotai
and the few remaining civil officials in keeping some sort of order
and, more importantly, in collecting the taxes without which the
rank and file gamblers, or New Regiment as they were now
officially called, could not be paid. The whole of the 1·3 million
taels which had formerly been remitted to Urumchi annually was
now earmarked for local expenses including the cost not only of
the 800 gamblers at Kashgar but of about 1200 others who had
flocked to the colours at towns as far north-east as Aksu and south-
east as far as Keriya. The Turki population who paid the taxes did
not object; so long as the demand was not raised they did not
care which of their Chinese masters had the money. And it was a
fact that the civilian tax collectors whom the gamblers had
appointed were content with much less 'squeeze' than their predecessors of the imperial regime.

The new respectability of the gamblers was connected with the
fact that towards the end of May the Taotai had received a telegram from President Yuan Shih-k'ai that the leaders of the New
Regiment would not be held responsible for the murders at
Kashgar, but that if there were any more murders of officials they
would be declared enemies of the Republic. This was the amnesty
for which the pork butcher and his men had bargained while their
swords still dripped with blood on the morning of 7 May.
Macartney was more nonplussed than ever. Was it possible that
the republican government had been behind the movement all
along and that the reactionary attitude of the gamblers was a

blind to mask the real objectives of the murders? Or was the whole business a Russian plot?

What Macartney did not know till many months later was that the assassinations at Aksu and Kashgar and the unsuccessful Honanese attempt at Urumchi on 28 December 1911 were the work of the secret society, the Ko-Lao-Hui. Whereas on the coast the revolution was more a matter of raising republican flags, and whole provinces joined the republican cause led by their generals and governors, in the west the Ko-Lao-Hui led a real rising of the Chinese against their rulers which was accompanied by much more bloodshed. The revolution was particularly violent in the north-western province of Shensi where local lodges of the Ko-Lao-Hui organized a rising at Sian, the provincial capital. Hundreds of Manchus and several missionaries were massacred by mobs and the Ko-Lao-Hui took over the administration of the province. They appointed one of their own leaders as provincial governor and applied to the President of the Republic for his approval.

It is not surprising that Macartney was puzzled by the circumstances of the *coup d'état* at Kashgar. Communications with China proper, slow and tenuous enough under the Manchus, had practically ceased to exist since November 1911, and he had no means of knowing what was going on even in Kansu beyond the Gobi, much less in Shensi still further east. If he had known he could not have failed to be struck by the parallel between the course of events in Shensi and that in Sinkiang up to the Russian intervention. In 1919 the activities of the Ko-Lao-Hui were described in Szechuan, Shensi and parts of Kansu by Sir Eric Teichman, Oriental Secretary to the British Minister at Peking:

The Society appears to exist for the purpose of practising blackmail and terrorism and securing mutual protection in the commission of every variety of crime. Among its members are special bands expert in gambling, kidnapping, piracy, robbery and similar pursuits. Others join merely in order to secure immunity from the depredations of more active members. Offences against the rules of the Society are drastically dealt with by punishments such as death, mutilation, gouging out of eyes, etc., carried into effect by members specially told off for the purpose; while should these avenging angels fall by some mischance into the grip of the law, the Society will see to it that they do not come to any harm and are well supplied with wine and opium while in prison. The Ko Lao Hui has many aliases and they are brigands one day, patriot rebels the next, regular soldiers the next and so on.

Had it not been for the restraining influence of Russian prestige and the moral support and advice Macartney gave to the respectable elements among the Chinese officials this description might well have applied to the gambler regime in Kashgar for many months in 1912 and 1913. Just as the Ko-Lao-Hui in Shensi had secured Yuan Shih-kai's provisional approval of their regime by presenting him with a *fait accompli*, so in southern Sinkiang the society had attained its objective; with the authority of the President of the Republic it ruled Kashgaria.

Then came the Cossacks. The Ko-Lao-Hui had hoped that if it gave the Russians no excuse for intervention they would leave the southern oases alone. But now not only Ili, where the Russian Consul's escort was about to be reinforced by regular troops, but Kashgar, unoccupied even in the Yakub Beg period, was at the mercy of the Tsar's forces. The Russian Consul-General had already renewed his tactics of infiltration which had been interrupted by the risings; his arrogant and hot-headed secretary was at Yarkand encouraging bogus Russian subjects to defy the Chinese officials. Something had to be done quickly to reassert Chinese authority against the hated foreigner. Two tough members of the Ko-Lao-Hui, Hsiung Kao-sheng and an assistant called Chaos, were sent post-haste down the Khotan road to organize resistance to the Russian drive.

TWELVE

The Chira Crisis

By the end of May 1912 the Ko-Lao-Hui leaders and their tools, the gamblers, had taken over the administration of the southern oases and Kashgaria had become more or less independent of the provincial government at Urumchi. But at that very time two things happened which were to have far-reaching consequences. The Russians put into action their plan for military intervention in Kashgaria and the President of the Chinese Republic formally appointed the Chief Justice of the province, Yang Tseng-hsin, to act as Governor of Sinkiang in place of the discredited Yuan. Macartney only mentioned this last event casually in his reports to the Resident in Kashmir. He had little use for far-off mandarins anyway, and no knowledge of Yang's character or the extent to which he had already stepped into Yuan's shoes. But it was Yang who, eighteen months later, won the last round of the triangular contest for control of the New Dominion.

The struggle between the other two parties in that contest, the Ko-Lao-Hui and the Russian Consulate-General, began with a riot at Chira in the Keriya district on 24 June 1912, just three days after the arrival of the Cossacks at Kashgar 350 miles away. The case became known in diplomacy as the Chira Incident and it would not have happened but for highly provocative action on the part of Secretary Behrens during his tour of the southern oases in the autumn of 1911. Everywhere he went he had encouraged the Andijanis to defy the Ambans and feelings were soon running high between Russian Muslims and loyal Turkis.

Near the small town of Chira, three marches beyond Khotan, there lived an Andijani landowner called Syed Haji who had an irrigation dispute with a Turki neighbour. When the case came to court in February 1912 the local magistrate pronounced judgement against him, so the Syed decided to make use of his Russian nationality. He organized a mob of about 100 peasants who had been registered as Russian subjects by Behrens the previous autumn and announced that he was not going to pay his grain tax unless the Amban changed his mind and decided the irrigation case in his favour. The magistrate stuck to his guns and sent bailiffs to the Syed's house, whereupon he and some of his men rode insolently into the inner courtyard of the *yamen* and demanded to see the Amban. This was the worst possible 'face' for the magistrate and he ordered his men to turn them out. A scuffle followed in which loyal Turkis joined and the Andijanis got the worst of it. But Syed Haji remained truculent and the affair made such a stir that Sokov had to agree to a joint inquiry into the case with the Taotai at Kashgar. Judgement went against the Syed, but in the confusion of the revolution he was released and in May he returned to Chira more cock-a-hoop than ever. As he arrived outside the town he was received by his followers with a salute of three guns as if he were the Amban, and three more guns were fired as he entered his house. This was rebellion in Chinese eyes, but the Amban, cowed by fear of Russian reprisals, did nothing.

When Secreary Behrens marched down the road again soon after the May assassinations he met Syed Haji and many other Russian subjects, genuine and spurious, at Khotan, and no doubt encouraged them in their belligerent attitude. At about the same time a large party of the Chira townspeople who were hostile to Syed Haji and the Andijanis marched into Khotan and complained to the Amban of the Syed's activities. It was their complaints, added to the reports of officials at other towns about Behrens's provocative behaviour, that decided the Ko-Lao-Hui chiefs at Kashgar to send two of their toughest members as *wei-yuans* (executive officers) on behalf of their nominee, the Taotai, to organize the gambler forces and to assert the authority of the Republic in the southern oases.

Hsiung Kao-sheng, senior of the two *wei-yuans*, seems to have been an educated man of ability and courage, if not of many scruples. He soon saw that Syed Haji's was a test case. If the man could be caught and executed or, failing that, killed in a battle of his own choosing, the pro-Russian rot might be stopped. At Khotan Hsiung was awaited by the complainants from Chira. He heard what they had to say and sent five of his soldiers back with them to Chira as a token that he was coming to redress their grievances. Three days later he followed them, and with a mixed rabble of 'old' and 'new' (i.e. gambler) soldiers collected from local garrisons, arrived at Chira on 23 June, two days after the Russian occupying force reached Kashgar.

Meanwhile Syed Haji had been to his estate in the country to collect peasantry to reinforce his partisans in the town. The largest house in Chira belonged to his father-in-law, Abdul Aziz Qari, and he made it his headquarters, flying Russian flags from the rooftop and manning it with more than a hundred of his followers, armed with rifles, swords, spears and clubs. In a speech to them the Syed was defiant; he was not afraid of Hsiung and would fight him if necessary. To bless his struggle against the Chinese infidels he hired twelve boys to intone the Prophet's words night and day.

Hsiung's arrival at once put heart into the opponents of Syed Haji and he soon found that he had the majority of responsible townspeople behind him as well as a sizeable mob of gambler riff-raff. But the Andijanis were numerous, determined, strategically placed and, by local standards, well armed. Diplomacy and bluff were the only alternatives to bloodshed and hours passed while deputation after deputation of elders, headmen and Begs pleaded, cajoled, threatened and bargained with the Syed. All was in vain; he refused to budge. If the *wei-yuan* wanted to see him, let him come and talk. One of the emissaries came back with a message so rudely worded that the interpreter toned it down to save Hsiung's face, a fact that was not lost on some of the onlookers. Hsiung and the gamblers in the crowd were furious, but they agreed to one more effort for peace; five of the town's most respected men did their best to persuade the Syed to surrender without bloodshed, but with no more success than their predecessors.

The situation seemed to have reached deadlock for Hsiung's force was not strong enough to storm Syed Haji's stronghold. He broke the deadlock in a peculiarly Chinese way. He announced that he could not waste any more time at Chira; he had business to do at Keriya, three marches farther to the east, and on his way back he would look into the townspeople's complaints. At once there was an uproar; he must not leave the town, they would be at the mercy of the Andijanis; if the *wei-yuan* did not act they would fight the Syed themselves. Before Hsiung could stop them (if, indeed, he tried) a large mob ran shouting through the streets to the house of Abdul Aziz Qari. Hsiung waited a little, then sent a sergeant and ten men after them with orders to quell the riot. But before the soldiers could get there a loyal Turki and a Chinese had been killed, the former by an Andijani with a sword, and the latter by Syed Haji himself with a rifle-shot from the house. On this the sergeant sounded the attack by bugle call and fighting started in earnest. Many of the Syed's followers ran away so he locked the doors of the house from the inside to prevent the rest, between thirty and forty in number, from deserting him. With rifle-fire from the windows they killed the Chinese sergeant and two soldiers as well as three or four more Turkis.

The mob and the soldiers, infuriated, avenged the deaths of their comrades in the only way they could; they set fire to the house, which, as everywhere in the hot south-eastern oases, was built of wood except for its outer brick walls. The place was quickly an inferno and everyone in it was burnt alive except Syed Haji himself and three or four of his friends, probably members of his father-in-law's family, to whom the house belonged. They knocked a hole in the back wall and escaped into the darkness. It transpired afterwards that two horses had been waiting in readiness for the Syed's escape and that he was seen twice next day riding through distant villages – on his way, men said, to the Russian frontier.

It was not till the end of June that Wang Taotai received the news of the Chira incident. Before the First World War the only telegraph line in all southern Sinkiang linked Kashgar with Urumchi via Aksu north of the Tien Shan; word from the oases in the south-east could only come by mounted courier. The news from Chira must have come as a most unpleasant shock to both the Taotai and the Titai. This was the very disaster, bloodshed and worse between the gamblers and Russian subjects that they had all feared and tried so hard to prevent. What would the Russians do now?

The first Macartney heard of it was on 1 July when Sokov called on him and read him a letter he had just received from the Taotai describing the affray, strongly condemning Hsiung 'for interfering with a Russian subject' and promising an early inquiry on the spot. The Consul-General was indignant; it was more than likely, he said, that he would be ordered to proceed at once to Chira with an escort of a couple of hundred Cossacks. Macartney calmed his colleague down, deprecating hasty action; the Taotai, he thought, was doing his best and should be given a chance to do justice. It was a pity that the row was over Syed Haji, a man whom Sokov himself had called a 'brigand' in connection with the first Chira incident in February. Macartney hinted that but for Secretary Behrens's provocative behaviour on his tour to Khotan the previous autumn the Syed would probably not have come into the news at all.

A few days later, when a detailed report dated 28 June came from the Indian Aksakal at Khotan, Badruddin Khan, Macartney sent Sokov a translation of it and tackled the Taotai and Yang Hsietai. They took a much firmer line than the Taotai had at first taken with Sokov; the two *wei-yuans*, they said, had gone to Yarkand and Khotan to 'restrain the gamblers' and had on the whole done their job well. Their only mistake was to go beyond their instructions and inquire into the conduct of a Russian subject. Macartney advised the Taotai earnestly to do justice himself so as not to give the Russians an excuse for taking the law into their own hands.

Telegrams then took a week or more to reach St Petersburg and Peking via Irkestam on the Russian side of the Ferghana frontier which was 120 miles by courier from Kashgar. The news of Chira broke on 14 July at the Russian capital. The *Novoe Vremya* came out with a lurid account of the burning alive of 100 Russian nationals in the house of 'Said Effendi' by a Chinese official from Kashgar called 'Sun'. Mr George Buchanan, the British Ambassador at the court of the Tsar, telegraphed a translation of the article next day to the Foreign Secretary, Sir Edward Grey, and *The Times* published it on 16 July. Two days later, the British Minister at Peking, Mr John Jordan, reported that the Russian government had demanded an apology for the outrage, reparation for the loss of Syed Haji's house and the killing of seventy-five Russian nationals, and the punishment of the officials responsible.

It was the middle of August before instructions were received by Sokov from his Legation and by the Taotai from Urumchi on the action to be taken in the case. The Russian charges against the *wei-yuan* Hsiung and his gamblers of responsibility for the riot were to be tried by a court of inquiry presided over by the Taotai; Secretary Behrens was to proceed to Chira with a strong guard of Cossacks of the consular escort to collect evidence, take bonds from witnesses and otherwise prepare the case for the prosecution. Sokov was not to be on the bench with the Taotai but would attend the proceedings as an observer. He assured Macartney that the court's sentences would be enforced, if necessary, by the troops of the detachment. He was very bitter against Hsiung, not without reason, as appeared later when a further report came in from Aksakal Badruddin. The man whom the Russians regarded as the villain of the piece not only confessed his guilt but claimed credit for what he had done as a triumphant assertion of Chinese sovereignty. In a proclamation at Khotan after the riot he said that the men of Chira, who, misled by Syed Haji, had taken out Russian nationality certificates and defied his authority, were traitors and rebels who deserved to be punished with death. He assumed the entire responsibility for what had been done at Chira.

Hsiung's words caused a resurgence of national feeling among the Chinese of the southern oases. Later, at Yarkand, he received an ovation from his compatriots as their champion against interference by foreigners in their affairs. The part played by him in the burning alive of more than thirty of China's unfortunate subjects did not detract from his achievements; 'Turban heads' were expendable in a good cause such as the frustration of Russian plots to take over the province. The skill with which he had managed the riot so that the mob, not his soldiers, had set fire to the house was doubtless admired as an instance of the superior intelligence of the ruling race. But among the Turkis dread of Russia was more than ever dominant. The Russian Akasakals of Yarkand and Khotan, whom Sokov had ordered to go to Chira and make a preliminary investigation, had no difficulty in completing it. The Muslims, dazed by the tragedy they had witnessed, not only cooperated and gave the Aksakals all the names they wanted but signed affidavits as one man testifying to the good character of Syed Haji.

In diplomatic circles the Russians had gone out of their way to assure their British colleagues in St Petersburg and London that they had sent troops to Kashgaria in response to a request from the Chinese who felt unable to guarantee the safety of Russian subjects. Russia had no intention of occupying Kashgar permanently. The Foreign Office in London, though sceptical, accepted these assurances, but the government of India took a different view. They learnt from Macartney's reports that the tenfold increase in Russian military strength at Kashgar had been neither requested by the Chinese nor approved as a precautionary measure, and also that the reinforcements were in no sense part of the consular guard but were under independent military command. Then came news of the Chira riot, just the sort of 'incident' that Macartney had foreseen. On 27 July the Viceroy telegraphed to Lord Crewe, the Secretary of State for India:

Russians evidently taking advantage of disorder in New Dominion to push policy of peaceful penetration which if unchecked will lead to permanent occupation and be a menace to Indian interests. We trust it will be possible to secure withdrawal of Russian troops. We have been considering Macartney's request for Indian infantry guard at Kashgar. We thought it a good idea to stultify Russian argument that increased garrison is necessary for safety of British Consulate as well as their own, and that it would demonstrate that we are not prepared tacitly to surrender our interests in the New Dominion. On the other hand military objections are very strong and deter us from recommending step on purely political grounds, the safety of the British Consulate-General being assured under existing conditions.

The India Office agreed with the government of India about the inadvisability of giving Macartney a consular guard, but about nothing else. To them at this period Sinkiang was of little importance compared with Tibet. Since Britain had agreed with Russia in 1907 not to interfere in Tibetan affairs China had again invaded and subdued her old vassal state and deposed the Dalai Lama. But with the outbreak of the Chinese revolution the Dalai Lama was again in power and Tibet would soon be independent. India could not afford to let the passes over the Himalayas fall into potentially hostile hands and the India Office wanted Russia's cooperation in arriving at a new agreement. This was more important, the India Office thought, than the frustration of hypothetical Russian designs on Sinkiang. In any case, Britain was not involved directly in the Russo–Chinese dispute at Kashgar and there was no plausible case for diplomatic action to get the occupying force withdrawn. The Secretary of State for India suggested, therefore, that Russia be given a free hand in Sinkiang in return for her cooperation over Tibet.

The government of India did not agree and thought that Russian concessions over Tibet, even with safeguards for Hunza's rights in Raskam and the Taghdumbash, were outweighed by the disadvantages of a Russian occupation of Sinkiang. It so happened that the Russian Foreign Minister, Sazanov, was visiting London at the end of September and when the question of Sinkiang was raised with him he was vehement in denying any intention of occupying the New Dominion. If there was ever to be a question of a Russian advance in that region, he said, it would only be in the neighbourhood of the northern boundary, by Kuldja and the Ili river, where the frontier was easy to cross and where incidents might take place on either side. It was only 'barbarous treatment of Russian traders at Kashgar' that had caused 'the increase in the Russian force at that place' and the Russian government had no wish to leave it there. There was no question of a move into any part of Chinese Turkestan without informing His Majesty's government beforehand.

There had been no case of 'barbarous treatment' of a Russian subject at Kashgar and the Chira massacre had taken place several days after the arrival of Colonel Bobrov's column. British officials were agreed on treating M. Sazanov's assurances with some disbelief. Nevertheless, if Russia intended to take over the province there was nothing to stop her there and then from sending more troops and making the utmost use of the Chira incident. But in Kashgar Macartney saw no signs of the Russians tightening their hold on the province. He reported only the growing power of the gamblers and of the Ko-Lao-Hui.

Throughout July and August the whole situation continued to puzzle him. Though less violent in their behaviour, the gamblers were getting visibly richer, dividing the spoils with the officials they had nominated. They demanded and obtained lucrative jobs; at Khotan, for instance, the new collector of customs dues was one of the men who had murdered the Taotai. Some of the officials were 'hunting with the gamblers and running with the Republic' as Macartney put it. Tsou, the gambler-appointed Prefect at Yangi Hissar, was a case in point. He gave out that he had been forced against his will to accept the post but when the new

Governor, Yang, in what Macartney described as 'a feeble attempt to assert his authority' appointed another official named Ku in his place, Tsou flatly refused to hand over his post. The key to the puzzle was of course the Ko-Lao-Hui; the officials who hunted with the gamblers and ran with the Republic were members of the society; those who ran with the Republic were not.

Encouraged by their success at Chira, the leaders of the Ko-Lao-Hui now set themselves to undermine the prestige of the Russians at Kashgar. A good way to do this was to make trouble between Sokov and the officers of the detachment. Intelligence agents paid by the Russians but employed also by the Ko-Lao-Hui may have been used for this purpose. This, at any rate, is the most likely explanation of an extraordinary and, as it turned out, highly comical incident which occurred in the Chinese quarter of the Old City on 26 August. It was the day of the annual paper burning festival at which bonfires of paper were burnt to warm the spirits of the departed. At about 7 p.m. a Jewish agent reported to Sokov that there was a fire in the walled city. He at once sent fifteen Cossacks of his escort, under a Captain Vagin, to help put it out. The party found the paper bonfires in the rice bazaar and insisted, in spite of protests, on pouring water on them. In the fracas that ensued a Chinese greengrocer was wounded by a Cossack sword thrust, but he was the only casualty. No gamblers were involved and the matter would probably have been amicably settled next day if one of Kashgar's rare thunderstorms had not suddenly come on. There was a shattering clap of thunder and the fifteen horses, left unfettered by their masters, panicked and galloped riderless through the streets back to their stables.

Sokov and the commandant were naturally alarmed, and more so when another Jew came with the news that Captain Vagin had been wounded in a fight with the gamblers who had been let loose from their stronghold. The bell of the Russian church tolled, the whole detachment 800 strong turned out and went to the rescue of their comrades. By this time the gates of the city were shut as it was long past closing time, 8 p.m. This did not stop the Cossacks; they blew a large gap in the North Gate with dynamite and marched through drenching rain into the town. Not a soul was to be seen for it was dark and everyone, including the fifteen Cossacks, was sheltering indoors from the unaccustomed downpour. The detachment infantry searched in vain till midnight, then bivouacked on, of all places, the flat roof of the Friday Mosque. At dawn Captain Vagin and his men appeared, unharmed and surprised at the fuss that had been made about them. They and the detachment troops marched back to their respective quarters leaving a platoon to guard the damaged gateway.

The first Macartney heard of the affair was at breakfast-time, when an agitated Yang Hsietai called to ask what it all meant. Had the Russians declared war? As a precaution, he said, he had ordered troops to be brought over from the New City and a gun to be mounted on the Old City wall and trained on the Russian Consulate compound in which the commandant had now made his headquarters. Macartney persuaded him with some difficulty to countermand these orders and so averted what might have turned into a very ugly incident. All ended happily with the Russians mending the gate they had blown up.

The officers and men of the detachment resented being made to look foolish by the hasty and ill-advised actions of the Consul-General. Relations between them had been cool from the outset but now a serious split developed. It was common knowledge that Colonel Bobrov and his officers were bored at Kashgar and wanted to go home, and they blamed Sokov for causing them to be detained there. Sokov on his part made no secret of his hope that sooner or later he would be instructed to go to Chira with 200 or 300 cavalry to restore order and see that justice was done. At an official dinner on the Tsarevich's birthday neither the Colonel nor any of his officers was present and the Consul-General retaliated by boycotting a lunch party given by Bobrov which was followed by Cossack sports on 7 September, the centenary of the battle of Borodino. Against Sokov's wishes Macartney and his brother, unwilling to take sides, attended the lunch and were rewarded by a remarkable frankness on the part of their host about Sokov.

The Colonel told them that he had recommended to his Commander-in-Chief at Tashkent the withdrawal of his force before the winter but this would not now be feasible because Consul-General Sokov wanted to make Chinese Turkestan a province of the Tsar's empire with himself as Governor-General. Hence the registration of hundreds, nay thousands, of bogus Russian subjects, and hence the Chira affair. An exposure of Sokov's goings-on would shortly appear in a St Petersburg newspaper. The Foreign Ministry, he knew, did not approve the tough line he was taking about Chira and wished the dispute to be settled amicably with the Chinese authorities. This talk must have embarrassed Macartney, for he was grateful to Sokov for his cooperation throughout the crisis and it was important to retain his confidence. He had to admit that Bobrov's strictures were justified, but these civil matters were no concern of the military, and anyway how did the Colonel and his officers come to know so much? Unknown to Macartney Sokov's position was far from secure; within two months disloyalty and intrigue among his own staff came to light which might well have cost him his post.

September passed quietly at Kashgar after the excitements of August while the three protagonists, Colonel Bobrov, Consul-General Sokov and the Taotai Wang awaited further orders from their respective higher commands. The first indication that the Chinese government was under strong pressure from Russia over Chira came in mid-September when Behrens, escorted by a Cossack lieutenant and twenty men, started off down the road once more to Khotan and Keriya. His mission this time was to complete the dossier of the Chira case and send as many of the accused as he could get hold of back to Kashgar for trial. Judging by the reports of the Indian Aksakals en route, the Chinese in the Yarkand district at any rate were much less easy to intimidate than on either of his previous tours. At Goma the Amban whose face he had caused to be slapped just a year before avenged the insult by ostentatiously refusing either to receive him or to call on him, remarking publicly in a loud voice that he was going to have no nonsense about Chinese subjects becoming foreigners at Goma. In a long report, part of which Sokov translated later to Macartney, Behrens magnified this incident into an attempt on his life. At Khotan the two Russian Aksakals who had been investigating at Chira met him with their report and lists of accused and witnesses. There and at Keriya the officials had been strictly instructed by Urumchi to cooperate with him and they did so in spite of their resentment of his bullying and browbeating tactics. With their help Behrens was able to send back to Kashgar escorted by some of his Cossacks thirty-six Turki and Chinese prisoners, including two officials of the Keriya district. Syed Haji, who had come out of hiding at Goma and joined the party, was also sent to Kashgar where he lived in Behrens's own quarters at the Consulate-General until the case was finally settled.

From Khotan Behrens went on to Chira and Keriya and here he discarded all restraints. Disregarding his orders not to inquire into any cases jointly with Chinese magistrates, he and the Amban of Keriya jointly tried two Chinese subjects for actions alleged to have been taken against Syed Haji's fleeing partisans after the riot. One of them was sentenced to a heavy fine and 2000 strokes which Behrens insisted on having administered on the spot with eight armed Cossacks standing by. From the sixty or seventy surviving 'pseudo-Andijani' followers of Syed Haji he took away their certificates of Russian nationality and issued new ones, his object being to destroy documents that could be used against Syed Haji at Kashgar. Behrens's last exploit was to burn the government granary at Keriya with its contents, apparently because a claim by an Andijani to the site had been dismissed by the District Magistrate. But the melodramatic reports he had been making to Sokov about the success of his tour proved to be Behrens's swansong in the New Dominion.

Early in October Macartney heard news which made him realize that the new Governor at Urumchi was not as 'feeble' as he thought. Tsou, the gamblers' nominee for Prefect of Yangi Hissar, submitted to pressure from Urumchi and handed over his office to the Governor's choice, Ku. But there was more to come. On 6 October Wang Taotai and the Hsietai came to the Consulate with the startling news that under orders from the Governor the whole New Regiment was leaving for Urumchi in a fortnight's time. Macartney found the news hard to believe, but it was true. The Titai, it seemed, had telegraphed to the Governor asking for cancellation of the orders, but Yang merely repeated them, adding that the Titai himself was to command the force in the north. It was needed to reinforce an expedition of 'Confucian' troops being sent against rebellious Mongol tribesmen in the Kobdo region.

The news that Kashgar was to be rid of its gamblers was welcome to Macartney but less so to his Russian colleague who came round next day, very worried, to discuss the announcement. It was obvious to Macartney that Sokov's first thought was that the departure of the gamblers would strengthen the case for an early withdrawal of the Russian detachment. The more dangerous the situation seemed, the better it suited his book. One evening about this time Macartney happened to be dining with a former army surgeon called Lavrienti who had been sent to Kashgar by the

Tsar's government to construct and operate a seismological station. In conversation this officer let himself go about Sokov. 'Il croit, il veut croire, et il veut faire croire au danger' was how he put it.

Exactly a fortnight later, on 20 October 1912, the Kashgar New Regiment, the strength of which had by now dwindled to about 490, was ready to march. That morning Macartney was surprised to receive a message from pork butcher Pien asking if he and his second in command, the pawnbroker Wei, could come round and say goodbye. Macartney had never seen or had anything to do with either of the assassins and he consulted the Taotai. It appeared that they feared punishment, perhaps death, if they put themselves in Governor Yang's power and they hoped that the British Consul-General would give them a letter of recommendation to him. Macartney did not oblige. But though he did not bid the gamblers farewell in person he did them an unplanned service that very evening: he saved them from what would certainly have been an unpleasant parting encounter with the Cossacks of the detachment, and perhaps saved Kashgar from being the scene of another Russo–Chinese 'incident'.

Macartney and his brother Donald had gone for their evening walk which that day took them past the Russo–Chinese Bank where they were surprised to see about 200 mounted Cossacks waiting. Colonel Bobrov and Sokov were there talking. Macartney strolled up to Sokov and asked him casually what was happening. He was told that they had been set as an exercise night manœuvres along the Maralbashi road. The brothers said goodnight and went on, but cut short their walk, very worried. The whole town knew that the gamblers were marching out by the North Gate after dark and along the Maralbashi road. Macartney guessed, correctly as he heard next day, that the rest of the cavalry had already ridden out by the same road and were waiting for the gamblers. Returning to the Consulate he at once sent his Chinese secretary to warn the Hsietai and advise him, firstly, to inform the foreign consuls which of the gates would be opened for the New Regiment when it left; secondly, to defer the departure of the troops till daylight; thirdly, to ride with them himself until the whole column was well clear of Kashgar. Hours later an orderly came with the Hsietai's red paper visiting card and a message that the troops would march out at 8 a.m. next day by the *East* Gate. The man went on and delivered the same message at the Russian Consulate-General. The

Macartneys went to bed relieved and hopeful, but still anxious. Next morning all was well. The gamblers had gone and the Cossacks were back in their billets. What the Colonel said when he realized that his exercise had missed fire and the gamblers had given him the slip is not on record.

The New Regiment duly arrived early in January at Urumchi where they were incorporated in a force of Confucian (old style, non-Muslim) troops of not much more military value than themselves. The Titai, Chiao, who since the Kashgar assassinations had been a mere puppet of the gamblers, followed them to Urumchi and commanded them on their expedition against rebellious Mongols in the remote Kobdo region. Governor Yang, whose power was by this time firmly based on Dungan cavalry from Kansu, thus killed two birds with one stone; he made a show of protecting the capital from rebel hordes, and at the same time disembarrassed himself of much useless and opium sodden soldiery. As for the arch-assassins Macartney some months later mentioned that Pien was acting as military Amban at Hami, 300 miles east of Urumchi, and was reported to be a reformed character.

Kashgar's riddance of the gamblers must be seen in the context of the Sino-Russian diplomatic crisis which had come to a head in the autumn of 1911 over the renewal of the Treaty of St Petersburg. Despite two years' diplomatic pressure, including an ultimatum with a large-scale frontier mobilization in 1911 and the military occupation of Kashgar the following year, the Chinese had stood firm and refused the further commercial concessions demanded by Russia. Article XV of the 1881 Treaty laid down that if, within six months of the expiry of a ten-year period, either party did not want a revision the commercial clauses would remain in force. In October 1912 the Tsar's government acknowledged defeat and announced that the existing commercial stipulations of the Treaty would remain in force for another ten years. The only change the Russians secured benefited both sides: a free trade zone on either side of the frontier, inhabited almost exclusively by smugglers, was abolished.

The diplomatic defeat had to be countered by concessions to Russian prestige and Governor Yang evidently decided that the removal of the gamblers from Kashgar was essential to this end. Not only were they a threat to his own authority but while they ruled the roost in Kashgar it was difficult to make the conciliatory gestures to Russia which were a cheap price for the renewal of the existing Treaty of St Petersburg and the withdrawal of the Russian force. A full-scale inquiry into the Chira Incident was the first step in this direction but since this was likely to take a long time the Chinese gave in to the Russian demand for a public apology by the highest-ranking Chinese official south of the Tien Shan. Accordingly on 12 October 1912 the Titai, Chiao, as Commander-in-Chief and second only in rank to the Governor, apologized publicly to the Russian Consul-General for the action taken against a Russian subject and for the burning of his father-in-law's house.

Yet another concession to Russian pressure was the arrest of the villain-hero of Chira, Hsiung Kao-sheng. He was the Ko-Lao-Hui leader of the 800 strong gambler regiment at Yarkand, and he returned to his headquarters in that town in triumph after the Chira riot. Sokov had more than once complained to Macartney that the Chinese were sheltering Hsiung, and Macartney had urged the officials to arrest him and bring him to Kashgar, but the Taotai, who feared the Ko-Lao-Hui and dared not use force, took no action. His excuse was that if Hsiung came to Kashgar there might be a popular demonstration in his favour as there had been at Yarkand. The departure of the gambler regiment changed all that and three days later Hsiung arrived unheralded for the trial.

This was good news to Macartney but another Russian move was ominous. One day when he was calling on Sokov he noticed in the background a youngish, well-dressed Andijani whom he had not seen before. He was startled to learn afterwards from the Taotai that the man, Mustafa Khan, was no other than the grandson of the famous rebel Yakub Beg, ruler of Chinese Turkestan from 1864 to 1877. Yakub's son and heir, Beg Quli Beg, had succeeded him for a few months after his death in May 1877 but when the victorious Chinese army threatened Kashgar he fled to Russian Ferghana. There he was still, calling himself King of Kashgar and drawing a Russian political pension. His son, an employee in the offices of the Governor-General of Russian Turkestan at Tashkent, had come to Kashgar ostensibly to recover a large sum of money from the heirs of a man who had been his grandfather's treasurer, Hashur Hakim Beg. It was alleged that after the death of the Amir and the flight of his son to Russian territory Hashur Hakim Beg had bought lands with what remained of his master's treasure; he was now dead but his widow held the land in trust for his children and Mustafa Khan's claim was against her.

Macartney perhaps recalled to mind one of his earliest conversations with Petrovsky at the very outset of his career in Kashgar when the Russian in an expansive mood had talked of a possible Kirghiz revolt against Chinese rule and had discussed the claim of Beg Quli Beg to lead it. More recently he had listened to Behrens's views that Chinese rule was decadent and should be swept out of Sinkiang and be replaced by a Muslim state. In Behrens's opinion it would not pay Russia to annex Sinkiang but it was to her interest to see it become an independent buffer state, too weak to resist Russian exploitation. Macartney's brief telegram on the subject caused a minor sensation in Whitehall. Could it be that the Tsar's agents in Central Asia were planning a Muslim revolt in southern Sinkiang with the grandson of Yakub Beg as its figurehead? Macartney certainly suspected something of the kind towards the end of October 1912, especially when Sokov told him that the situation in Khotan and Keriya districts was so disquieting that he was thinking of sending 300 troops there.

However, an unexpected change then came over Russian politics in Kashgar. During the first week of November, 150 of the 350 Cossack cavalry rode out of Kashgar on their way back to Russian Turkestan. It was said that the men were time-expired and would be replaced, but the reduction in the strength of the detachment was the subject of much hopeful comment. Next, Macartney noticed a change in his colleague's attitude towards Colonel Bobrov, with whom he seemed to be completely reconciled. There was also a new scepticism in Sokov's references to Behrens's melodramatic reports from Khotan. Then came the startling news that a Russian general of high rank, called Metentzov, had crossed the Terek Pass on his way from Tashkent to Kashgar with an escort of 100 Cossacks. No explanation was forthcoming from the Russian Consulate about the reasons for his visit. Could it be the first Russian move to put Mustafa Khan on the throne of Kashgar?

General Metentzov arrived in Kashgar on 17 November and

was received at the Russian Consulate by the Titai, the Taotai and a number of other Chinese officials. The following day he visited Chini Bagh accompanied by Sokov, and Macartney found himself agreeably surprised. The General arrived ablaze with decorations and escorted by 100 Cossacks, but he was far from being the bombastic, fire-eating type Macartney expected. He spoke French well and was dignified, rather reserved in manner, if a little peremptory, but the total impression was of a man far superior in breeding to most Russian officers. He made no mention of the reason for his visit to Kashgar and did not refer to the political condition of the country, a silence that Macartney reciprocated. The General's visit lasted for seven days during which time he was treated with marked respect by the Chinese officials. But as far as Macartney knew he did not discuss any political questions with them. Altogether he met Macartney four times and only once referred to the situation in Kashgar when he asked if foreigners had suffered at all during the recent troubles. Macartney replied that the Chinese had studiously confined their disputes to themselves and no British interests had suffered appreciably. When Metentzov left for St Petersburg on 24 November Macartney was no wiser about the purpose of his visit or his views on the political situation in Kashgar: 'The world in Kashgar only knows that, though General Metentzov has come and gone, there is still no talk of the withdrawal of the Russian Detachment.'

It was Christmas before the full story behind Metentzov's visit was revealed to Macartney. Soon after the General left, Macartney discovered in a conversation with Sokov that the Consul-General was thoroughly disillusioned about his secretary, Behrens, who was still in Khotan collecting evidence for the Chira trial. His reports were highly sensational and gave the impression that Russian lives and property were in imminent danger. So bitter, Behrens said, were the Chinese against the Russians that a St Bartholomew's Night might at any time be the fate of Russian subjects. He recommended that a whole regiment of Cossacks should be stationed at Khotan and that troops should also be quartered at intermediate towns on the road there. The Andijanis at Khotan, he said, were clamouring for the establishment of a Russian consulate in their midst. He had insisted on some Chinese soldiers being beaten at Khotan for an alleged assault on Andijanis while on patrol duty. By way of apology for this he had tried to force the Chinese

military authorities to lower their regimental banners before the
Russian flag in his presence and that of his twenty-five Cossacks.
He had not succeeded and the Chinese refusal was a grievance to
Behrens. According to him Syed Haji was a martyr whose suffer-
ings at Chira should be avenged by at least fifty executions. Sokov
said that he had sent these reports to headquarters, but had been
careful not to endorse the views expressed, for he had no wish to
be thought at one with his secretary. What worried him was lest
they should prejudice the prospects of the detachment's withdrawal which he, Sokov, had recommended. Moreover, he was
now in doubt about how to proceed with the Chira trial, for he was
convinced that the Chinese were not so much to blame as he had
at first been led to believe.

After these astonishing revelations Macartney was not surprised when three weeks later Behrens returned from Khotan and
word went round that he was leaving very shortly for St Petersburg. At his farewell call on Christmas Eve he treated an embarrassed Macartney to a lengthy harangue. Seldom has an intriguer
given himself as well as his victim away more thoroughly; he must
have thought Macartney more than usually gullible, for he
ascribed to Sokov all the sins he had committed himself. He said
he had been summoned to the capital about the Chira affair; he
had written privately about it to a friend at the Ministry of Foreign
Affairs contradicting the Consul-General's reports, and his letter
had been effective. Since the outbreak of the Chinese revolution
Sokov and the Governor-General of Russian Turkestan had aimed
at pushing Russia into occupying Kashgaria. So far as Behrens
knew there was nothing in Sokov's instructions from the Ministry
at St Petersburg to indicate a 'forward policy'. He had systematic-
ally exaggerated the danger to Russian interests. When the Chira
Incident had happened he had given it a sensational turn, saying
that more than thirty Russian subjects had been massacred by the
gamblers. The truth was that there had been only two genuine
Russian subjects among the fifty or so Chira people killed; the
others were all either loyal Chinese nationals or people who,
through the agency of Syed Haji, had been forced by Sokov to
take out Russian nationality certificates. These men had all been
born in Chinese Turkestan and their fathers too. If their ancestors
had come from Ferghana at all (a doubtful point) it could only
have been before the Russian conquest of the province.

In view of Sokov's doubts about the forthcoming Chira inquiry Macartney found what Behrens had to say about it particularly interesting. 'Why', he asked rhetorically, 'does M. Sokov not proceed with the trial? Because he cannot whip up enough Russian subjects to appear as accusers. In all Chinese Turkestan there are not more than 200 *bona fide* Russian Muslims, but M. Sokov has issued 2000 nationality certificates; his object is to embitter the Chinese against us and at the same time to cause friction with Britain by heaping up Russian interests on the Indian frontier. Thanks to my reports he has been called upon for an explanation.'

Sokov must have heard of his secretary's interview with Macartney and guessed at its contents, for next day, although it was Christmas, he went round to Chini Bagh and gave his version of the story. In October, he said, he had been asked by the Foreign Ministry if he could explain some fantastic allegations made against him by a member of his staff. He was accused of trying to arrest the gambler leaders, Pien and Wei; of bribing gamblers to light the fires that caused the paper burning fiasco; of engineering the Chira incident from start to finish; of embezzling 9000 roubles of government money and of staging an accidental fire to destroy the evidence. Although Sokov had not been on good terms with Colonel Bobrov at the time his first reaction to these accusations was to go round and ask if he knew who was responsible. The Colonel had told him that the denunciatory letter had been sent by Behrens in collusion with the seismologist Dr Lavrienti (the man who had said of Sokov to Macartney 'Il croit, il veut croire, et il veut faire croire au danger'). As Kashgar was specially in the news at the time owing to the Chira crisis the Tsar had specially commissioned General Metentzov to go there on a visit of inspection to report on the situation. He, Sokov, had had no difficulty in refuting Behrens's calumnies; his talks with the General had cleared the matter up and Behrens had been summoned to the capital to answer for his perfidy.

The whole story was now clear. Secretary Behrens had joined the Consulate-General in June 1911 at a critical period in Sino–Russian relations over the 1881 Treaty, and in September that year he started down the Khotan road on his stormy tour of the southern oases. It is hard to believe that the appointment of Behrens, young, ambitious, energetic and experienced in political work, at such a juncture, was a mere matter of routine. It seems more than likely that his appointment and his filibustering policy were Russia's way of bringing pressure on the Chinese to agree to new concessions in the Treaty of St Petersburg. The Chinese revolution and the seizure of power by the gamblers in Kashgar upset Sokov's and Behrens's calculations although it gave them every opportunity to urge the annexation of Kashgaria. There was probably a great deal of truth behind Colonel Bobrov's accusation that Sokov wanted Chinese Turkestan as a province of the Tsar's empire with himself as Governor-General. It was also possible, as Behrens said, that he was supported in his schemes by the Governor-General at Tashkent. But they had underestimated the toughness of the new Chinese regime. The republican government had refused to give in to demands for a revision of the 1881 Treaty while Governor Yang's skilful concessions made it difficult for the Russians to exploit the Chira Incident.

Macartney's reports, which resulted in the discussion between Sazanov, the Russian Foreign Minister, and Lord Crewe, the Secretary of State for India, in September 1912 possibly alerted the Russian Foreign Office to what its agents in Kashgaria were trying to do. Since the days of Petrovsky the St Petersburg Foreign Ministry had striven to restrict Russian policy in Kashgaria to one of exploitation rather than annexation and when Behrens's letter denouncing Sokov arrived at the Ministry they lost no time in dispatching General Metentzov to Kashgar to give a true report on the situation. On his part Behrens probably feared that he had overplayed his hand in the Chira Incident and that when some of the true facts came to light Sokov might repudiate him. He thought it best to get his blow in first and denounce his chief. But his intrigue had rebounded on himself and his career in Kashgaria had come to an abrupt end.

THIRTEEN

The Contest for Sinkiang

With the new year 1913 the three-cornered struggle for the control of Chinese Turkestan entered a new phase. For the first time the Chinese contestants, Governor Yang Tseng-hsin at Urumchi and the Ko-Lao-Hui in Kashgaria, temporarily allied against Russia, found their star in the ascendant. The strength of the detachment had diminished by a quarter; the Treaty of St Petersburg, innocent of revision in Russia's favour, was again in force for another decennial period; preparations for the Chira inquiry were going well from the Chinese point of view, whereas Secretary Behrens who had been in charge of them on the Russian side had been recalled.

Sokov, deserted and betrayed by a trusted lieutenant, awaited anxiously his government's reactions to Behrens's revelations. His personal situation was certainly difficult. What was he to do about the trial? If he pursued it vigorously he would have to identify himself with the very forward policy which Behrens now denounced. Moreover, without Behrens to conduct the prosecution he did not know whether he would be able to persuade the Chinese judges to convict their own officials. Even if he did, would his Foreign Ministry approve? On the other hand, if he stood aside and let the Russian case go by default his own and Russia's prestige would sink and his career would suffer. All he could do was to postpone the trial while he awaited instructions from his government. He thereby lost the initiative and gave the Chinese plenty of time to work up their case against Syed Haji, which they did to such effect that when the proceedings at last opened in the third week of February Sokov found the tables turned and the officials whose execution Behrens had demanded acting as counsel for the prosecution.

Meanwhile, Macartney's services in the cause of peace and sanity throughout the disturbances caused by the Chinese revolution were rewarded in the New Year's honours list where his name was among the Knights Commander of the Indian Empire. Macartney probably owed this recognition to the influence of Sir Aurel Stein, the archaeologist, who stayed with him on some occasions in Kashgar. Both men held each other in great esteem and it seems that several times Stein was quietly able to use his influence with the government of India to forward Macartney's views. The honour made no difference to the Macartneys' style of life. A much grander building had risen on the site of Chini Bagh, but the new Lady Macartney still cooked in the kitchen in the absence of reliable help. Twenty-two years had passed since Macartney had arrived in Kashgar as Younghusband's reserved and diffident assistant; the experience of those years had given him self-assurance, but Sir George Macartney remained the unassuming quiet observer whose tact and readiness to listen now drew the rival confidences of Behrens, Sokov, pork butcher Pien, the feeble Taotai, and the respected Hsietai of Kashgar.

The faith of the British-Indian residents in their Consul was described in a report made to the Foreign Office in February 1913 by Miss E. G. Kemp, a remarkable traveller, who crossed the Karakoram from India and stayed for three weeks with the Macartneys. At Yarkand she found 1500 British Indians who begged her to tell Sir Edward Grey that 'if it had not been for Sir G. Macartney Russia would long ago have swallowed the whole country. The Chinese depend entirely upon him for advice, and it has only been by his wise counsel that they have been prevented from giving the Russians the opportunity which they have long been seeking of picking a quarrel.' Miss Kemp also put to the Foreign Office Macartney's disadvantage in having no Vice-Consul to help him whom he could send to Yarkand or other places where there were disturbances. Asked if Macartney himself had mentioned this she said no, but he had been much disappointed when his request for an escort had been turned down.

Despite his honour and Miss Kemp's good opinion Macartney was not without his critics. There was some raising of eyebrows at lower levels in the Foreign Office when his reports of his talks with the Taotai and Sokov after the Chira Incident were received. It was suggested that he was advising the Chinese how best to oppose Russian encroachments. A senior official minuted:

This is a delicate situation and it may lead to trouble. It is for consideration whether the Consul should not be warned that it is not his duty to give such advice but that he should restrict himself to reporting what is going on and if necessary soliciting instructions.

On this the Foreign Secretary's orders were:

I do not see that he has done more than use his influence to prevent the Chinese from giving provocation or cause for legitimate complaint to Russia. I think it would be a good thing if he was instructed carefully to keep within these limits and not to encourage any objective tactics or attitude on the part of the Chinese against Russia.

Macartney himself anticipated criticism of his advice to Sokov when they discussed together Behrens's behaviour on his Khotan tour. He concluded his December dispatch with the following apologia:

My plea is (1) that the subject was always opened by Sokov; (2) that no offence was taken; (3) that if it is in our interest that Russia should be prevented so far as possible from filibustering, it is as well that they should be made to see that we are watching them. Personally I think that had there been no British consul at Kashgar to play the role of spectator – and of reporter to his government – before now Sokov might have thrust a quarrel on the Chinese and, by exaggerating, forced the Russians to an even more serious undertaking than has hitherto been carried out.

Macartney was not boasting when he pointed out the significance of his own reports in restraining Sokov's attempts to adopt the role of *agent provocateur*. His experiences of Petrovsky had shown him how an ambitious and unscrupulous consul could bring Russia to the brink of annexing Kashgaria, and he was quick to warn his government of Sokov's every move. But his twenty-two years in Kashgar had given him little hope that Russian designs would ever be checked by China herself. At a distance of 800 miles from Urumchi, which in the days before motor transport could only be covered in a journey of fifty-one stages, he had little means of reporting on or assessing the new Governor and his regime. He was never in a position to leave Kashgar for the four months needed to visit the capital and had to rely on the occasional news letter from the missionary, the Reverend George Hunter, and on the gossip of the Kashgar *yamens* and bazaar. Successive Taotais and Titais had long been accustomed to play down Urumchi in conversation with Macartney, pretending that in all but routine matters they were in direct touch with Peking. It was therefore some time before he had any realization that in Governor Yang the Russians had for the first time in his experience met a Chinese whose intelligence, skill and ruthlessness were equal to their own.

The Governor was always to remain a shadowy figure in Macartney's reports and few Europeans ever saw him. The German archaeologist, G. N. Roerich, who interviewed him in 1926 described him as 'robust and well built with a long grey beard, dressed in a very plain grey coat and wearing a black skull-cap. He spoke slowly in a low tone, and then would suddenly raise his voice and thunder.' Another observer was impressed by his strong face and the remarkable dignity he showed in all his actions. 'One felt that in him was a man possessed of a capacity for administration of a high order.' According to a Chinese writer, A. K. Wu, who visited Sinkiang as an official of the Nationalist government in 1932 after Yang's death, the Governor was about forty-six years old when he took over the administration of the province. His appointment was at first merely temporary after the resignation of Governor Yuan, and from A. K. Wu's account, Yuan Shih-k'ai, the new President of the Chinese Republic, was urged to supersede him and to appoint one of his own entourage in his place. But the President was so impressed by Yang's dispatches, which were concise, accurate and respectful, that he told his officials who coveted the post, 'There is not one of you who can come near him. This Yang has the greatest mind in China today.' Wu goes on to describe how Yang built up his power in Sinkiang from the days of the revolution:

> He knew the minds of Chinese politicians and was an adept at diplomacy. Trading upon the mutual rivalries of the leaders, making all possible concessions to their dignity, and basing his appeal upon his fame as a just ruler, he won over the rebels

without bloodshed. Following upon this first triumph he never faltered, but slowly increasing his hold upon the province he ruled with such wisdom that for seventeen years, while wars raged in the outside world and Republican China was torn by conflicting factions, in Sinkiang there was absolute peace.

A. K. Wu's admiration for the Governor's achievement perhaps made him a partial historian but there can be no doubt that Yang's greatest asset in his rise to power and in his subsequent government of the province was his own acute intelligence. This gave him the diplomatic skill and subtlety to play one faction off against another and to combine both ruthlessness and conciliation in his methods. In the early days of his rule, when he was surrounded by enemies, conciliation was the only course open to him. His most immediate task was to establish his own authority and to bring back order to the province, which was threatened not only by Russia but by the Ko-Lao-Hui in Kashgaria and the Russian-backed separatist movement in Ili. There was also a possible danger from the nomadic tribes of the mountains and northern steppe, the Kirghiz, Kazakhs and Mongols, who could be organized by Russian agents or dissident Chinese into pillaging bands or a cavalry force capable of overrunning the province. To deal with this situation Yang had one strength only: the Dungan troops whom his predecessor, Governor Yuan, had brought into the province in his attempt to contain the first outbreak of the revolution.

Yang, who was a Yunnanese by birth, had spent much of his career in the predominantly Muslim province of Kansu and had acquired a reputation for his understanding of and ability to manage Dungans. This now stood him in good stead, and with about 2000 Dungan troops behind him he was able to negotiate with the Ili rebels. Their leader was Brigadier Yang Tsuan-hsu, the garrison commander at Kuldja, whose men had started the revolution in Sinkiang by storming the fortified Chinese town of Kora and killing the last of the 'Tartar Generals' of Ili. Governor Yuan's troops had failed to subdue them and there was grave danger that the rebels would break away from the provincial government and let the Russians into the much-coveted Ili. Yang realized that he was not strong enough to master them by force so he used his diplomatic skill to buy the alliance of their leader.

212

The price was a high one. Brigadier Yang Tsuan-hsu was made Titai of Kashgar, and, as such, commander-in-chief of the province and senior official south of the Tien Shan. On the face of it the appointment was a risk, but, as it turned out, in one brilliant stroke Governor Yang had divided his enemies by the simple expedient of sending the northerners to the south and the southerners to the north. The gambler regiment of Kashgar and the old Titai, Chiao, were removed from the only environment in which they were dangerous and were replaced by the Ili leader with a mixed force of 400 Dungans, Shibos and Turkis. Cut off from his local base and placed among people with an outlook different from his own, it was easy for the ambitious young Titai to make mistakes, a course that was perhaps not unanticipated by the wily Governor at Urumchi. The removal of the gambler troops from Kashgar also prevented their staging a confrontation with the Russians, and in the interest of further neutralizing the Russian danger the Governor risked loss of face by ordering the Titai Chiao to apologize to Sokov for the Chira Incident. The apology, though, affected the Titai's prestige more than that of the distant Governor, a fact that, again, was perhaps not unanticipated in Urumchi.

Skilful though the Governor's handling of the situation was his own ability and the support of the Dungan troops could not by themselves have kept him in power. No one was more aware than he that the Dungans could be a double-edged sword. Not only had they to be conciliated and their leaders given positions of power but the troops had to be paid. In the state of Sinkiang's finances this was no easy matter. The provincial revenues were still seriously deficient and the finances of the new Republic gave no hope of an increased subsidy from Peking. Yuan Shih-k'ai had about a million men under arms whom he could not pay, feed or clothe, and many of them had already taken to mutiny and plundering. The country was defaulting on its repayments of previous loans and indemnities and the President was desperately casting about for fresh money from abroad. In this situation it is unlikely that any funds from the central government trickled into the provincial treasury at Urumchi. Yang seems to have survived financially by adopting the methods of his predecessors. Stringent attempts were made to squeeze more taxes out of the people, but the chief recourse was to the manufacture of paper money. By

January 1914 the notes in circulation were six times the amount of the provincial revenues.

Although Yang knew that he could look for no help from outside and must somehow finance his own administration he consistently followed a policy of supporting the Peking government. He was ruthless in stamping on plots to make Sinkiang a separate republic even when it was proposed to make him head of it. Yang had nothing to lose by this policy. In every way that mattered he was an independent ruler and he soon set about putting his own relatives and friends in all the key posts of Sinkiang. But he knew that if he was to avoid becoming the tool of Russia he needed the authority and international standing of the Peking government behind him. Moreover, all his sympathies and those of the majority of his officials lay with Yuan Shih-k'ai and the President's ambition to proclaim himself emperor. The democratic policies of Sun Yat-sen and the Kuomintang in the south seemed only to lead to social and political anarchy hateful to one of Yang's temperament and training. Yuan Shih-k'ai, on the other hand, was a man of his own kind and the higher Yuan's fortunes rose the stronger Yang felt his position would be.

His new Titai, Brigadier Yang Tsuan-hsu, did not share the Governor's outlook. He himself had risen to power as the leader of the revolutionaries in Sinkiang and his star was firmly linked to the republican cause. He arrived in Kashgar on 28 January 1913 with his 400 troops, all without queues and dressed in Cossack fleece overcoats. Macartney had already heard from Dr Morrison, formerly *The Times* correspondent at Peking, of Brigadier Yang's intelligence and smart appearance, and when the Titai paid his courtesy call at Chini Bagh he was at first favourably impressed. He made his entry to a fanfare of foreign bugles, escorted by 100 of his own troops and wearing a uniform of foreign style covered with orders of unknown institution. Macartney knew of his blood-spattered career at Ili but he thought that the Titai talked well, modestly, and with dignity. Here perhaps was someone who could counterbalance and control the Ko-Lao-Hui which, in the absence of any other Chinese authority, still held sway in Kashgar.

It was obvious, though, that the Titai would not find his way easy and that the Ko-Lao-Hui would oppose any attempt to oust their society from power or to create a rival republican party in Kashgaria. At the time of the Titai's arrival Macartney reported that a section of the Chinese population, including those gamblers who had not left with the New Regiment, were holding frequent public meetings in which they criticized the officials and urged each other to join various political clubs and societies. They also put up placards on the *yamen* walls at night saying that four men were worthy of death for having cut off their queues and adopted foreign dress. These reactionary sentiments were supported by most of the Chinese population. They showed their dislike of republican changes by refusing to join the *yamen* officials in celebrating the new year on 1 January instead of on the old date.

Macartney was aware of the strength of conservative and reactionary opinion and was therefore alarmed by the Titai's talk and behaviour when he returned his call on 4 February. Yang received him with a display of European culture. He wore a Russian general's peaked cap above his foreign-cut uniform, and his guard of honour presented arms in the English manner. During dinner a band of fifteen musicians played marches tolerably well on European instruments. Yang was extremely friendly but he was clearly trying to impress Macartney with his personality and power. He spoke as if he had only to make a sign and his order would instantly be obeyed, not only by the military but by the civil officials, whom, contrary to all precedent, he claimed a right to control. The impression he gave was that he was a dictator in Kashgaria, responsible for all its affairs, civil, military, foreign and social. Macartney thought that he meant well and that he wanted to work for the good of the country and not solely for his private ends, but he detected under his energetic appearance a certain inexperience and immaturity of judgement.

The Titai found the Chinese at Kashgar very much behind the times compared with Ili. They needed hustling; they must be made to accept the republican regime whether they liked it or not. The queue belonged to the Manchus and should disappear with them. As for the troops, his idea was to encourage recruiting among the Turki population. He would like to buy from Europe by the Indian route two field guns and 3000 rifles; Chinese supplies were too distant and it would be useless to expect any help from the Russians. He had heard on all sides how friendly Macartney was with the Chinese and would be glad of his good offices in the matter. The Kashgar troops were very badly equipped because the last Titai had taken with him all the arms that were of any use.

Macartney advised his host to hasten slowly, especially over the queues of the 'old-style' troops. He suggested a compromise; instead of cutting them off let the men wind their queues round their heads on parade. As for the guns and rifles, he emphasized the political objections to importing them through Indian territory and the physical difficulties of the long and mountainous Ladakh route. But he was all in favour of the garrison being properly equipped, and if later on the Titai wished to speak to him again on the matter he would consider it seriously. This was a mistake; two days later the Titai, encouraged, summoned the merchants of Kashgar to his *yamen*, told them his plans, and proposed that they should raise 250,000 taels (£37,500) for the purchase. That evening (6 February) Macartney met Sokov's secretary at a party and mentioned the matter to him casually. Needless to say the Titai did not get the money and no more was heard from him on the subject, but anticipating possible trouble Macartney paid a special call on Sokov on the 8th and told him that if the Titai renewed the subject he would refuse to discuss it with him unless the Russian Consul-General was a party to their talks.

Macartney had acted too late to protect himself. Sokov had already seized the opportunity to make capital out of the affair. A fortnight later the Counsellor at the Russian Embassy in London informed the Under-Secretary of State for Foreign Affairs that the British Consul-General at Kashgar had been requested by the Chinese to obtain 3000 rifles for the Chinese army. The Russian government was sure that these could only be intended to use against the small detachment of Russian troops at Kashgar, which was the only force able to protect the Europeans in the district, and they requested that the arms in question should not be supplied. In reply to a telegraph inquiry Macartney told the Foreign Office exactly what had happened, and in a letter dated 19 March 1913 Sir Edward Grey was able to assure his Russian counterpart that M. Sokov had been aware throughout that he would be consulted before any further steps were taken. The assurances were accepted and the matter was dropped. But soon after this incident the Russian detachment was restored by fresh reinforcements to more than its original strength. Sokov had found Macartney's lapse a useful excuse for strengthening his forces.

Despite the Titai's failure to equip his troops with satisfactory weapons – Macartney thought that without their Cossack overcoats there was nothing inspiring about them – he quickly established his position in Kashgar and the gamblers made no open attempt to defy him. The Taotai, Wang, had forfeited the popular favour that had given him his post and there was even vague talk of murdering him. Wang was frightened and ineffectual and it was not difficult for Yang Titai to usurp his authority. But the Ko-Lao-Hui was not entirely quiescent. At the beginning of March Macartney reported that Yang had discovered a plot against his own life and had tried a sergeant and ten others who were implicated. He ordered the sergeant to be shot, which was done without any public stir.

Macartney was finding it difficult to give any coherent account of Kashgar politics. He could only guess at the underworld of the Ko-Lao-Hui and at the political currents in the province as a whole. The one thing he could say with certainty was that any respect for constituted authority had largely disappeared. Wang Taotai and Yang Titai had themselves risen to power through revolutionary disorders and others envied their position which brought with it wealth if nothing else. 'The present condition of things,' Macartney reported, 'is one eminently favourable to adventurers who, so long as their personal ambition remains unsatisfied, care nothing for the welfare of the community, but who range themselves, for their own protection, on the side of law and order.' Yang Titai, though, was showing every sign of successfully consolidating his position. His relations with Urumchi appeared to be good, although it was apparent that he no longer disputed the Governor's supremacy in matters of general administration. He was centralizing the military control of southern Sinkiang in his own hands, and his popularity was growing. This was largely due to the stand that he and the Provincial Governor were taking against Russian demands and to the turn of events in the Chira inquiry.

For the first time for many years in Central Asian history China was meeting Russia on her own ground and on equal terms, in a Chinese lawcourt with Chinese judges who were not sharing their authority with a Russian consular official. Sokov took it for granted at first that he would at least sit on the bench with the judges, but he was disappointed, for one of the few points on

217

which the Chinese got their way in the preliminary negotiations at Peking in the autumn was the composition of the court; the Russian Consul-General was prosecutor and could not be one of the judges. The trial opened on 21 February in Kashgar before three judges, Wang Taotai, Yang Titai, and Chang Chifu of Kashgar New City. Sokov was present with two of his dragomans to watch over the interests of the complainants, twenty-six real or fictitious Russian subjects. The accused were Hsiung Kao-sheng, the gambler leader, Tang Ta-jen, the former Chifu of Khotan, who held office when the Chira riot occurred, and some seventy natives of Chira. The Russians were in the position of accusers but Sokov had apparently found it difficult to frame specific charges and left it to the Chinese judges to question their own people. The accused, though, were not to be intimidated, and soon turned the trial into a denunciation of Syed Haji and his pro-Russian activities. He had, they said, incited the Chira people to cast off the Chinese yoke and urged them to escape taxation by becoming Russian subjects. He had forced them to buy Russian nationality certificates at prices of 25 to 50 taels apiece and had himself set fire to his house in which thirty people died.

Macartney had no official part in the case and in fact leant over backwards to avoid giving Sokov any grounds for suspecting that his sympathies lay with the Chinese. Privately he must have enjoyed the spectacle of the accused turning into accusers but there were dangers in the Chinese success; it might go to their heads and lead to provocative actions which would give the Russians grounds for refusing to withdraw their troops. By the middle of March the slow progress of the trial and its unexpected developments were producing the effects that Macartney feared. On 10 March Sokov had told him he had no complaints about the behaviour of the judges, but nine days later he was accusing them of partiality. This was because Wang Taotai had been seen in friendly conversation with one of the accused, Tang, the former Chifu of Khotan. Tang had not been imprisoned during the trial so Sokov used this as an excuse to release Syed Haji from his confinement in the Consulate and encouraged him to parade about the town as a hero. He told Macartney at a dinner on 19 March that the Chira prisoners were denying the charges and making counter-accusations 'de sorte que je serai obligé de prendre la justice entre mes propres mains'.

This remark and his observations of Sokov's behaviour convinced Macartney that the Consul was on the brink of provoking a crisis which would be as much an attempt to solve his own personal problems as to bring the Chira trial to the desired conclusion.

> From what I can see, I believe that M. Sokov, who nervously is a wreck, is in a desperate mood. The disclosures which Mr Behrens, now in St Petersburg, may make against him at the Russian Foreign Office are preying on his mind, and here, in his conduct of the Chira case, he feels, no doubt, that he has to stake not merely the prestige of Russia, but his reputation also with his own government.

There could be little doubt that Sokov had been writing highly coloured reports of the Chira affair and that when the evidence recorded at the trial was forwarded to St Petersburg the Russian government would begin to suspect its Consul of gross exaggerations. Syed Haji's indiscriminate issuing of Russian nationality certificates would also be an awkward point to explain away. In this situation it was only natural that Sokov should try to throw the trial proceedings into confusion by incriminating the judges. Macartney described his behaviour like that of 'a chess player who, seeing that the game may go against him, overturns the table'. He would try to persuade his government that he was being badly used and tricked and that 'another dose of the mailed fist should be administered to the Chinese'. What form this would take Macartney could only guess but it seemed likely that more Cossacks would be poured into Kashgaria.

Sokov's intrigues, as Macartney pointed out, were of no interest to the British government if its policy was to allow the Russians *carte banche* in Kashgaria. With only a hint of irony His Majesty's sole representative in Sinkiang explained to his superiors that he was kept completely in the dark about the policy he was supposed to be executing on his government's behalf. He did not know, he said, if Britain had bargained away her interests in Kashgaria in return for Russian goodwill in Tibet, but if this was not so the Foreign Office should try to influence the Russian government in the direction of restraining their agent in Kashgar. The Ambassador in St Petersburg could throw out hints about the real difficulties of the Chira case, which, coupled with Behrens's disclosures, might cast doubt on the wisdom of Sokov's policies and the truth of his reports. Otherwise the Russian government could find itself dragged into a situation in which it was compelled to absorb Kashgaria although it had no real wish to do so.

The Resident in Kashmir, to whom Macartney addressed his views, recommended them to the government of India, and they were eventually passed on to the Foreign Office in London with rather lukewarm support from the Secretary of State for India. Lord Crewe thought it desirable that the Tsar's ministers should be reminded from time to time that the British government was interested in the course of events in Chinese Turkestan and that if Sir Edward Grey saw no objection the British Ambassador could inquire unofficially in St Petersburg about the progress of the Chira case. But by this time the date was 6 June and the situation had developed at Kashgar in a way that strengthened the case for a more normal approach to the Russian government.

During March and April relations between the Russian Consulate-General and the Chinese officials, especially Wang Taotai, grew steadily worse and tension built up over other matters besides the Chira inquiry. Sokov was furious with Wang for failing to satisfy the claims of Mustafa Khan, the grandson of Yakub Beg, and he threatened to break off relations with him. He also found himself frustrated in his plan to link Kashgar with the Russian telegraph system at the frontier station of Irkeshtam. He tried to hustle Wang into giving permission for the scheme by hinting vaguely that this was the *quid pro quo* for the withdrawal of the Russian detachment. But Wang referred the matter to Urumchi and was told that Governor Yang could not give his consent without orders from Peking. The Governor, like Macartney, saw the scheme as another sample of Russian diplomacy designed to strip the Chinese of their independence, and he had no intention of permitting 'another coil round the Chinese body politic'. It was Wang, though, who bore the brunt of Sokov's frustration.

The biggest bone of contention between the Russians and the Chinese continued to be the registration question which in the course of time threatened, in Macartney's view, to bring the entire tax-paying population under Russian jurisdiction. This had become for the Chinese the main issue at stake in the Chira inquiry, and to make his position clear Governor Yang had taken steps a

220

few days before the proceedings opened to force the issue not only with the Russians but (lest there be complaints of discrimination) with the British too. The Ambans of Goma and Karghalik, the two largest oases between Yarkand and Khotan, simultaneously sent notices to all the British and Russian subjects in their districts ordering them to sell their land, houses and goods and to leave the country within six months.

This raised a difficult question for Macartney. His own conscience was clear, for he had issued no British nationality certificates since before the revolution. But he had already received letters from the Ambans of Yarkand and Khotan complaining that certain Indian Aksakals had given British subjects unauthorized certificates over their own signatures exempting them from the payment of likin dues. Macartney feared that this would cause the British Consulate-General to be tarred with the same brush as the Russian and he wrote at once to the Taotai disowning the certificates and apologizing for the Aksakals' action. He also did something that showed that he was no longer under any illusion about who governed Kashgaria. He telegraphed directly to Governor Yang at Urumchi saying that the periodical registration of British subjects had not yet begun, that he objected to the orders issued by the two Ambans, and asking whether the officials were acting on the Governor's orders.

Within a fortnight the Governor's reply came by telegram through the Taotai. It was in the form of courteously worded, almost identical letters to both the consuls-general, but every line gave evidence of a strong hand controlling Sinkiang and of the Governor's determination to resist further foreign encroachments. The reply was unambiguous: the Chinese government would never tolerate the purchase by the natives of southern Turkestan of foreign nationality certificates in order to become foreign subjects. The Governor would nullify the notices issued by the Ambans of Goma and Karghalik but on condition that those Turkis who had acquired foreign nationality certificates without the permission of the Chinese government should still be regarded by the foreign consuls as Chinese subjects and not be claimed by them as their own nationals. The Governor wrote in his letter to Macartney:

I have always held in high respect your sense of justice. You know our language well and you are well acquainted with the condition of Southern Turkestan, wherein you have resided for more than a decade. You will, I am sure, settle this nationality question with Wang Taotai, so that the friendship between the two countries may be cemented.

Macartney knew that despite the unauthorized actions of some British Aksakals the Governor's quarrel was not with him but with the Russians, and, provided the threat to expel British subjects was withdrawn, he was in full support of Chinese policy. In his reply to the Governor he managed to convey not only an indignant denial that he had sold nationality certificates to Chinese subjects but a condemnation of the Russian policy which was behind the trouble. The British Consulate, he said, was not a shop and British nationality certificates were not articles of merchandise. He had not yet begun to issue them, but when he did they would only be to people who were British subjects *ab initio*.

Sokov's reaction to the Governor's message was very different, and he called at Chini Bagh on 21 April to enlist Macartney's support for an uncompromising stand. He insisted that all those who had been registered by him in southern Turkestan were real Russian subjects, adding in a tone of determination 'Ils le seront'. The two consuls exchanged translations of their replies to the Governor, and the Russian's reply, far from repudiating the registration policy, justified it, ending with the words:

> Those to whom this Consulate has given registration certificates are *ab initio* Russian subjects, their origin having been duly attested by reliable witnesses, and Russian subjects they must remain.

By the beginning of May the Chira trial had become the battleground on which the two sides fought out the registration question, the Chinese with growing belligerence. The conduct of the Chinese case was now in the hands of Yang Titai, as Sokov was showing his disgust with the Taotai by refusing to have any dealings with him. It was a tactical mistake on the Consul's part which he discovered too late. Yang saw his chance to seize effective control of the Kashgarian administration and to increase his popularity by humiliating the Russians. Sokov had demanded the execution of Tang, Hsiung and two other men for their part in the Chira affair, but the Titai retorted by asking what was to be the fate of Syed

Haji. Sokov said he was innocent, whereupon Yang asked him why he was making all the fuss since twenty-nine out of the thirty people killed were Chinese subjects whom the Consul had no business to register as Russians. It was for the Chinese to complain and no one else. The Titai seized every opportunity to express his anti-Russian sentiments. Colonel Bobrov's troops were at this time quartered outside the Russian Consulate and Sokov applied to the Governor for permission to house them in a large government building near the East Gate of the town which was intended for a school. The Titai promptly put his own troops from Ili into it and telegraphed to the Governor that it could not be spared.

Relations between the two sides, like the Chira inquiry, had reached an impasse. Either the Russian government must order their Consul to make a friendly compromise or they must attempt to overawe the Chinese by military force. On 2 May Macartney wrote a long report on the situation in which he expressed his view that the Russian government did not want to annex the country but that Sokov showed every sign of trying to force his government's hands. If St Petersburg were determined on annexation Macartney was prepared to accept the situation but he declared himself unwilling to see British interests disturbed through the personal ambition of Sokov.

> Kashgaria is now at the parting of the ways. Either it will remain what it was a year ago – namely a region where Russian influence, though preponderant, is not supported by military force, or it will follow the fate of North Manchuria – and that will be its fate if the Russian troops do not withdraw.

If their withdrawal was to depend on Sokov's recommendation then it would never happen as he would always claim that only their presence stopped the Chinese from maltreating Russian subjects.

On the very day that he wrote this report Macartney was informed of the Russian choice. Sokov's secretary, Hagelstrom, called at the British Consulate and Macartney questioned him about the truth of bazaar rumours that Russian reinforcements were on their way. Hagelstrom replied that the 150 time-expired Cossacks who had returned to Russia the previous autumn were to be replaced, but when the Terek Pass was properly opened 'others' would be coming. On the strength of this news Macartney sent a cypher telegram via Russia on 2 May to the Resident in Kashmir warning him that considerable Russian reinforcements were expected and concluding 'I fear annexation.' Next day he cancelled this by a further telegram after he had paid a visit to Sokov. Sokov denied that the size of the detachment was to be increased and went on to say that he could not understand why the whole force was not withdrawn as he believed that the Russian government had no intention of keeping troops permanently in Kashgar. Macartney had his doubts about the sincerity of Sokov's assurances as there was every sign that the detachment was preparing for a long stay. They were converting a house into a club for the officers; a tennis club was shortly to be opened; two new officers had arrived to study the Chinese language, and four others were expecting their wives to join them from Russia. But in the face of Sokov's denials he felt he had no alternative but to cancel his telegraphed warning of reinforcements.

On 23 May he learnt the extent of Sokov's deception. The 'replacements' arrived and instead of 150 there were 300 infantry and cavalry, bringing the strength of the detachment up to 1000. The mere rumour of their coming was apparently enough for the Titai. Without waiting for orders from the Governor he apologized to Sokov and began serious talks with him about the Chira dispute. On 7 May at a regimental fete held by the Cossacks he whispered to Macartney that the Chira case was practically settled as he had made substantial concessions to the Russians. Hsiung Kao-sheng and two local Chinese officials were to be imprisoned with hard labour, and Sokov himself was to deal with Syed Haji and would inform the Titai of his decision. The families of the men who perished in the flames would be compensated by the Chinese authorities without prejudice to the question of their nationality which could be settled later.

Macartney did not share the Titai's optimism about a settlement of the Chira case, rightly as it happened, because the Governor turned down the draft agreement and snubbed the Titai for interfering in the negotiations without authority. The Titai's settlement certainly fell short of Chinese demands since Syed Haji would go free while Hsiung and the two Ambans were to be severely punished. Also Sokov had given no undertaking that he would discontinue the registration of Chinese Turkis as Russian subjects.

Once more deadlock was reached and there were no further proceedings in the Chira case for the next two-and-a-half months.

During this period the Chinese became more and more intransigent. In the middle of June Macartney reported that in some country towns the Ambans were handling the Andijanis roughly. Some of them had Russian nationality certificates taken away from them and others were beaten or imprisoned. Hagelstrom told Macartney that the Consul-General was receiving petitions from Russian subjects all over the country, but he was not dealing with them 'owing to the nationality impasse'.

The Chinese attitude, which could become dangerously provocative, owed more, perhaps, to the anarchical spirit and general air of levity about the future, which Macartney saw as one of the results of the revolution, than to any dogged determination to resist the Russians. What struck him most in this period about the Chinese in Kashgar was their lack of any unity of purpose or patriotism. The revolution had dissolved the old bonds of society but it had not swept away the corruption and self-seeking which had flourished under the Manchu regime. The officials had cut off their queues and some of them had adopted badly fitting European clothes but they remained preoccupied with their personal enrichment. The one difference was that whereas formerly they had fawned on and cringed before their superiors, now they openly criticized and even vilified them. The Taotai, Wang, 'sickly and invertebrate', was looked on as a mere figurehead by his subordinates who did not consult him or pay any attention to his orders. Wang had repeatedly submitted his resignation to the Governor and constantly told Macartney of his wish to leave the country, almost flee from it. It was still rumoured that there would be attempts on his life, and Macartney could not help seeing that if these were made the Titai must be held responsible.

Macartney was on good terms with both men and although he accepted that Wang was a mere figurehead in Kashgar he had nourished hopes that the Titai, young and energetic, would prove to be the strong man needed to bring order and resolution into the administration. He had to confess his disappointment. The Titai had his troops under control but he had done nothing to improve them. He had given up his attempts to drill them on foreign lines, and, with the first revolutionary ardour dissipated, they had sunk back into their pre-republican condition. Yang was an inveterate opium smoker so he made no attempt to suppress opium smoking among his men. Despite his addiction Macartney thought him still capable of the energy and strength necessary to introduce reforms, but without money or arms and neglected by Peking he thought 'the sheer force of inertia seems too great for him to overcome'. Whatever his hopes had been on first coming to Kashgar, by the summer of 1913 Yang Titai was enmeshed in Kashgar politics and an underworld of plots and counterplots in a personal struggle for power.

He had won the first round of his campaign for the control of Kashgaria by virtually superseding the Taotai in relations with the Russians, but his open disparagement of Wang led Macartney to warn him that if an attempt were made on Wang's life the responsibility for it would primarily rest on his shoulders. The Russians were bent on making Wang the scapegoat for their frustration in the Chira inquiry. This suited the Titai but he was aware that the Russians could make his own position difficult. Reflection on these lines no doubt led to Yang's concessions to Sokov when the news of the detachment's reinforcements showed that the Russians were bent on solving the Chira deadlock in their own way.

But the Russians were not the only enemies Yang had to contend with. What Macartney called the 'chaotic condition of things' in the official hierarchy was intensified by the activities of the secret societies, chief among them the Ko-Lao-Hui, which flourished among all classes of Chinese. The Ko-Lao-Hui were said to have 500 members in Kashgar and 400 in the New City; in Yarkand they were 800 strong. The secret societies had been proscribed by the Manchus as dangerous and anarchical but since the revolution every Chinese had declared himself a member of one or another. Like the Jacobin clubs in revolutionary France they rivalled each other in what Macartney described as their 'tumultuous writings' and in their denunciations of officials. The officials found it best to join them in the interests of their own safety. If they submitted to blackmail and shared the profits of office they maintained their popularity but if they refused they were the object of murderous threats.

So far the secret societies and their gambler adherents had shown themselves to stand in awe of the Titai but even he could not feel secure in the general atmosphere of intrigue, plots and violence. He had already executed one of his own men for allegedly plotting against his life, and all round him he was aware of others jockeying for personal power. The immaturity of judgement that Macartney had early detected in Yang Titai now came into play and by one rash move he brought about his own downfall. On 20 July he brutally murdered Major Li Kuan-tai, the commander of his Ili troops, on the grounds that Li was plotting against him. The event closely followed another of a similar nature in which the Amban of Khotan had instigated the murder of a member of a secret society whom he accused of plotting against his life. Macartney saw the hand of the Ko-Lao-Hui in this, perhaps intriguing to bring the Amban to his own ruin, and it is possible that they played on the Titai's fears in the same way. Perhaps Major Li had planned to supersede his chief, although this seems unlikely, as Urumchi and Peking would have had to agree to his appointment. But whoever encouraged the Titai to murder his second in command almost certainly calculated that this would alienate Yang's Ili troops from their Commander-in-Chief. In the event the Ko-Lao-Hui, the Russians and Governor Yang at Urumchi all gained by the removal of the one man who at one time, it seemed, might seize control of Kashgaria.

Five days before Yang murdered his subordinate the Russians made a decisive move to end the Chira deadlock and to force the Chinese to accept the draft agreement which Sokov had negotiated with the Titai in May. On 15 July the Russian Minister in Peking presented a demand for the dismissal of Wang Taotai and a satisfactory settlement of the whole Chira affair. In President Yuan Shih-k'ai's mind as he considered this demand was the situation that had developed in Manchuria where the Russians were pressing for the dismissal of the Governor of Tsitsihar because of his refusal to do justice in cases brought before him by Russian subjects. When the Russians found their demands ignored they moved a brigade of Cossacks to within 20 miles of the provincial capital and the Chinese were obliged to submit. The thought of a similar move against Urumchi was enough to persuade the President that it was wise to make concessions. On 23 July Sokov informed Macartney that he had received a telegram from his Minister in Peking saying that President Yuan Shih-k'ai had appointed Yang Titai to settle the Chira affair with the Russian Consul-General and that Wang Taotai was to be dismissed for his dilatoriness in the case.

At the official level all was now set fair for a settlement of the Chira case on the basis of the May agreement between Yang and Sokov, but the Titai's assassination of his subordinate brought Kashgar to the verge of a new crisis. Yang's Ili troops, the only Chinese forces of any military value in Kashgaria, were incensed by the murder of their commander and were on the point of mutiny. The Titai had to lock himself away in his own head-quarters and dared not go out, even to negotiate with Sokov. The situation was highly dangerous for the Chinese. A mutiny might start a new wave of revolutionary violence and invite further Russian intervention.

Fortunately for Kashgar there was at hand one Chinese officer who had not joined in the scramble and intrigues for personal power. This was Yang Hsietai, commander of the 'old style' troops in Kashgar Old City who had played a key role in the events of May 1912 and was on close terms of friendship with Macartney. It was he who had installed Wang as Taotai after the murder of Yuen Hung-fu and since then he had been a prominent figure in Kashgar. He was below the Titai in rank but by reason of his age and the general respect in which he was held he had acquired a fatherly ascendancy over his chief. Macartney said of him, 'single-mindedly he has worked for the peace and tranquillity of the country; and if any Chinaman in Kashgar merits the character of patriot, it is he'. He now came forward with disinterested loyalty to shield the Titai from the anger of his own men. It was almost certainly due to his diplomatic intervention that the death was announced of the Titai's father in far-off Hupei. This event obliged the Titai to put his *yamen* into mourning and while it evoked some sympathy for his bereavement it also made it possible for him to live in the security of his inner apartments until the anger of his troops should cool.

Macartney visited him there on 5 August to express his con-dolences and found him with the Hsietai and Wang Taotai whose dismissal had not yet been announced. Macartney urged them to settle the Chira dispute without delay and pointed out the lesson of Russian intervention at Tsitsihar which he had read about in newspaper reports. The Titai confirmed that he had been in-structed by Peking to treat with the Russian Consul-General on the basis of the settlement they had drafted three months before. In China's weak condition, he said, it was impossible to expect fair treatment from the Russians and there was no other course but to yield. Within a few days the dismissal of Wang Taotai was announced and his place was taken by Chang, the District Magistrate of Kashgar New City, who three years previously had received the order of St Anne for services to Russia. Yang Titai also found himself obliged to resign because he no longer commanded the confidence of his men, and the Hsietai was promoted in his stead. Sokov told Macartney that he was glad of the Hsietai's appointment as his predecessor seemed to be setting himself up in opposition to the Russians and it was a nuisance having him menacing the peace so near the Russian border.

Macartney was relieved that the deadlock was to be resolved without bloodshed or annexation even though the chief concessions were made by the Chinese. He was not aware of it at the time but the telegrams he had sent in May when he had heard of the Russian reinforcements had played some part in ensuring that Sokov's powers of provocation and intervention were kept under restraint. The telegrams he had sent on 2 and 24 May in which he had reported the reinforcements reached London in June, but his telegram of 3 May, in which he cancelled his warning of annexation, never arrived in Whitehall. The British government therefore went on uninterruptedly, if leisurely, considering its reactions to the Russian reinforcements throughout June and July. On 15 July Sir Edward Grey agreed that it was desirable to warn the Russian government of Sokov's possible exaggerations and perversions of fact and that the reinforcement of the Russian detachment provided the right occasion. The decision was made on the same day that the Russians presented their ultimatum in Peking, and between then and 21 July, when the British Ambassador in St Petersburg broached the subject, the Chinese had conceded the Russian demands. The British initiative therefore had no part in ending the Chira deadlock but it did ensure that the Russo–Chinese *détente* should have some permanence.

The British Ambassador's tactful inquiries from M. Sazanov about the reason for Russian reinforcements going to Kashgar revealed that the Foreign Minister was not well informed on the subject. Sir George Buchanan managed to convey the British government's view that the Chinese had done everything in their power to satisfy the Russian Consul-General but Sokov appeared to be suffering from an attack of nerves and was sending home reports of a far more alarmist nature than the situation warranted. He warned the Foreign Minister of Sokov's possible exaggerations. Sazanov promised to make inquiries and agreed that Sokov was a nervous man. But he assured Buchanan that he need have no anxiety over Kashgar. Russia had not, as he put it, 'a policy' in Kashgar as she had in Ili, Mongolia or Manchuria. She would confine her attention to the protection of her subjects and would take no action of a political nature in Kashgar except in agreement with the British government. Buchanan took this last statement to mean that if Britain sought to revise the Anglo-Russian agreement over Tibet to her advantage Russia would ask for counter-concessions in Kashgaria. The whole interview, though, impressed him with the sincerity of Sazanov's assurances. Apart from some doubt about how the Russians intended to interpret the term 'Russian subject' in Kashgaria, and therefore what policy was involved in their protection, the British government felt confident of Russia's pacific intentions.

Macartney's reports, however, had served an important purpose. Exaggerated as they were by the non-delivery of his telegram of 3 May they had yet made sure that Sokov's chances of mischief-making were reduced to a minimum. The Russian government was made fully aware of its Consul's powers of distortion and also that the British government was closely watching the situation in Kashgaria. The note that Sazanov later sent to Buchanan about the Russian reinforcements showed that the Foreign Minister was misinformed about the size of the detachment. He put it at 150 less than its minimum number and 350 less than Macartney's estimates. It is possible that Sazanov was trying intentionally to deceive, but more likely that he was misled by his colleagues in the War Office whose aggressive designs the Foreign Office often found difficult to control. Kashgar's danger lay in an alliance of Sokov with these martial elements in St Petersburg and Tashkent, and some of Macartney's most valuable services lay in keeping their activities under observation and restraint.

The Chira agreement which Russian pressure in Manchuria forced on China was initialled by Sokov and Yang Titai in the middle of August and was finally signed after the agreement of their governments on 1 October 1913. Macartney did not see a copy of the document but he learnt from Sokov and the Chinese officials that it censured Wang Taotai for official incapacity in deputing Hsiung Kao-sheng to Khotan and Chira. The District Magistrates of Khotan and Keriya who had held office at the time of the riot were fined large sums which were to be paid as compensation to the families of those who had been killed. Hsiung Kao-sheng was to be imprisoned for twelve years, but without hard labour. The forty Chira men who were accused of burning down the house belonging to Syed Haji's father-in-law were imprisoned for terms of four to ten years. Syed Haji was to be banished from Sinkiang and tried in Russian Turkestan for killing two men in the fight and for inciting the natives of Chira to revolt. Finally, the question of the nationality of those burnt to death was left undecided but the Chinese government was to pay their families 70,000 taels in compensation.

There could be no doubt that superficially Russia had emerged as victor from the affair, but although no decision was made about the nationality of the riot's victims the important thing for China was that Sokov made no attempt to continue his registration policy, and his successor preferred peaceful cooperation with the Chinese over the whole nationality question. In October, at a dinner celebrating the agreement, Sokov told Macartney that he had no doubt that his government would order the withdrawal of the Russian detachment and that he himself would shortly be going on leave. On 16 October, the Turkestan Rifles, about 420 strong, marched for the last time out of the North Gate and along the road to Andijan. No orders had been received about the Cossacks and they stayed on until after the arrival of Sokov's successor in December. On 24 October, Macartney, his mind relieved of anxiety, set off on a long-planned tour of the southern oases, his first escape from his office for nearly two years.

FOURTEEN

The New Regime

The departure of Sokov and the signing of the Chira agreement brought to an end the systematic registration of new Russian subjects in Kashgaria. But Macartney was taking no chances and the chief purpose of his six week tour of the southern oases was to register British subjects. If the Russians should resume their policy, which the Chira agreement had done nothing to prohibit, Macartney had no intention of allowing them to draw British subjects into their net. The Chinese cooperated with Macartney despite their experience with Behrens, and he was accompanied on his tour by an official of the new Foreign Affairs Office which the Governor had established at each of the three towns in the province where there was a foreign consul. Behind the Chinese cooperation with Macartney were several factors: they found it useful to have a British community and a British consul to counterbalance the Andijanis, and the Chinese officials no doubt realized how much they had been helped in resisting Russian pressure by the presence of Macartney. It was also in their own interest to put an end to interminable wranglings by establishing who precisely could claim exemption from customs dues. Thirdly, their experience of Macartney gave them every confidence in his moderation and justice, and they could be sure that he would make no attempt to copy Behrens's tactics. This was borne out by Macartney's behaviour at Yarkand where in deference to the Amban's wishes he accepted for registration only children of immigrants whose fathers had died less than ten years before or who were themselves less than forty years old, on the grounds that those who did not so qualify had given up all intention of returning to India.

In registering children of British Indian immigrants and not just those who were born under British jurisdiction Macartney had acted on his own initiative without the sanction of the government of India. But as he explained in a letter from Yarkand, without the registration of second generation immigrants the numbers of British subjects would be very small and their interests 'in the event of our wishing to have a say as to the future of this part of the New Dominion, would scarcely give us a broad basis'.

Another problem his tour raised was the position of the Afghans. Afghanistan had no diplomatic or consular representation in China but Britain claimed in her own interests the right to protect Afghans. Macartney found Governor Yang unwilling to recognize this claim and his own government had been reluctant to force the issue. But as customs dues were now being levied with increased severity he was convinced that unless Britain could secure their exemption the Afghans would turn themselves into Russian subjects. Even Persian and Turkish Armenians were getting exemption with the help of Russian Aksakals. Rather than see this happen Macartney took a risk and registered the Afghans without first securing his government's approval. But the India Office and the Foreign Office were persuaded by his arguments and in November 1913 they agreed to issue new instructions to Macartney.

The result was that in April of the following year Macartney found himself appointed as an Additional Assistant Judge of the British Supreme Court in the Shanghai concession with instructions to register as British subjects in Sinkiang not only immigrants from India but their sons who had been born on Chinese soil, even in cases where the father had died in Sinkiang without ever having been registered as a British subject. He was also empowered to register Afghans, Bajauris, Chitralis and other tribes on the northern frontiers of India, together with their children (but not grandchildren) born on Chinese soil.

These instructions gave the gloss of official approval to Macartney's tour in which he registered 209 British subjects at Yarkand, including twenty-eight Afghans; he also registered fifty at Karghalik, mostly Afghan carriers from Wakhan, forty at Goma, and seventy at Khotan, half of them Afghans. The large majority of the new registrations in Yarkand and Khotan were second generation landowners. If these had been disqualified there would only have been a dozen Bajauri and Kashmiri farmers and twenty Punjabi merchants, an insignificant number compared with the size of the Andijani population of Yarkand. Before the Behrens era the Chinese would never have permitted registrations on this scale, but when he returned to Kashgar Macartney found himself complimented by high Chinese officials on the moderation he had shown. That this was not sarcasm on their part was shown by Governor Yang's recommending him for a Chinese decoration. The Governor's motive may have been purely political but there was the note of sincerity in the record of Macartney's services that the Kashgar officials submitted to Urumchi: 'The Hon-Consul-General has been a long time in Kashgar. His conciliatoriness and justice in the treatment of affairs are eulogized alike by officials, merchants and ordinary people.'

Macartney's return to Kashgar followed closely on the departure of Sokov, and in December 1913 Prince Mestchersky arrived to take up the position of acting Russian Consul. An aristocrat, a man of great height and charming manners, Mestchersky's general knowledge of the world was above that of the average Russian official, but he was by no means an able man and was disinclined to hard work. Nevertheless he was an easy colleague to get on with and made no secret of the fact that he intended to avoid all friction over the nationality question. He had orders, he said, to return to the Chinese all their subjects whom Sokov had registered on insufficient evidence. He remarked ruefully to Macartney that the unpleasant duty devolved on him of repairing the damage done by his predecessor. It was evident that since their failure to secure a revision of the Treaty of St Petersburg in their favour, and with growing tension in Europe, the Russians had lost interest in an aggressive policy in Sinkiang. By April 1914 Mestchersky was complaining to Macartney that he could not get any support from his government over a question that had previously led the Russians to threaten a military demonstration. The Chinese had returned to their old tack of refusing Russian subjects permission to marry Turki girls or to acquire land in any towns except Kashgar. When Mestchersky telegraphed to his government he received the answer that the land question was a difficult one and he must do his best to keep on friendly terms with the Chinese. The Sokov era had passed with a vengeance.

Although Sinkiang's prospects were brighter to this extent, the relaxation of Russian pressure coincided with a deterioration of affairs within the province. The economic situation worsened as the provincial government continued to finance itself by issuing paper money. District *yamens* were refusing to exchange tael notes for coins and in the north depreciation had reached 50 per cent.

By March 1914 Macartney was telegraphing the British Minister in Peking that unless the Peking government would come to the help of Sinkiang by sending cash and guaranteeing the par value of the tael notes the province would be bankrupt.

Politically, affairs were no healthier. There was still a strong secessionist movement in Ili which was led by two senior officials. Governor Yang at length dealt with it by his own ruthless methods; he arranged for the assassination of the leaders by a Dungan and then forcibly incorporated Ili under the control of Urumchi. In Kashgar the gamblers were again lifting up their heads, emboldened by the departure of Yang Titai of whom they had stood in some awe. They were the more dangerous now than at the time of the revolution for they had ceased to be merely a gang of bloodthirsty ruffians and had acquired leaders of education; military officers, some disbanded and others still serving; literati without employment; pawnbrokers and shopkeepers. They were united by their common addiction to the gambling tables and by their intention of living as parasites on the Ambans. They were a law only to themselves and no official could touch them. When two Kashgar Begs offended them the gamblers secured their dismissal at sword and pistol point, and there was an alarming rumour at the end of December that they would set fire to the town. The Kashgar officials found themselves obliged to repair their gambling den and to hand over the district gaol to them as the means of recovering 'debts of honour'. Hsiung Kao-sheng, who had played such a prominent part in the Chira affair and who under the subsequent agreement with the Russians should have been serving twelve years' imprisonment, was still living openly in Kashgar and was conspicuous as the leader of the gamblers. It seemed likely that the withdrawal of the Russian detachment would only encourage the Chinese to break the Chira agreement and there were signs of increasingly intransigent behaviour towards the foreign consuls, encouraged, no doubt, by pressure from the gamblers.

In February 1914 the gamblers went beyond the threats that had previously been enough to terrorize the Kashgar officials and murdered the Amban of Karghalik. The Amban's offence was that he had seized and burnt some opium which was on its way to the gamblers at Charchan. But in this murderous defiance of authority the gamblers found they had gone too far. The Governor had either to punish the criminals or acknowledge them as a rival power. Once again he turned to his Dungan troops for help, and they suppressed the Karghalik gamblers without much difficulty or mercy. The lesson was not lost on Kashgar. The Titai summoned the gamblers and warned them that if they did not give up their blackmail and intimidation he would call in the Dungans. The threat was enough to secure their submission and they promised to cease pressing the officials for money. One of their leaders was arrested without the gang showing any resistance, and soon renewed proclamations were out prohibiting the sale of opium and the planting of *charas*. There was even talk of suppressing the gambling dens.

Macartney welcomed this turn of events, but from the first he had feared the power that was being put into the hands of the Dungans. There were now twenty regiments of them in the north of the province and they were the only troops garrisoning Urumchi. The danger was obvious and he pointed it out to his superiors:

> The question is how the policy adopted heretofore with success by the higher authorities in Urumchi, of playing off Muhammadan Dungans against Confucian Chinese will answer in the long run. So long as the former are well paid and are given military commands, and so long as their coreligionists in the neighbouring province of Kansu remain quiescent, no disorder need be apprehended. None the less the Dungans are at present the controlling factor in the situation of the New Dominion; and the Chinese officials are, to a dangerous degree, dependent on their good will.

For the first part of 1914 Macartney was chiefly occupied in registering further British subjects. By July there were 651 and he had arranged that people in the north of the province claiming to be British subjects should travel to Kashgar to have their nationality inquired into. He had also interested himself in the plight of the many pilgrims who passed through Kashgar in the hope of making the journey to Mecca. He suggested the setting up of 'Haj committees' in the southern oases to provide information for travellers, to collect subscriptions for the stranded, and to persuade the destitute among them that they were not obliged to undertake the pilgrimage. The Chinese, though, did not welcome his suggestions, which they chose to look on with suspicion, and they turned them down with no thanks for his pains.

The intransigence Macartney had noted in the officials since the withdrawal of the Russian detachment became more marked as the months passed. The customs officers began to question the rights of British subjects to exemption, a question that Macartney had hoped his registration policy would settle once and for all. The Taotai was also showing signs of restiveness as the numbers of registered British subjects slowly mounted. There was even a hint that the Chinese might soon take a more aggressive view over their claims to Hunza; when the Mir of Hunza sent the customary present of gold the Taotai returned patronizing messages enjoining him to be diligent in the discharge of his duties and to see that his subjects had no cause for complaint. He was also showing reluctance to recognize Kanjutis as British subjects.

The real trouble, though, arose over the Afghans. Despite the Foreign Office's promise to obtain recognition of Afghans as British subjects Macartney found when he inquired of the British Minister at Peking that he had received no instructions to raise the question with the Chinese government. This was a serious setback to Macartney's hopes and in November 1914 he found himself at odds with the Taotai. The Yarkand customs officials were refusing to allow the Afghans exemption and the Taotai gave them his support. Macartney telegraphed to his Minister urging a speedy declaration that the Afghans were British subjects, but the Minister replied that Peking was bound to consult first with the Kashgar officials which might not help the British case. Macartney agreed to a delay and commented in his diary that a new spirit was coming over the Chinese officials: 'The revolution has given an opportunity of service to a class of men, comparatively young, and very self-assertive where foreigners are concerned.' Several of this type, including the Taotai of Kashgar (or Taoyin as he was known from August 1914) held key posts in the province, and they were not slow to see that the European war had diminished the power of the foreign consuls in Kashgaria.

In September 1914 the Russians began to withdraw men from their posts in Shignan and Murghabi, and trade between Kashgar and Russian Turkestan was dislocated. The following month it was reported that even the consular guard at Ili, which until recently had been 300 strong, had also left for Russia. It was obvious that the sympathies of the Chinese and Kashgarians were with anyone who could humble the Russians and they welcomed news of Russian defeats. The Muslim population looked to Turkey as its champion and although they knew little of the Germans they supported their cause because they were fighting the Russians. The British, whom they knew almost solely from Macartney's dealings with them, aroused no hostile emotions, but Macartney soon found himself hampered by his country's alliance with Russia.

The two consuls-general were brought up against their changed position at the beginning of 1915. Russian creditors, acting under the instructions of Prince Mestchersky, had sealed up shops belonging to their debtors, but the District Magistrate of Kashgar intervened and told the Prince that there was to be no interference with Chinese property without his consent. Again, the Russian officer at Tashkurghan had tried to repeat the tactics of his predecessor, and finding himself short of firewood had felled fourteen trees in a private garden. In Sokov's time the Chinese had remonstrated in vain but now the Taoyin took up the case strongly and demanded heavy compensation from the Russian Consul-General.

Macartney, too, found himself in difficulties. A good deal of opium smoking still went on in the *yamens* but when a British subject was caught selling the drug the Taoyin made a great issue of the case. However, the chief source of trouble continued to be the registration of British subjects. In Khotan and Maralbashi the officials were bringing pressure on the people not to register and the Taoyin caused a proclamation to be posted in Yarkand that Chinese subjects registering as foreigners would be shot as traitors. Macartney found himself compelled to seek the aid of his Minister in Peking, but it was doubtful how effective such pressure would be. The Governor's attempts to raise foreign loans to solve his financial difficulties might have offered a better hope of restoring the consuls' position, but Russia was now unable to give financial aid and Mestchersky had to refuse the Chinese requests.

A new threat to the consuls' troubled relations with the Taoyin was the appearance in Kashgar in February 1915 of a party of five Turks. China, as a neutral power, had no reason for excluding Turks from her territory, but Macartney knew that the Turks intended to travel in the spring to Afghanistan, another neutral state but one which could easily swing to the German-Turkish cause, with disastrous results for the British. Turkish agents could not only foment trouble in Afghanistan but they could also use Sinkiang as a base to stir up the tribes on the borders of India or the Muslim peoples under Russian rule. Nevertheless, Macartney and Mestchersky had to tread warily. There had already been a clash with the Taoyin when the Russian Aksakal at Keriya had asked the local Amban to arrest two Turks whose activities he suspected and to send them to Kashgar. The Amban had obliged, but the Taoyin reacted angrily to this interference and maintained that the Turks were doing no harm. Macartney hinted as diplomatically as possible that if the Turks used China's neutrality to start an agitation against Britain and Russia the allies would have a grievance against China. He suggested the Taoyin could do no better than keep the Turks under his observation in Kashgar. The Taoyin did not seem averse to this policy and promised that the Turks would not be allowed to leave Kashgar without his permission.

There Macartney had to leave the matter because in April 1915 he left Kashgar to escort his family home. They had been about to leave in the summer of 1914 so that the older children could go to school in England (Eric was now twelve and Sylvia eight) but when they had already sent off their heavy luggage news of the outbreak of war and the cancellation of all leave forced them to stay on. Miss Cresswell, their governess, had already left so Catherine Macartney had to take on the task of teaching her children as well as cooking for the household in a situation made much more difficult by the shortage of European stores and the general dislocation of trade. In preparation for their leave they had actually sold off a lot of their possessions at an auction, but when the Kashgaris became aware of their plight such was their loyalty and friendship that they returned all the goods to the family.

In April 1915 Brigadier Sir Percy Sykes, accompanied by his sister, arrived to relieve the Macartneys, and they hastily set off on their journey before the closing of the Terek Pass should make for further delay. The usual crowds gathered to say goodbye. Catherine Macartney intended to return with her husband but as she left Chini Bagh she had a premonition that this was the last she would see of Kashgar. The family arrived safely in England after a nightmare journey but when the time came for their return after six months' leave women were not allowed to travel and Macartney had to go back alone for the last three years of his service.

In his absence Sykes had had to cope with the problem of the Turks in Kashgar. Contrary to his implied promise the Taoyin had visa'd their passports and had given them permission to leave for Sarikol and Afghanistan. This was just before Macartney left Kashgar and he telegraphed to India saying that he felt unable to interfere. There could be no doubt that the Taoyin was acting perfectly within his rights. But on 16 April Sykes received instructions from the government of India to try to prevent the Turks from leaving Kashgar. It was too late for this, so Sykes consulted Mestchersky and the two consuls jointly pressed the Taoyin to have the Turks brought back to Kashgar. Somewhat unexpectedly the Taoyin agreed. Despite his dislike of anything that could be seen as foreign interference the Taoyin was equally averse to Turkish intrigues among his Muslim subjects. There was no news of the Turks' whereabouts but Mestchersky sent instructions to the Russian officer at Tashkurghan and to the Pamirsky post to arrest the men if they could be found. Four stages from Tashkurghan a party of Cossacks came upon them and sent them under arrest to Osh. There was an outcry from some Turkish subjects in Kashgaria about the Cossacks making arrests on Chinese soil but the Taoyin declined to act and did not raise the question with either of the consuls. He was, no doubt, glad to have the problem settled for him.

There was no change, though, in the Taoyin's general anti-foreign views and in the policy of his officials to prevent the registration of new Russian and British subjects and the sale of land to them. Kazis were dismissed for legalizing sales and sellers were beaten and threatened with execution. Before Macartney left Kashgar the Chinese were bringing pressure on the Afghan Wakhanis who lived at Dafdar to declare themselves Chinese subjects under threat of expulsion, and in a memorandum he wrote in London Macartney said he was also expecting trouble in Raskam. The previous year the government of India had encouraged the Mir of Hunza to send cultivators to Raskam with the idea that this was the best way of protecting British interests in the area. But Macartney believed that the Kashgar officials were taking steps to evict them and a clash was to be expected. With Russian goodwill he believed that both these questions could be settled amicably, as it was the Russians who had always prevented an agreement over Raskam. The wartime alliance between Russia and Britain provided in his view the ideal opportunity for a convention between Britain and Russia on their joint aims and interests in Sinkiang which would bring to an end their years of rivalry.

In the memorandum he drew up on this theme, dated 23 August 1915, Macartney again proposed that the British government should try to agree with the Russians on spheres of influence. The Russians would recognize Hunza, the Taghdumbash Pamir and Raskam as part of the British sphere and in return Britain would promise not to seek for herself, or any other power, interests in the province north of the Tien Shan. Both Russia and Britain should have a free hand in Kashgaria where he estimated there were roughly 10,000 Russian and 4000 British subjects. He also suggested mutual concessions giving freedom of travel to each other's subjects in Russian Turkestan and India and the same taxation as that levied by each on Chinese citizens and their goods. This would mean that British goods could enter Russia free of the crippling duties that then hampered her trade. Fundamental to the whole scheme was Macartney's support for the policy that under no circumstances should the Indian border be pushed beyond the Mustagh watershed provided British influence could be maintained in Raskam and the Taghdumbash Pamir as the means of excluding foreign intrigues among the tribes of the Hindu Kush.

If Macartney had been in Kashgar in May he would have found encouragement for his proposals from a conversation Sykes had with Romanoff, the secretary at the Russian Consulate. Romanoff said quite openly that all Russian officials were working for the annexation of the Chinese districts of Ili, Tarbagtai and Urumchi for the reason that if China became strong 'it would be undesirable to allow her such a suitable base as these provinces, if developed, would become'. Russia, at least, knew where her interests lay, if the British Foreign Office could never make up its mind about its own. Macartney's memorandum met the fate of most of its predecessors and was filed without comment, its subject obscured by the cataclysmic events then shaking Europe.

He returned to Kashgar in November 1915. The British Consulate building was now spacious and dignified but without his wife and children it must have seemed a desolate place. The homeliness of Chini Bagh and the congenial company of Father Hendricks in Macartney's first years of loneliness must at times have seemed preferable to the honours and position that were now his. It was true that he could now count on the friendly cooperation of the Russian Consulate, but this was offset by the growing hostility of the Chinese. Most of it was inspired by the Taoyin whose one aim seemed to be to assert himself against the foreign consuls. It showed itself in a persistently obstructive policy towards British and Russian subjects which was often clumsily carried out by his underlings. Some of these officials were actively hostile to the foreigners but in Macartney's opinion the majority did not want to go beyond the stage of recovering rights which they had lost in the past through foreign aggressiveness. They were now regretting that they had ever permitted the registration of Chinese subjects who mostly had only technical grounds for claiming foreign citizenship. The tens of thousands of acres owned by them had become a sore point, and the Chinese clearly intended that they should acquire no more.

Macartney tried to soften the bad impression which the Russo-British alliance had on the Chinese in Kashgar by explaining that it had no connection with Chinese affairs and aimed only at destroying the power of Germany. The Kaiser, he said, now threatened to dominate the whole world, including China herself. He tried to show that the alliance would benefit China since the Kaiser posed as the champion of Islam, and China, as well as Russia and Britain, had Muslim subjects whom, he implied, could also be incited to rebellion.

Since the excitement caused by the new educational policy had died down the Chinese felt no alarm on account of the Turkis, but they needed no reminder of the presence of their other Muslim subjects, the Tungans. Almost every month brought evidence of their growing power in Sinkiang. The new District Magistrate of Kashgar Old City was a Tungan and at the beginning of December something happened that the Chinese in Kashgaria had long feared: the new Titai arrived from Urumchi, and proved to be a Tungan, Ma Fu-sin.* He was accompanied by 300 Tungan levies. Ma was sixty-four years old, of a coarse but jovial appearance and was quite illiterate. He had lived near Urumchi in obscurity as a farmer until he managed to put himself at the head of the Tungan levies which had been raised on the first outbreak of the revolution. Since then he had been employed in shooting down Chinese sedition-mongers and riffraff of the gambler type, a task that he and his troops had found congenial.

With Ma's arrival and the appointment of the Tungan District Magistrate a new element of unpredictable violence entered the Chinese administration, all the more frightening because it was mostly irrational but was chiefly directed against Confucian Chinese. The District Magistrate had signalled his appointment by the summary execution of six Chinese who were said to be members of a secret society. He had them seized and brought to the *yamen* without charge or trial where they were put up against a wall and shot. Not to be outdone the Titai marked his first full day in Kashgar by arresting and shooting three men who appeared to be innocent of any possible crime. The Taoyin protested at this behaviour but the District Magistrate advised him not to interfere. Besides the 300 men Ma had brought with him the troops in Khotan were also Tungans so there was already a strong nucleus of them south of the Tien Shan. Macartney predicted in his reports that other Chinese Muhammadans from Urumchi and Kansu would collect round them and perhaps in time would oust the Confucian Chinese from the army. The Tungans, he said, had been used effectively as bulldogs in the cause of the republican government, but they were now to be feared as a power in the province, 'undisciplined, ignorant and ferocious'.

Any republican flavour that the provincial government and its officials had assumed in the first turmoil of the revolution had been quickly discarded, and in Kashgar as in Peking there was soon little to distinguish the officials of the new regime from their predecessors under the Manchus. Only the dress was different. Yuan Shih-k'ai had nothing to fear from Sinkiang, reported Macartney in December 1915, if he should proclaim himself emperor. The officials had never favoured republican sentiments as these placed

* See the 'Ma Titai' mentioned in chapters VI and XVI of C. P. Skrine's *Chinese Central Asia.*

them too much on a footing of equality with the ordinary people and exposed their peculations to open criticism. After the arrival of the Tungans the life of any Chinese expressing republican views was no longer safe in Kashgar; he ran the risk of being shot instantly on the pretext of being a member of a secret society. So great was the terror inspired by the Tungans that the gamblers and the Ko-Lao-Hui disappeared from the public view and from Macartney's reports. On 10 January 1916, as he had predicted, the proclamation of Yuan Shih-k'ai as Emperor was made in Kashgar without a voice being raised in protest against it.

A subtle power struggle between the Titai and the Taoyin then began, as had happened before in the time of Yang Titai. It came to centre on the anti-foreign campaign conducted by the Taoyin, not because Ma Titai had any particular liking for foreigners but because he had to place himself in the opposite camp to that of the Taoyin. Macartney had been driven to complain to the Provincial Governor at the beginning of the new year about the Taoyin's obstructiveness over the collection of debts owed to British subjects. But on 1 February the Taoyin brought his campaign to a climax by ordering the Tungan District Magistrate of Kashgar to distribute a proclamation throughout the Kashgar circuit in which he told people to resist all claims by the heirs of the Andijanis who had come to Kashgar as robbers many years back. The proclamation generated a great deal of excitement as was no doubt intended. The whole town was astonished; the Chinese had never openly dared to refer to the Russians in such terms before. Gleefully the Kashgarians seized the opportunity and openly insulted Russian subjects; one of them even threw a brickbat at a Cossack.

The proclamation, as it proved, was a bold but almost despairing move by the Taoyin to strengthen his own position. The Dungans, in the persons of the Titai and the District Magistrate, had shown that they intended to seize effective control of Kashgaria, and with 400 Tungan troops quartered in the new City the Taoyin was not in a strong position to resist. His chief hope lay in winning popular support among the officials and the Chinese population by playing on their anti-Russian feelings, the only sentiments capable of uniting them. He was gambling, though, on receiving support from the Provincial Governor, without realizing, perhaps, the extent to which Yang had made himself dependent on the Tungans, and his continuing weakness in the face of foreign pressure. When the Russian Consul telegraphed to the Governor asking if the proclamation had been issued by his order the reply came in the negative from Urumchi.

Immediately this was known the Tungan District Magistrate went in person to the city gates on the night of 5 February, accompanied by a few men carrying lanterns, and tore down the proclamation. The following day the Titai made his opposition to the Taoyin clear by inviting the foreign consuls to see him. Macartney had no intention of being drawn into the power struggle and advised Mestchersky to be in no hurry to accept, but to agree to pay a friendly call after an interval. He then heard that the Provincial Governor had telegraphed the Titai to restrain the Taoyin's anti-foreign campaign, and he accepted the Titai's invitation to dinner for 8 February. Immediately he knew of this the Taoyin asked the consuls to dine with him on the same date and at the same time. In fact the dinner with the Titai proved to be a purely social occasion, but the Taoyin realized that without support from the Provincial Governor he was defenceless. On 14 February he called on both consuls and announced the withdrawal of all his opposition to foreign subjects' buying land. Two days before, Macartney had heard from the Governor that he had instructed the Taoyin to give all the necessary cooperation to the consuls and to see that his officials behaved in the same way.

From 14 February the anti-foreign agitation in Kashgar stopped abruptly, but the Taoyin's change of front was too late to save him. The complaints of the Russian Minister in Peking did not carry as much weight as they had done before 1914 but they no doubt reinforced Governor Yang's determination to dismiss his subordinate. He could not then afford a breach with the Tungans, least of all the Commander-in-Chief of the army, and he could not profit from any confrontation with the foreign powers. On 8 March the Russian Consul heard from his Minister in Peking that Yuan Shih-k'ai had ordered the removal of Chang Taoyin. The Taoyin affected to know nothing of his dismissal but he set about organizing a monster petition for his retention in office. To bolster his popularity he also sent out new instructions to his subordinate officials who renewed their anti-foreign campaigns in Yarkand, Aksu, Goma and Karkhalik. When this showed no sign of averting his fate the Taoyin asked the Governor for permission to retire so that his dismissal could not be interpreted as the result

of the foreign consuls' pressure. But his plea was unavailing and
the Governor announced that his successor was on his way to
Kashgar. The lesson was not lost on his subordinates and the
Ambans of Goma, Karghalik and Yarkand quickly became as
meek as they had been arrogant before.

The Titai had now no rival in Kashgar but he continued to
show every sign of friendliness to the consuls while carrying on
with his summary executions of those Confucian Chinese who
were supposed to have taken part in the 1912 disturbances.
Macartney found his aims transparent enough: he had risen to as
high a rank as he could ever expect to reach and he intended to
keep it. The best way of ensuring this was to make himself feared
by suppressing any form of agitation: 'For him, any form of
government in China is good enough, so long as under it he remains Titai and he is given a chance to line his at present lean
pockets.' His religion counted for little and the fortunes of the
Sultan of Turkey were immaterial to him. He intended to give
foreigners no occasion for complaint because that might endanger
his position, and in any case, as a Dungan, he had no particular
sympathy for Chinese national feelings.

The Titai's policy suited Governor Yang well enough as he had
no use for any cause or sentiments that threatened the precarious
peace of Sinkiang. He had been steadily strengthening his personal
position since the revolution by filling official posts with his relatives and fellow Yunnanese, but in February 1916 this policy
threatened to cause trouble. In the previous December the
province of Yunnan had rebelled against the Peking government
and several Yunnanese officers in Sinkiang planned to involve the
province in their cause by forcing Yang to declare its independence, supposedly under his own rule. Yang discovered what was
afoot and made his own preparations. On 16 February he invited
the rebel leaders to dinner and in a macabre imitation of a party
game had them shot there and then, one by one. The Chief of
Police, the officer in charge of the arsenal, and the chief of the
military department were all arrested and deported. Yang, like Ma
Titai, would tolerate no movement that threatened his personal
position, and while Peking did not interfere with him he saw
every advantage in according it nominal allegiance.

When the death was announced in Kashgar on 18 June of
Yuan Shih-k'ai Macartney recorded that no one showed any

emotion save that of relief. The common opinion was that with the advent of a new President things might quieten down in the rest of China. In Kashgaria there would be no change. Macartney summed up the position in one of his reports: the men in power intended to remain so:

> And anyone, be his political creed what it may, who attempts to disturb them, they will seize and summarily shoot down. At present the Governor and the Titai wield extraordinary powers; and I doubt if any Chinese authority, not even that from Peking, can remove them, barring the one derived from the knife of the assassin. For the moment Sinkiang appears to stand as a self-contained entity.

FIFTEEN

War and Counter-Intelligence

By June 1916 when Yuan Shih-k'ai died Governor Yang had succeeded in bringing peace and a precarious stability to Sinkiang
which he ruled with autocratic powers, despite his nominal
allegiance to Peking. The autonomy of the province rested on the
preoccupation of the Chinese and Russian governments with the
war and their own internal problems and Yang saw to it that
neither should be provoked into showing any interest in Sinkiang.
But although he had succeeded in repressing Chinese revolutionary
and republican elements in his province there were still internal
threats to the stability of Yang's rule. One was the economic weakness of Sinkiang, and the other, though scarcely yet discernible,
was a danger that Yang was too intelligent not to recognize.

The war and Turkey's part in it had given an added impetus to
Turki nationalism, and in north Persia, Afghanistan and
Turkestan this had inspired the pan-Turanian movement which
was bent on restoring the glories of the old Turkish empire. These
stirrings of Turki nationalism, already evident in the pan-Islamic
movement before the Chinese revolution, were capable, if cleverly
directed by German and Turkish agents, of causing untold trouble
to the British authorities in India and to the Russian government,
which had more Turkish-speaking people within her border than
Turkey herself. But Governor Yang also recognized that the whole
fragile fabric of his rule rested on the quiescence of his Turki subjects and he dealt carefully with any issue that might stir up
religious or nationalistic sentiments.

Some years before, Kashgar had come under the influence of
Hosein Bai Batcha's pan-Islamic ideals and his efforts to educate
and improve the Turki population. In 1915 a Turkish subject,
Ahmad Kamal, started a school in Kashgar where the pupils were
taught to look to the Sultan of Turkey as their head. The Chinese
officials in Kashgar closed the school and imprisoned everyone
associated with it. This had caused a good deal of ill-feeling among

the Turki population and the following year their elders petitioned Urumchi to allow its reopening. Yang saw the danger of the Turkis nursing a sense of grievance and he gave his permission, but he made sure that his officials kept a close watch on it and that all signs of allegiance to the Sultan of Turkey were removed. He also added the Chinese language and military drill to the curriculum, which apparently so discouraged the pupils that the numbers soon fell from forty-five to eighteen. Without appearing oppressive Yang effectively brought under control a potential source of agitation against his rule.

The danger from German agents, though, was a much more real and pressing one in the summer of 1916. There had been a few small alarms in the first years of the war when German or Austrian prisoners of war had escaped from camps in Russian Turkestan and crossed to Sinkiang. Prince Mestchersky had become very excited over a Bavarian baker who had been given refuge in Kashgar by the former Taoyin as a way of venting his spite towards the consuls. Macartney had to calm him down and point out that any attempt to abduct the German would cause a great deal of unnecessary trouble since the man was only a harmless nonentity.

In the beginning of 1916 there was a more serious case in which a German agent called Syed Hamza, who claimed to be a Turkish subject, arrived at Goma, accompanied by a party of Afghans, on their way from Afghanistan. Both consuls asked Hsu Taoyin to arrest him as a rebel Russian subject, claiming on somewhat slight authority that the man was a Bokhari. The Taoyin refused the request as there was no definite proof of Syed Hamza's nationality but he agreed to send him under escort to inner China.

These cases highlighted the difficulties of dealing with German and Turkish subjects while China continued to be a neutral country. As Macartney had told Mestchersky over the case of the Bavarian baker the German Legation at Peking was watching for any chance of accusing the Chinese of a breach of neutrality which they would use perhaps as an excuse to install an *agent provocateur* as German consul in Kashgar. Once there, his aim would be to make as much trouble as possible between the allies, the Chinese, Dungans and Afghans. Therefore everything must be done to avoid attracting the Germans' attention to Sinkiang while denying their agents the power of working mischief.

249

In the summer of 1916 Macartney's nerve and skill as a counter-intelligence agent were put to the test when he had to deal with the dangerous Von Hentig Mission. Von Hentig was a German who spoke Chinese well from the years he had spent training soldiers for the Chinese government. The Indian authorities never knew what his object was but it seemed safe to assume that it was to bring Afghanistan into the war on Germany's side. He had set out from Germany with a large staff which included an Indian revolutionary and several German companions. They travelled across the Persian desert, a journey that cost the lives of several of the party, and entered Afghanistan. Here they spent several months, meeting the Amir about once a fortnight. Despite the Amir's hospitality he was disinclined to enter the war on either side until he could be sure which was going to win. Von Hentig had to admit defeat and decided to split the mission up into small parties to return to Germany. He himself, accompanied by two Germans, one at least of whom spoke English, Turkish and Persian, an Indian sepoy, and a Badakhshi, chose to cross into Sinkiang, either because he thought the Chinese route the safest or because he saw the chance of stirring up trouble for the British and Russians.

In July they arrived without any attempt to conceal their identity in Yarkand where they showed every sign of settling down for a long stay, and began intriguing among the Afghans. Macartney and Mestchersky could not help but be alarmed, and they immediately sought to bring pressure on the Chinese to remove the Germans to inner China. The Taoyin at first protested Chinese neutrality but at length he agreed to place Von Hentig under polite restraint at Yarkand while Macartney sought orders from Peking for his removal. The German was confined for some time, and in a rage he wrote a challenging letter to Macartney. Nothing that the consuls could do, he said, would intimidate him: 'Je suis un diplomate et officier allemand qui ne disparait pas sans bruit et qui sait bien se defendre soi-meme . . . j'ai pris precaution que nulle injustice ne se passe sans vengeance.' He was always ready, though, he said, to cultivate personal relations and was even prepared to visit Sir George Macartney in a private capacity in Kashgar.

Von Hentig's threats were far from being idle boasts and Macartney knew as well as anyone that it would be difficult to remove him without provoking awkward consequences. He tried the usual channels of protest, at first apparently with success:

Governor Yang sent orders to the Taoyin to arrange for the Germans to travel under strong escort to inner China, provided this was done without any embarrassment to Chinese neutrality. Short of using actual physical force the local Chinese officials did their best to carry out these orders, but faced by the Germans' adamant refusal to move they soon found themselves at a loss. Ma Titai asked for the consuls' advice on how he should act and Macartney tried to persuade him to accept the view that since the Germans had entered Sinkiang without a passport the Chinese would be justified in using force to remove them.

Already he was aware that the possible consequences of using force were outweighed by the damage done by the Germans' presence. The hospitality they had received in Afghanistan could allow the Chinese to doubt how far the Afghans were under British protection. Von Hentig was sending letters to Badakhshan and might establish regular communications with the Afghans. In August Macartney heard through official channels that Von Hentig was claiming that several hundred German troops had already reached Afghanistan, and rumours were circulating in the bazaar that the Germans would soon have a consul in Kashgar. Under pressure from the British Minister at Peking Governor Yang sent orders that the Germans were to be compelled to move. But on 10 August Macartney reported, 'It is quite evident to me that, however much the Chinese may argue with the Germans, they will never dare to apply physical force to them.'

He and Mestchersky made one last effort to persuade the Governor that he must act, in his own interests as much as in theirs. In a joint telegram sent on 11 August they said that all reports spoke of the Germans' increasing influence and dangerous propaganda. They were claiming that Turks, Afghans, Wakhanis, Badakhshis and Persians were under German jurisdiction, and they were intervening on their behalf with the Chinese authorities. They would encourage the hundreds of Turks in the province to gather round them despite the fact that since Turkey had no treaty with China all Turkish subjects were amenable to Chinese jurisdiction. The consuls' joint telegram concluded with the words, 'We hope you will exercise your powers as master in this province. All the warnings we have given you are on record; and if hereafter there be trouble, please do not attribute blame to us.'

Unknown to Macartney, while he was composing this telegram,

trouble was already on its way, and in the most dramatic form. On 9 August Von Hentig, accompanied by an Austrian soldier, a Badakhshi and a Turk, suddenly escaped from Yarkand and was one day's march on the road to Kashgar before the Amban of Yarkand knew he was gone. Macartney heard of the German's approach only four hours before he arrived in the New City. He lost no time in sending a message to Ma Titai and in securing five Cossacks to guard the British Consulate. The Titai rose to the situation as though a whole German regiment was marching on his city. With a great deal of commotion he called out all his troops and sent detachments flying in every direction to intercept the Germans. One of these stopped them in a side road when they had already passed the New City and were within a quarter of an hour's walk of the British Consulate. The Chinese officer politely asked Von Hentig to accompany him to the quarters which were prepared for him in the New City, but Von Hentig insisted on going on his way. When the Chinese troops barred the road the German threatened to shoot, but when he was warned that the troops would reply in kind he had to submit. He allowed himself to be taken to the Titai's *yamen* where he was kept a prisoner in the garden. He remained there for a week while 100 men guarded him night and day.

In the meantime messages were passing backwards and forwards between the consuls and the Taoyin. Macartney and Mestchersky demanded that Von Hentig should be disarmed and made to leave immediately for inner China, but the Taoyin was still fearful of using force and Von Hentig refused to move. However, after a few days' confinement, and threats from Ma Titai that he would be taken out into the courtyard and shot, Von Hentig was persuaded to change his mind. At first he held out for one day's liberty in Kashgar but the consuls warned the Taoyin that he would probably use the opportunity to take refuge in one of the Swedish mission houses which would raise the whole question of Swedish neutrality.

In the end Von Hentig and his party left for the interior under strong guard on 17 August. With this victory won Macartney set about trying to detach the two Asians from the German party. He telegraphed Governor Yang asking him to send the Indian sepoy and the Badakhshi back to Aksu on the grounds that both were British subjects. As he told the Resident in Kashmir, it was essential that the two men, both of whom had knowledge of Indian conditions, should be made to give up their role of decoys for Von Hentig, as the German seemed intent on trying his luck either on the Yunnan–Burma border or in Tibet. Macartney's efforts, though, met with no success. The Governor denied that there was an Indian with the Germans and the British Minister in Peking was unable to help Macartney. The Peking government merely repeated Yang's denial and since it was known to have practically no control over Sinkiang there was nothing more that could be done.

Von Hentig had been foiled in Kashgar but he had made things difficult for Macartney. What precisely the German's aims were in his secret dash from Yarkand to Kashgar was never revealed. Macartney told the Taoyin that he suspected an attack on the British Consulate which Von Hentig knew was unguarded, but since there seemed little to be gained by such folly it seems more likely that the German was seeking asylum in one of the Swedish missionaries' houses. The Swedes tended to be pro-German because of their dislike of the Russians, and it is significant that one of them, a missionary called Tornquist, who was strongly pro-German, was Von Hentig's only visitor during his confinement in the New City. Protected by Swedish neutrality Von Hentig could have made his plans and his contacts at leisure, and since he left two of his party behind at Yarkand it seems likely that his removal to Kashgar was intended not only to secure his freedom but to widen the scope of his operations.

Macartney had been able to frustrate Von Hentig's plans only through the ready cooperation of Ma Titai who for reasons of his own went out of his way to cultivate friendly relations with the consuls. It was fortunate for Macartney that Von Hentig was safely disposed of in the middle of August for in September a new Taoyin arrived unheralded in Kashgar and announced his appointment in place of Hsu Taoyin. He was none other than Governor Yang's brother, but an unprepossessing figure, about forty years old, lanky and opium-emaciated with a perpetual sleepy look. There was some mystery about his arrival, for Hsu Taoyin was not disgraced and it appeared that the Governor was merely anxious to find a place for his brother. The effects of the change, though, were soon felt by the consuls. The new Taoyin was a confirmed opium smoker and was never to be seen before 2 p.m.

He delegated most of his work to the Kashgar District Magistrate, the Dungan Ma, who was clever, energetic and covertly anti-foreign. As a result, most of the cases that the consuls referred to the Taoyin for settlement were merely shelved. The new Taoyin also joined his Dungan District Magistrate in hostility to Ma Titai, and Macartney suspected that through them Governor Yang was working to remove the Titai from office. Ma Titai evidently had the same impression for he went out of his way to seek Macartney's and Mestchersky's support which he hoped would stand him in good stead at Peking.

The consuls were not averse to a private alliance with the Titai if only, as Macartney said, 'to make use of him as a counter-poise to the ever-increasing power of the Governor who is nominating none to office but his own relations, personal friends and pupils, all inclined to be rather anti-foreign. . . . Little by little, the whole provincial administration is passing into the hands of the Governor's family or henchmen.' According to the common opinion of the Chinese the Governor was bracing himself for a stand against his enemies in Peking, the chief of whom was the former Titai, Yang Tsuan-hsu, now an influential adviser of the new President of the Republic.

If Governor Yang had nominated his brother as Taoyin to strengthen his own position it evidently did not take him long to discover his mistake. The new Taoyin had been involved in shady intrigues in Peking and his journey to Urumchi was in reality a stealthy flight from the capital. If the Governor was at first unaware of these circumstances he evidently realized quickly enough that his opium-sodden brother was no use to him as Taoyin of Kashgar, and he dismissed him from the post at the end of 1916. The Taoyin tried to resist at first, but at length found himself forced to yield, and in March 1917 a new official, Chu, took over the post.

Yang's dismissal came as a relief to Macartney, for the ascendancy of the anti-foreign Kashgar District Magistrate had renewed his anxieties about the effects of Von Hentig's mission and the activities of other German-Turkish agents. In September 1916 two men who claimed to be Norwegian mining engineers and spoke Chinese well arrived at Khotan. Macartney became suspicious when it was reported that they had left for the Raskam valley and he telegraphed inquiries to Peking about their identity.

The Norwegian Minister knew nothing of them so Macartney arranged for the Indian authorities to dispatch some Hunza scouts to waylay them in the Raskam valley. This was done and the two men were taken to Gilgit where one of them was found to be the Secretary of the German Legation in Peking. In December 1916, before Yang's dismissal as Taoyin became known, Macartney wrote to the British Minister at Peking expressing his fears that if Von Hentig arrived in Peking he would send fresh parties of Germans to Sinkiang from among those who were trapped by the war in Peking and Shanghai. Since the Japanese had command of the sea their only hope of getting back to Europe was through Sinkiang along the unfrequented southern route of Lop Nor and Khotan. From there they could steal through the Raskam gorge to the Taghdumbash and thence into Afghanistan, or they could stay in Kashgaria to foment trouble between the consuls and the Chinese.

With Yang as Taoyin, and the Kashgar District Magistrate in charge of affairs, Macartney saw that it would be far more difficult than in the past to stop the intrigues of the Germans and to remove them from the province. Some of the Chinese officials with strong anti-foreign views had seized with relish on Von Hentig's propaganda and were themselves trying to detach the Afghans from the British cause. They had always resented Macartney's claims to protect Afghan subjects and it seemed they were now trying to open up a direct communication with Afghanistan. The Chinese at Yarkand were doing their best by intrigues and blandishments to win over the sympathies of the Afghans and it was possible that for their own purposes they might harbour or even encourage the Germans.

So seriously did Macartney look on the situation in view of the Chinese attitude that he decided to risk something which in all his long years at Kashgar he had never dared to do. Towards the end of 1916 he wrote to Macpherson, the Political Agent at Gilgit, and suggested the dispatch of a few Hunza Scouts to the Kukturuk valley which was part of Chinese territory leading up to the Wakhjir Pass and Afghanistan. From there they would be able to hold up travellers going to Wakhan. Macpherson obliged, but the Amban of Sarikol, highly indignant, reported their arrival to the Taoyin, and Yang, in a rage, demanded from Macartney what he meant by bringing British troops on to Chinese territory.

Macartney argued that there were already Russian Cossacks stationed at Tashkurghan with the consent of the Chinese and he claimed that if the Taoyin looked up the files of his predecessor he would find an agreement which he had made with Macartney that the British had the same rights as the Russians to keep troops at Tashkurghan.

The Taoyin simmered down but in December 1916 Macartney had to fight again for the right to keep fourteen Gilgit Scouts on the Taghdumbash for the winter. As he told the Political Agent at Gilgit the trek of enemy agents to Afghanistan had not ceased. Six Turks were at Kucha and Syed Hamza, whose activities had alarmed the consuls earlier in the year, and who they supposed to be safely out of harm's way, arrived back in Khotan. He carried a passport given him by the German Consul at Hupei who claimed to protect him as a Turkish subject. Hamza had more than ordinary powers of mischief-making since he was popularly supposed to be a member of the old ruling family of Bokhara. Macartney again asked the Taoyin to remove him to inner China and not to allow him to ridicule the previous orders for his deportation. The German Consul, he argued, had no right to protect Turkish subjects in Chinese territory and the passport he had issued had no Chinese visa. If the Taoyin permitted this Macartney threatened to issue passports himself without Chinese visas, even to non-British subjects throughout the length and breadth of China. Since the beginning of the war the Peking government had not issued passports for Sinkiang to any subjects of countries at war with the allies, and surely, he said, it was the duty of the authorities in Sinkiang to act in harmony with Peking.

Macartney's mixture of threats and persuasion had no effect on Yang Taoyin. He looked up the records of his predecessor and said that Macartney had permission to station only two officers and a few couriers in Sarikol and that his action in summoning troops without giving notice to the authorities was contrary to international law. China was neutral and was obliged to give equal protection to all belligerents. The Sinkiang authorities had already gone beyond what was required of them to oblige the British and Russian consuls. He demanded the immediate recall of the Indian troops from Sarikol. It looked as though Macartney's initiative in summoning the Gilgit Scouts would end in a humiliating defeat for British prestige, but before Yang could take any action he was dismissed from his post and Macartney left the Scouts where they were in the hope that the next Taoyin would be more amenable.

In March 1917 the former Taoyin of Aksu, Chu, became Taoyin of Kashgar. Macartney found him a man with pleasant manners and thought there was a good chance that he would be less hostile to the consuls than his predecessor. But at Yarkand the Amban, Lew, was doing his best to undermine British influence by giving every encouragement to Mulla Maqsud Gul, an Afghan who had befriended both Von Hentig and Syed Hamza. Maqsud aimed at placing himself at the head of the group of Afghans and Bajauris in Yarkand, and he pressed them to renounce their British status. He was deeply involved in the smuggling of opium from Badakhshan to Yarkand which had become a centre for the illicit distribution of the drug all over Sinkiang and Kansu. Lew was fully aware of the fact that his *yamen* had become a secret opium market and there could be little doubt that he profited by it. He also shared Maqsud's hostility to the British and Russians, and he recognized him unofficially as agent for the Afghans, even going so far as to send him cases for settlement. Macartney knew that any protests he made would be ineffectual as Lew was the brother-in-law of the Governor and therefore a very powerful man. It was another instance of what he had reported the previous month, that the administration of Sinkiang was being run practically as a family concern by Governor Yang, and that all the officials, including the new Taoyin of Kashgar, realized that it was far more important to stand well with the Governor than with the British Consul.

Macartney realized that Yarkand could become a centre for Afghan disaffection and intrigue against the allies. He was all the more worried when he discovered in March that there was a steady, clandestine trade in rifles and cartridges from the Kashgar military stores, many of which found their way into Afghan hands. The consuls protested to Ma Titai and to Governor Yang. The Titai was probably involved personally as part of the process of lining his own pockets, but the Governor acted promptly to suppress the traffic. The prospect of his subjects arming themselves was not one that he could tolerate. Nevertheless, it was too late to recover the rifles which had found their way over the passes to Afghanistan.

Macartney's worries about the intrigues in Yarkand came at a time when the news of the Russian revolution had struck a blow at Russian prestige which necessarily affected her ally, Britain. Mestchersky remained staunch to the Tsarist cause but henceforth his influence counted for little in Kashgar, and Macartney alone bore the responsibility for keeping German agents out of Afghanistan. Fortunately for him the news of the Russian revolution reached Kashgar at much the same time as the announcement that China had severed diplomatic relations with Germany so his task became suddenly much easier. He was able to enlist the help of the Chinese Postal Commissioner in Urumchi, a British subject called Tudhope, in censoring any German letters sent from China to the Swedish missionaries. Macartney suspected that Von Hentig in Peking was keeping in touch with Afghanistan by sending letters which certain Swedish missionaries delivered to disaffected Afghans in Yarkand. The chief suspect was a Swede in Yarkand called Arel who was a friend of Mulla Maqsud Gul.

When China severed diplomatic relations with Germany Macartney found a new ally in the Taoyin, Chu. In May 1917 Chu suggested that he should meet Macartney and Mestchersky once a week at the house of each in turn, partly as a social occasion and partly to discuss local topics together. Chu further showed his readiness to cooperate by rounding up the Turks who were still at large in Kashgaria and interning them at Turfan. He also gave every help when Macartney discovered that secret German propaganda against the allies was being circulated in Kashgar in pamphlets printed in Turki, Arabic and Hindustani. On 21 August Macartney received a telegram announcing that China had declared war on Germany, and almost simultaneously one of his anxieties was relieved by the news that the Governor had ordered the deportation of Mulla Maqsud Gul to Afghanistan. The Kashgarians' pro-Turkish sympathies were stronger than ever and they had little sympathy with China's new alignment, but the cordiality between the Chinese officials and the two consuls increased. Mestchersky left Kashgar on leave for Russia in September 1917. His country's prestige was at its nadir but the Prince was personally popular both with the Chinese and the Muslims.* His secretary, Uspensky, acted for him in his absence.

* Macartney last heard from Mestchersky in Paris in 1930 to which the Prince and his wife had escaped from the Russian Revolution. They were

258

The expulsion of Mulla Maqsud helped to demonstrate in Yarkand the continuance of British influence, and the Taoyin brought some pressure on the Amban, Lew, to cease giving special protection to the Afghans. Lew himself realized that with China's involvement on the allies' side he could no longer support the Afghans against the British, and when Macartney visited Yarkand in October 1917 the two men met and parted on cordial terms. Macartney knew, though, that Lew's anti-foreign sentiments had not changed and at the beginning of 1918 he had to report that Lew showed his bias in the settlement of his cases. Lew made no attempt to suppress the smuggling of Badakhshi opium, in which the traffic increased daily. But in this he was not alone because Chinese officials generally were the chief smugglers, and Sarikol, Kashgar, Aksu and Urumchi, as well as Yarkand, had become opium markets.

With 1918 began Macartney's last year in Kashgar. After twenty-eight years of alarms, intrigues and revolution the last few months before his retirement passed in comparative tranquillity. But his diplomatic career was to end in the same atmosphere of secrecy in which it had begun. On 7 June three British officers, Colonel Bailey, Major Etherton and Captain Blacker arrived in Kashgar and stayed there for six weeks before Bailey and Blacker left for Tashkent which was now under Bolshevik rule and had become a centre for the training of communist agitators. From Tashkent agents were being sent all over the Middle and Far East, India and Afghanistan, to preach Bolshevism. The situation in the area between the Caspian Sea and Chinese Turkestan was in flux and the authorities in India were fearful of a combined German and Turkish attack through Afghanistan. They needed accurate information about the political situation so that they could devise the best policy for protecting India's northern borders. They had hopes of exploiting the autonomous sentiments which they believed to be strong in Russian Turkestan, or, failing that, they at least planned to start effective propaganda to combat Bolshevism. First, though, it was essential to make contact with the Tashkent Soviet and to discover the true facts of the situation. For this part

---

in desperate circumstances working as a waiter and a chambermaid in a hotel. Macartney was able to help them with money.

of their mission Macartney was appointed as guide and inter-
mediary while Etherton acted in his place in Kashgar.

It was to be Macartney's final service to the government of
India and meant his saying goodbye for the last time to Kashgar.
At the customary farewell dinners Etherton recorded that many
proofs were given of the goodwill of the local community and of
their genuine regret at Macartney's going. On 11 August the
British subjects, the whole Russian colony, the Swedes and the
Chinese turned out *en masse* to see him leave and Etherton wrote
in his official diary, 'It would be difficult to imagine more genuine
cordiality and esteem than that displayed on Sir George's departure, and it testifies to the extraordinary influence and popularity he had acquired.' Macartney himself left no record of his
feelings as he said goodbye to the place that had been both his
career and his home throughout his working life. Once his last
entry was made in the Kashgar diaries the reticence that had
always been so marked closed round him and his career.

The mission to Tashkent succeeded in doing some important
intelligence work but it was unable to make any headway with
the Tashkent Soviet. In a letter to *The Times* in November 1922
Captain Blacker wrote of Macartney's part in it, 'Sir George's
modesty prevents him from making clear that it was his personality, his knowledge, his experience of Turkestan, and his prestige
with the Soviet that made him the unquestioned head of the
Mission in Tashkent,' although officially this was not so. It was
soon clear that there were no prospects of cooperation in Tashkent,
and finding it impossible to return to England through Russia
Macartney had to ride back to Sarikol and from there to Gilgit
and India.

It was typical of the many ironies of his career that while he
was making his way to the Indian border there arrived on 22
September the first British troops to be seen in Kashgar. For
twenty-eight years Macartney had protected British interests in
Sinkiang through all kinds of dangerous situations without the
help of a single soldier. Now when he was leaving behind him an
impressive Consulate-General, and an unquestioned position for
his successor, in a Kashgar where Russian influence had ceased to
exist and where order was kept by the strong hand of Governor
Yang, a British consular guard arrived from India, while the man

who for so many years had been denied its support slipped away quietly into retirement.

The Macartneys made their home in retirement in the Channel Islands. Unlike several other travellers and residents in Sinkiang Macartney wrote no book about his experiences, although his wife described their life in Kashgar in her book *An English Lady in Chinese Turkestan*. Reticent to the last, his personal papers had nothing to add to the official letters and reports he wrote from Kashgar which stand as his only memorial. When the Germans invaded Jersey during the Second World War Macartney found himself reliving some of the experiences of his first years in Sinkiang, with a real threat of deportation to Germany hanging over him. The qualities that had enabled him to survive before under alien rule stood him in good stead now, but as so often in his life he had not long to enjoy the triumph of liberation and victory. He died after a long illness at the age of seventy-eight on 19 May 1945, only a few days after Germany admitted defeat in Europe.

The record of George Macartney's career in Sinkiang is one of a remarkable personal achievement. Few men could have succeeded as he did in representing British interests, almost unsupported and in the face of determined opposition, for twenty-eight years in one of the most inaccessible posts in the service of the British government. His ability and courage were matched by his modesty, which concealed his achievements from all but a few government officials and travellers who read his reports or benefited from his advice.

The Kashgar diaries and letters form a relatively insignificant part of the vast bulk of Political and Secret Records of the government of India. Often they have to be searched for among the indexes under miscellaneous headings such as 'Frontier Policy', 'China', or 'Consulates'. This aptly reflects the confusion and lack of consistent policy on the part of the British and Indian governments that was one of Macartney's chief handicaps at Kashgar. The government of India left him to formulate his own objectives and to sink or swim as he could. Moreover, they often kept him grossly ill informed about shifts in policy that vitally affected him. Macartney could never be sure when his whole work would be undermined or destroyed by a decision to abandon British interests in Kashgaria in favour of settlements with the Russians or Chinese elsewhere. He lived always with the knowledge that the divided counsels of the government of India, the India Office and the Foreign Office made any consistent policy almost impossible and that his work at Kashgar was usually at the bottom of diplomatic priorities. Despite this he put up with loneliness and hostility, and was able to win in the end the respect of the Chinese and the Russians for himself and the British consular post he had created.

What he was able to achieve at Kashgar was limited by the restraint imposed by his government. Without a single soldier to call on and separated by distance and the difficulties of communication from his superiors there was nothing that Macartney could do when the Russians decided to send troops to the Pamirs and Kashgar. For nineteen years he had no official status in Sinkiang so that even his work of protecting British trade was dependent on his skill and tact in handling the Chinese authorities. Yet he was able to make sure that British traders were never hopelessly handicapped by discriminating duties or prohibitions over and above their existing difficulties of transport and the privileged competition they faced from the Russians. One undisputed achievement, though, was the freeing of several hundred British-born slaves from captivity in Kashgaria which he accomplished almost single-handed and without alienating or embarrassing the Chinese.

Less tangible, but probably his most important achievement was in his role of observer and reporter to his government. In this capacity he undoubtedly restrained the expansionist ambitions of the Russian Consulate in Kashgar. Early British fears of a Russian annexation of Kashgaria were almost certainly exaggerated; responsible Russian policy-makers realized that the annexation of Kashgaria would not cover the cost of invasion and administration, and that it would offer an exposed frontier and long drawn out hostilities with China. But moderate and responsible counsels were not always in control of Russian policy, and there was the danger that a clever and unscrupulous consul, such as Petrovsky or Sokov, could manipulate or exaggerate events to force the hands of their government. An obvious occasion was during the Chinese revolution when Sokov and Behrens between them sought to use the Chira affair to this end. Macartney was able to counter their versions of events by accurate accounts of his own, which through British diplomatic channels kept St Petersburg in touch with the true facts of their Consul's activities.

Second in importance to his role of observer was the advice Macartney gave to the local Chinese authorities. Sometimes it was designed to stiffen Chinese resistance to objectionable Russian demands; at other times, when opposition was useless he pressed the need for pliancy and conciliation in the face of Russian threats and provocation. In this way he helped to avoid the confrontation that Behrens and Sokov sought to bring about. The role of unofficial adviser to the Chinese demanded the greatest tact and delicacy on Macartney's part. Not only had he to retain the confidence of his hosts and avoid officious interference, but he ran the risk of incurring the displeasure of his own government, as well as increasing the hostility of the Russians. That he was able on at least one occasion to write the Taotai's dispatches for him is an indication of his success, and the respect the Chinese had for his integrity.

Macartney's reports reveal most of the failings of Chinese rule in Sinkiang during the twenty-eight years he spent there. Administrative corruption, military inadequacy, ignorance and rapacity, were all obvious, and gave grounds for the Russians' openly expressed contempt and derision. But despite these glaring faults the Chinese were not only preferred as rulers by the Turkis, but they retained, even in the upheavals of the revolution, both their ability and their will to rule. They were past masters at the art of maintaining the appearance of power even when there was nothing to support it. Prevarication, delay and a combination of obtuseness and pliancy were their only weapons in the face of Russian bullying, but they used them with traditional skill. This, and the strength of their imperial tradition, which made them tenacious of every inch of territory they laid claim to, hinted that, once organized and armed, Russia would find China a formidable opponent.

Macartney's observations of Russian policy in Sinkiang show that even at their most arrogant the Russians were not unaware of future possibilities. Despite their professed contempt for what they saw of Chinese power they never lost sight of the desirability of strengthening their frontiers by acquiring territory such as Ili. Russia did not want the expense and trouble of conquering Sinkiang, but neither did she want to see a strong China occupying it. Her policy was to exploit it economically for her own advantage and to keep it weak politically. This accounts for

Russia's interest in fostering potential leaders of the Turki people who might wrest the province from China and set it up as a Russian satellite state. These ideas were clearly in Petrovsky's mind and at the present day this appears to be Soviet policy (*The Times*, 4 March 1970).

More than half a century has passed since George Macartney left Kashgar. In that time the defence of India's northern frontier has ceased to be Britain's direct concern, and China, which he left when it was pitifully weak and disorganized, has become one of the world's great powers. She now confronts Russia across the border of Sinkiang on equal terms. In the salty desert of Lop Nor her nuclear weapons point towards the Russian heartland. But the contest for Sinkiang continues, and in the nuclear age it is still illuminating to see its beginnings through the neutral but shrewd eyes of the first British Consul in Kashgar.

Bibliography

ORIGINAL SOURCES

INDIA OFFICE LIBRARY AND RECORDS

Political and Secret Home Correspondence (L/P & S/3) 1890–1918.

Political and Secret Correspondence (L/P & S/7) 1890–1918.

Political and Secret Subject Files (L/P & S/10):

2359/1904 *Chinese Turkistan, 1904–10.*

3537/1912 *Chinese Turkistan: Treaty of St Petersburgh, 1881; revision.*

124/1913 *Chinese Turkistan, 1910–15.*

2450/1914 *Kashgar: Consulate, 1914–21.*

2273/1919 *Kashgar: Monthly Diaries, 1912–20.*

4529/1914 *German War: German Agents in China.*

Political and Secret Files (L/P & S/11) 1912–18.

Political and Secret Memoranda (L/P & S/18):

A.79 (1888) Departmental Note, 'India Frontier Policy with remarks by Sir W. Lockhart on the Hindu Kush Passes'.

A.82 (1891) S. C. Bayley, 'The Pamir Question and the N.E. Frontier of Afghanistan'.

A.83 (1892) S. C. Bayley, 'The Complication with Hunza'.

A.86A (1892) S. C. Bayley, 'The Russian Expedition to the Pamirs of 1892'.

A.95 (1895) F. E. Younghusband, 'Northern Frontier of India; Roads and Passes'.

A.135 (1898) R. P. Cobbold, 'Report on his journeys on the Pamirs and in Chinese Turkistan'.

A.160 (1904) P. H. Dumbell, 'Frontier between Hunza and the Chinese Dominions'.

A.172 (1915) Sir G. Macartney, 'Chinese Turkistan: suggested Anglo-Russian Convention'.

A.173 (1915–6) German War: Presence of Germans in Afghanistan.

C.177 (1918) J. E. Shuckburgh, 'Central Asia: despatch of a British Mission to Turkestan'.

C.181 (1918) P. T. Etherton, 'Central Asia: The Pan-Turanian Movement'.

265

Political and Secret Department Library (L/P & S/20):
> A.56 Lieut. W. R. Robertson, *Routes from Russian Territory in Central Asia towards Afghanistan and India: Section 1 – The Pamir Line of Advance* (1893).
> A.108 Major S. Geoghegan, *Military Report on Kashgaria* (1907); revised by Sir G. Macartney.

European MSS.D.658:
> Papers, dating from 1918 to 1940, of Lieut.-Col. F. M. Bailey, concerning his mission to Tashkent in 1918 and the part played in it by Sir George Macartney.

PUBLIC RECORD OFFICE

FO 65 *Russia in Central Asia* (1890–1898).
FO 106 *Russia in Central Asia* (1899–1901).

CONTEMPORARY BOOKS

Anon, *Report on the Proceedings of the Pamir Boundary Commission* (Calcutta, 1896).

Blacker, L. V. S., *On Secret Patrol in High Asia* (London, 1922).

Bower, H., *Confidential Report of a Journey in Chinese Turkistan, 1899–90* (Calcutta, 1891).

Cobbold, R. C., *Innermost Asia* (London, 1900).

Curzon, G. N., *Russia in Central Asia in 1899 and the Anglo–Russian Question* (London, 1889).

Elias, N., *Confidential Report of a Mission to Chinese Turkistan and Badakhshan in 1885–6* (Calcutta, 1886).

Etherton, P. T., *In the Heart of Asia* (London, 1925).

Holdich, Col. Sir T. H., *The Indian Borderland, 1880–1900* (London, 1901).

Knight, E. F., *Where Three Empires Meet* (London, 1897).

Lansdell, H., *Chinese Central Asia*, 2 vols (London, 1893).

Macartney, Sir George, *Eastern Turkistan: the Chinese as Rulers over an Alien Race* (London, 1909).

Macartney, Lady, *An English Lady in Chinese Turkestan* (London, 1931).

Skrine, F. H. and Ross, E. D., *Heart of Asia* (London, 1889).

Stein, Sir Aurel, 'A Third Journey of Exploration in Central Asia, 1913–16', *The Geographical Journal*, vol. XLVIII, No. 2 (August 1916).

Younghusband, F. E., *Among the Celestials* (London, 1898).

Younghusband, F. E., *The Heart of a Continent* (London, 1897).

Younghusband, F. E., *The Light of Experience* (London, 1927).

SECONDARY WORKS

Alder, G. J., *British India's Northern Frontier, 1865–95: A Study in Imperial Policy* (London, 1963).

Anon, 'The Sinkiang–Hunza Frontier', *Journal of the Royal Central Asian Society*, vol XXXVIII (1951).

Beckmann, G. M., *The Modernization of China and Japan* (New York, 1962).

Boulger, D. G., *The Life of Sir Halliday Macartney* (London, 1908).

Dallin, D. J., *The Rise of Russia in Asia* (New Haven, 1949).

Davidson, B., *Turkestan Alive* (London, 1957).

Fleming, P., *News from Tartary* (London, 1936).

Fleming, P., *The Siege at Peking* (London, 1959).

Frechtling, L. E., 'Anglo–Russian Rivalry in Eastern Turkistan, 1863–1881', *The Geographical Journal*, a composite volume entitled *Central Asia and Afghanistan*, pp. 471–89.

Hudson, G. F. and Rajchman, M., *An Atlas of Far Eastern Politics* (London, 1938).

Jackson, W. A. Douglas, *The Russo–Chinese Borderlands: Zone of Peaceful Contact or Potential Conflict* (Princeton, 1962).

Lamb, H. A., *Britain and Chinese Central Asia: The Road to Lhasa, 1767 to 1905* (London, 1960).

Lattimore, O., *High Tartary* (Boston, 1930).

Lattimore, O., *Inner Asian Frontiers of China* (New York, 1940).

Pearl, C., *Morrison of Peking* (1967).

Pierce, R. A., *Russian Central Asia, 1867–1917* (Univ. of California, 1960).

Roerich, G. N., *Trails to Inmost Asia* (New Haven, 1931).

Skrine, C. P., *Chinese Central Asia* (London, 1926, reprinted 1971).

Sykes, Sir P., *The Right Honourable Sir Mortimer Durand* (London, 1926).

Stein, Sir A., 'Innermost Asia: Its Geography as a Factor in History', *The Geographical Journal*, vol. LXV, No. 5 (May 1925).

Teichman, Sir E., *Journey to Turkistan* (London, 1937).

Tien-Fong Cheng, *A History of Sino–Russian Relations* (Washington, D.C., 1957).

Tregear, T. R., *A Geography of China* (London, 1965).

Wu, A. K., *Turkistan Tumult* (London, 1939).

Wu, A. K., *China and the Soviet Union* (New York, 1950).

Yakhontoff, V. A., *Russia and the Soviet Union in the Far East* (London, 1932).

Index

Abdul Aziz Qari, 190

Abdur Rahman, secretary to M., 42

Abdurrahman Khan, anti-Russian Amir, 9

Afghanistan, 6, 26; Russian involvement, 7, 74, 138, 150; border intrigues, 7–8; Oxus frontier, 8, 34; gap in demarcation line, 9, 11, 13, 14–15; and Alichur Pamir, 60–1, 71; frontier delimitations, 71–2, 75–6, 80; lack of consular recognition in China, 233; Turkish travellers, 238–9, 240; pan-Turanian movement, 248; German agents, 250, 251, 255, 256, 259

Afghans, and Pamir gap, 16, 69; and Chinese in Somatash, 27–8, 41–2, 50, 54–5; and Russian aggression, 59; clash at Somatash, 59–60, 61, 65; receive Durand Mission, 65–6; Yarkand traders, 96; and British nationality, 133, 140, 233, 237, 251, 255; and German agents, 249, 251, 257

Afghan Wars, 7, 9

Ahmad Din, Munshi, clerk to M., 85; assaulted by Chinese, 86–7, 88–9, 91, 101; and Ko-Lao-Hui, 87; replacement, 103

Ahmad Kamal, Turki school, 248–9

Ahmadyar, Aksakal of Yarkand, and Indian traders, 98–9, 100

Ak-Baital river, 61

Aksai Chin country, 107

Aksu, 17, 87, 131; river, 61; Chinese revolution, 175–6, 185, 186; anti-foreign campaign, 245; opium market, 259

Aktash, 56; Russian occupation, 60, 65; destruction of Chinese fort, 61; disbandment of garrison, 154

Alder, G. J., *British India, Northern Frontier, 1865–95*, viii

Alichur, Russian claims, 34–5

Almati, Russian military depot, 143

Andijan, 97, 184; trans-Siberian extension, 79; roadway to Naryn, 147

Andijanis, 142, 225, 244; Russian traders, 25, 104, 105, 232; dispute with Hindus, 100, 149; incited by Behrens, 171, 188–9; and Syed Haji, 189–90

Aris, 152

Armenians, and customs exemptions, 233

Artush, 87; trading company, 156, 157

At Bashi, 143, 144

Azghur, Raskam valley holding, 109–10

Badruddin Khan, Indian Aksakal, 192, 193

Bai, ix

Bailer, Col., and Tashkent Soviet, 259

Bajaunis, 233, 257

Baku, 138

Baltis, and British nationality, 140

Baltistan, 171

Baluchistan, British control, 8

Bayik Pass, 82

Behrens, Edward, Russian secretary, relations with M., 168–9; on Kashgar regime, 169, 203; tour of Tarim Basin, 170, 171–2, 188, 192, 206; registration of Russian subjects, 171, 188–9; manipulation of Chinese revolution, 183, 189; in Yarkand, 184, 198; and Chira

Behrens, Edward—*cont.*
Incident, 192–3, 198–9, 204–5, 207, 208, 262; and annexation of Sinkiang, 203; farewell revelations, 205–6; denounces Sokov, 206, 207, 219; recalled, 208
Blacker, Capt., and Tashkent Soviet, 259, 260
Blue Lake, 16
Bobrov, Col., arrival in Kashgar, 184–5, 195; relations with Sokov, 197, 203, 223; and Chira Incident, 198; and departure of New Regiment, 200–1
Bokhara, Bokharis, 7, 8, 26, 249
Borland, James, father-in-law to M., 85
Boxer Rebellion (Society of the Harmonious Fists), 160; and Peking, 113–14; reactions to, 114–15, 117; relief of legations, 115; aftermath in Sinkiang, 125, 127
Bozai Gumbaz, 33, 34, 59, 61
British Government, interest in Sinkiang, 10; and Hunza, 13; and Russian aggression in Pamirs, 58, 72; and Raskam valley affair, 106, 129; and Russian reinforcements in Kashgar, 229–30; *see also* Great Britain
Buchanan, George, ambassador to the Tsar, 192; interview with Sazanov, 229–30
Bulungkul, 60, 66
Burma, 11; Commission, 63

Canton, 175
Central Asia, Russian conquests, 7, 36; Anglo-Russian spheres of interest, 8–9; urban characteristics, 19; struggle for supremacy, 26; Russian manoeuvres, 138
Chalt, 37, 42
Chang, General, 28, 45; Yonoff and, 35; and Somatash, 41, 55; and Hunza, 46, 47; ordered to defend Chinese territory, 50; exchanges with Russians, 51–2; returns to Kashgar, 56; relations with M., 60, 62, 65–6; and Chinese boundary in Pamirs, 70; and Raskam valley dispute, 104

Chang, manager of Foreign Affairs Office, 89, 90, 97, 103
Chang Chifu, judge at Chira inquiry, 218
Chang, District Magistrate, 176; murder, 177–8
Chao, member of Ko-Lao-Hui, 187
Charas (marijuana), 10, 96, 98, 103, 111, 120, 132
Charchan, 17, 87–8, 235
Chimkent, 152
China Inland Mission, ix, 152, 157
Chinese, scholar officials, 1; sense of cultural superiority, 1, 20, 116; domination of Kashgar, 19–20; racial exclusiveness, 20; characteristics of occupation troops, 21; hereditary civil and military service, 21–2; virtues of mandarin rule, 22–3; moribund empire, 23, 82; importance of 'face', 31, 54; and slave-owning, 64, 77; Muslim converts, 79; and Petrovsky, 90, 104, 120; suspicions of British encroachment, 92; dependence on Russian trade, 120–1; new economic measures, 132–3; concessions to British traders, 133; intermediaries between British and Russians, 145–6; economic and military reforms, 152–4; Europeanization, 158, 225; attitude to foreigners, 157, 234, 242; anti-revolutionary elements, 214–15; and registration question, 220; secret societies, 226 (*see also* Ko-Lao-Hui); sympathies in World War 1, 238; era of administrative violence, 243
Chinese empire, Manchu imperialism, 1, 2, 21, 153, 173, 175; defeat by Japan, 78, 79, 82; boundary demarcation question, 81; fear of Ko-Lao-Hui, 87; relations with Britain, 121; Opium War, 135–6; beginnings of revolutionary thought, 136; spirit of renewal, 152–3; socio-economic reforms, 154–5; chaotic currency, 155, 160; military reform, 156
Chinese Republic, 173; local institution, 175, 176; and Chira Incident, 192, 198; intransigent

Index

behaviour of Chinese, 225, 237;
Manchu-type officials, 243;
neutrality in World War 1, 249,
250; declares war on Germany,
258, 259
Chinese Revolution, repercussions in
Sinkiang, ix, x; initiation and
spread, 173–5; treatment of foreign
nationals, 179, 182; amnesty for
Kashgar murderers, 185; work of
Ko-Lao-Hui, 186, 195, 196;
massacres, 186, 191; positions held
by 'gamblers', 195; influence on
Chinese mentality, 225, 226–7, 237
Chinese troops, 65, 89, 163; at
Rangkul, 49, 51; in Sarikol, 65, 69,
73, 75, 106; assaults on M. and his
servants, 66, 68, 89, 99, 103;
immobility, 70; and Dungan
revolt, 86–7; reaction to Boxer
rebellion, 114; pay dispute, 118;
shortages and malpractices, 143;
military reforms, 156; riots among
foreign-trained, 163, 166; and the
revolution, 174, 175, 176, 178–9;
and foreign nationals, 182, 184;
New Regiment (gamblers), and
the revolution, 179–82, 185–6, 188,
189, 206; increasing power, 195;
posts held by, 195–6; ordered to
Urumchi, 199, 200, 213; departure,
200–1
Ch'ing, Manchu Prince Regent, 175
Chini Bagh, 16, 139; location, 19;
visitors and courtesy calls, 26,
57–8, 79, 214; M. and, 39–40;
British Consulate building, 168, 209,
242; and Chinese revolution, 176–7,
179–81
Chira, 182; Incident, 188–94, 262;
repercussions, 197–8; investigated
by Behrens, 198–9, 205–6; Chinese
apology, 202; official inquiry, 208,
217–18, 224; and registration
question, 220–1, 222–3, 224, 231;
attempted and final settlements,
224, 227–9, 230–1, 232; deadlock,
225, 226, 227
Chitral, 12, 58, 171, 233
passes, 7, 11, 61
Chow, Kashgar City Magistrate, 178,
179
Cobbold, Ralph, 116; and Petrovsky,

24, 25, 29, 32, 94–5; arrest in
Pamirs, 95; and M.'s humiliation,
96; on his position in Kashgar,
100–1
Confucianism, 243, 246
Congress of Berlin, 7
Cresswell, Miss, governess to M.s,
176, 180, 239
Crewe, Lord, Sec. of State for India,
194, 220
Customs dues, 156, 232, 233, 237

Dafdar, 140; Pass, 129; Afghan
Wakhanis, 240
Darwaz, 8, 75, 141
Davison, companion to
Younghusband, 31–2, 33, 35;
arrest, 33, 34; adventures, 34–5
Deasy, Capt., 103, 107, 116
de Lavroff, acting Russian Consul,
134, 138; consular secretary, 142,
187
Dufferin, Lord, 11
Dungans (Hui, Chinese Muslims),
19, 176; martial character, 19, 79,
114; origins, 79; Kansu revolt, 81,
86–8; used by Governor Yang, 212,
235–6; power in Sinkiang, 242–3;
era of violence, 243; anti-republican
views, 244
Dunmore, Lord, and Pamir frontier
dispute, 69–70
Durand, Col. Algernon, and Hunza
and Nagir, 38, 42–3, 45, 47, 53,
54; and Russian threat to India,
50, 71; and enslavement of British
subjects, 52–3
Durand, Sir Mortimer, Foreign
Secretary, 40; relations with M.,
45, 52–3; Afghan Mission, 75–6,
80
Dzungaria, 17

Eastern Turkestan, becomes Sinkiang
(see under), 1, 11; Muslim revolt
against Chinese, 10; Chinese
reconquest, 11; Mandarin rule,
22–3; communication with India,
71; Russian intentions, 194–5
Elias, Ney, visit to Yarkand, 11;
and Pamir gap, 14
Elliot, Mr, secretary at St. Petersburg
embassy, and Vrevsky, 35

Etherton, Major, and Tashkent Soviet, 259, 260; on M.'s farewell, 260

Ferghana, 26, 28, 95, 97, 202
Formosa, 80
Forsyth Mission to Kashgar, 10–11
France, banker to China, 80
Futai, the, Chinese Governor at Urumchi, 22

Gerard, Gen. Sir Montagu, and Boundary Commission, 80; on M., 82–3
Germany, agents in Sinkiang, 248, 249; and China's neutrality, 249
Ghazanfar Khan, f. of Safdar Ali, 58
Gilgit, 162, 171; British agency, 13, 116; roadway to Nomal, 37, to Chalt, 42; Durand's recommendations, 38; M. and installation of new Mir, 60, 62–5
Gladstone, W. E., and military adventures, 8
Gobi desert, crossed by Younghusband, 14
Goma, dismissal of Amban, 154, 166; and Behrens, 198; expulsion of British and Russian subjects, 221; registration of British subjects, 233; anti-foreign campaign, 245; German agent, 249
Gordon, General, and Taiping rebellion, 2
Gortshakov, Prince, agreement with Granville on Central Asia (1873), 8–9, 34
Government of China (Peking), and Russian aggression in Pamirs, 41, 55–6, 74; and Hunza, 47, 53; and M.'s official position, 67, 89, 99, 138, 151; cuts Sinkiang Subsidy, 79, 87, 127; and frontier demarcation, 80; and Dungan revolt, 86; and assaults on M., 91; condemned by Petrovsky, 92, 94; and Raskam valley dispute, 106–7, 109, 110, 112; reaction to Boxer rebellion, 114; and Japanese indemnity, 127, 130–1; centralized power, 153, 154; electoral reform, 154, and educational system, 154–5, 166; and Western taxation systems, 155; and Kashgar Taotaiship, 160;

US/European loan, 167; and Treaty of St Petersburg, 170; and Syed Haji case, 192, 198; post-revolution, 214, 227–8, 253
Government of India, 11; mission to Yarkand, 2; and Russian Central Asian activities, 13, 37, 38, 60, 125–6, 138, 194–5; effort to close Pamir gap, 14, 28; ridiculed by Petrovsky, 29–30; relations with M., 41, 119, 122, 261; and Afghan claims in Pamir, 60–1; and M.'s official position, 74, 83, 91, 96, 134–5, 140, 141, 146; and Raskam valley affair, 98; and British nationality, 133; and new Consulate, 158; and Chinese revolution, 174–5; Political and Secret Records, 261; *Moral and Material Progress Report*, 24
Granville, Lord, agreement with Gortchakov in Central Asia (1873), 8–9, 34
Great Britain, and Afghanistan, 7–9, 75–6; relations with China, 11, 99, 104; and Hunza, 30–1, 37, 38, 53; and Pamir dispute, 60, 71, 75–6; prestige in Kashgaria, 95–7, 158; aids China with Japanese indemnity, 99; Foreign Office and Central Asia, 11–12, 138, 141, 209; trading position in Kashgaria, 121, 127, 132, 133; and Russian encroachment in Sinkiang, 125–6; alliance with Japan (1902), 135; and Tibet, 138–9, 141; agreement with Russia, 150; wartime alliance with her, 238, 240
Great Karakul Lake, 56
Grey, Sir Edward, 192, 229
Gromchevsky, Col., 44–5, 49; relations with M., 6; arrival in Hunza, 13, 30; and Younghusband, 14, 36; in Yarkand, 15

Hagelstrom, secretary to Sokov, 223, 225
Hai Ta-Lao-yieh, and Pamir dispute, 70–1
Hakim Khan, and throne of Kashgar, 27
Hami, 17, 36, 54, 86
Hankow, start of revolution, 173

Index

Hashur Hakim Beg, 202–3

Hazrat Apak Khoja, patron saint of Kashgar, 27

Heath, Fanny, nurse to M.s, 137

Hendriks, Fr, Dutch priest, friendship with M., 39–40, 50, 103; Petrovsky's vendetta, 107–17; death, 146

Hindu Kush, 69; passes, 13, 31, 60, 71, 80; Russian expedition, 33, 36; routes to Gilgit, 36–7; limit of British expansion, 55, 81, 125, 241; Russian frontier, 117, exclusion of foreign intrigues, 241

Holditch, Col., and Boundary Commission, 80

Honan, assault on Urumchi, 174, 186

Hosein Bai Batcha, educational benefits, 157, 162; pan-Islamic ideals, 248

Hsiung Kao-sheng, resistance to Russian drive, 187, 189, 190; and Chira Incident, 190–1, 192–3, 202, 231; arrest and trial, 202, 218, 222; imprisonment, 224, 231; leader of Kashgar gamblers, 235

Hunan province, 73

Hunter, Rev. George, 152, 156, 176, 211

Hunza, 11, 61, 146, 183; Muslim state, 12; and Emperor of China, 12; and Kashmir, 12, 13; Younghusband's discoveries, 14; ultimatum from Indian government, 42–3; British annexation, 46–7, 53, 63, 71, 93; settlement of dispute, 54, 241; claims to Taghdumbash tribute, 55, 140, 237; installation of new Mir, 60, 62, 65, 72; grazing and cultivation rights, 92, 165; economic decline, 93; and Raskam grants, 109–10, 141, 165; Safdar Ali and the *jagir*, 126; Scouts and German agents, 255–6

Hupei province, 73, 228; German consul, 256

Ili, 23–4, 86, 87, 88; Russian threat, 167, 230, 241; and Chinese revolution, 173, 174, 175, 183, 187, 214; separatist movement, 212, 213, 235; murder of troop leader, 227,

228; withdrawal of Russian consular guard, (1914), 237

India, English society, 4; Anglo/Russian ambitions, 6; fear of Russian encroachment, 9, 50, 71, 258–9; trade with China, 10; with UK and Russia, 81, 131; outbreak of plague, 90, 118; danger from Turki nationalism, 248

Indian Civil Service, an élite corps, 3–4

India Office, 89, 91, 117, 125, 194

Indians, British (Hindus), traders, 19, 95–6, 116, 133; attacks on, 89; trading disputes, 98, 100; debt-collecting problems, 104–5; and British nationality, 133, 221, 232; post of Aksakal, 182, 183, 192, 198

Irkeshtam, 35; Chinese frontier, 184; Russian reinforcements, 73, 106, 168; telegraph, 79, 220

Japan, and China, 78, 79, 80, 86, 115; economic results of war, 97, 153; indemnity, 127, 130–1, 132–3; Russian convention, 150; and new spirit of reform, 153; and World War 1, 255

Jordan, John, 192

Kabul, 9, 55, 76

Kanjugan, oil grounds, 153

Kanjutis, 46, 58, 68; and Russians, 60; Raskam valley interests, 93–4, 98, 104, 106, 112, 117, 126, 129; tax levies on Wakhanis, 140–1; British subjects, 237

Kansu, 73, 186, 212; Dungans, 19, 79, 81, 85–6, 175, 236; opium smuggling, 257

Karakoram mountains, 209

Karakoram Pass, 10, 15, 32, 120; Chinese claims, 81; Hunza grazing rights, 92, 93

Karashahr, and Chinese revolution, 176

Karghalik, 78, 171; dismissal of Amban, 154; expulsion of British and Russian subjects, 221; registration of British subjects, 233; murder of Amban by gamblers, 235–6; anti-foreign campaign, 245

273

Karim Beg, 130, 147, 169
Kashgar, Russian factory, 10, 113;
Chinese rule, 11, 19–20, 28–9, 81;
105, 129, 150; roadways, 17, 49,
147; centre of government, 19;
architecture, 19; Russian consulate,
19, 23–4; Andijan Gate, 19;
claimants for the crown, 27;
ignorance of Japanese threat, 78;
Anglo-Russian politics, 81; and
Dungan revolt, 86; election of
Russian Aksakal, 97; appointment
of Amban, 100, of Mayor, 111;
Russian involvement and influence,
113, 124, 135, 156; reaction to
Boxer rebellion, 114; value of the
rouble, 126–7; landowners'
payments, 132; Russo-Chinese
Commission (1904), 139; character
of District Magistrate, 139;
unprotected frontier, 143; military
reforms, 154, 156; abortive *duma*,
155–6, 157, 162; petitions against
taxes, 155; trade guilds, 156, 162;
growth in gamblers and thieves,
161, 235–6; new ministries, 162;
impact of Chinese revolution, 174,
175, 176, 177–8 ff.; influx of
Russian troops, 184, 190, 196–7;
removal of New Regiment, 199–201;
physical separation from Urumchi,
210–11; office of Titai, 213; era of
violence, 243; pan-Islamism, 248; in
World War 1, 249; and a German
consul, 249, 251; anti-Allied
propaganda, 258; arrival of British
troops, 260
Kashgaria, 17; Turki people, 18, 52;
position of Chinese, 23, 38, 81, 88,
97, 162–3; presence of British
slaves, 48, 52; position and influence
of Russians, 52, 97, 119–23, 126–8,
132–3, 188, 193–4, 207, 223, 262;
new tariff regulations, 131, 132;
British position, 134–5; effect of
Japanese victory, 135, 139;
administration of Ambans, 153–4;
and Peking reforms, 155–6, 162;
and foreign trading rights, 157,
164; school-building programme,
162; administrative chaos, 166–7;
provincial independence, 188;
Anglo/Russian spheres of interest,

241; new era of violence, 243, 244;
pro-Turkish sympathies, 258
Kashgar-Ferghana frontier, 70
Kashgar-Naryn trade route, 142–3,
159
Kashmir, 5, 68; trade route, 10, 26;
Muslim border States, 12; Chinese
intrigues, 12–13; British Resident,
133, 146, 178, 220, 252–3
Kazakhs, the, 212
Kemp, E. G., traveller, tribute to M.,
209
Keriya, 17, 116, 144, 231; and Deasy,
103, 107; gold-mining, 133;
denunciation of Amban, 166; and
Chinese revolution, 182, 185, 203;
Behrens and, 198, 199; Turkish
activities, 239
Khiva, Russian conquest, 7
Khotan, 17, 115–16, 172, 183, 187,
221; garrison mutiny, 118; gold
deposits, 133, 153; denunciation of
Amban, 166; and Chinese
revolution, 187, 189, 190, 203, 227;
Behrens and, 198, 204–5;
registration of British subjects, 221,
233, 238; German agents, 254–5,
255, 256
Khyber Pass, 71
Kilian, trade route, 91, 94, 95–6, 131
Kirghiz, nomad people, 14, 212;
and the Pamir, 15, 19, 34–5, 59;
circular tents, 26; need for a
leader, 27; predicted uprising, 52;
and Russian troops, 65; cultivate
Raskam lands, 117
Kobdo region, 199, 201
Kokand, 7, 10, 191; Russian
annexation, 20–1, 34, 56
Kokcha river, junction with Oxus, 9,
34
Ko-Lao-Hui (secret society), 87, 88;
Kashgar membership, 87, 214, 217,
226; and Chinese revolution, 173,
174, 186, 196, 212; Russian
intervention, 187; and battle for
Sinkiang, 188, 189, 195, 196, 208,
214, 227; and Chira Incident, 202;
proscribed by Manchus, 226;
disappearance from public view,
244
Kolbine, Capt., and fuel supplies,
169, 170

Index

Kolokolof, position at consulate, 88, 138, 141; and Bombay plague, 90; relations with M., 90, 141–2, 145, 149–50; embassy secretary, 109; and Far East policy, 141–2, 150; negotiations with Taotai, 142–3, 144, 147; and Anglo/Russian commercial contracts, 145; and sale of land, 157–8: leaves Kashgar, 159; and revision of Sino/Russian treaty, 159

Kora, headquarters of 'Tartar General', 173, 212

Korea, Japanese ambitions, 78, 80, 135, 144

Kornilov, Capt., 112, 115, 126

Kostenko, Col., and Pamir gap, 11–12

Krasnovodsk, 138

Ku, and Yangi Hissar prefecture, 196, 199

Kuang Hsu, Emperor, imprisonment, 153; death, 160

Kucha, 17, 176, 256

Kuchar, 16, 146

Kugiar, trade route, 91–2, 93, 94, 95–6, 120

Kukturuk valley, 255

Kuldja, 23–4; and revolution in Sinkiang, 173, 212

Kunlun-Karakoram complex, 17

Kuomintang party, 214

Kwan, 'Tartar General', 173

Ladakh. 5, 26, 31, 94, 104, 183

Lake Victoria, 9, 34, 65, 78, 80

Lanchow, 81

Lansdowne, Lord, Foreign Secretary, 141, 210

Lar Wang, Taiping prince, 2

Lastochkin, Col., 142

Lavrienti, Dr, on Sokov, 199–200, 206

Leh, 5, 68;—Yarkand trade route, 10, 12, 13

Lew-Ching-Tang, former Provincial Governor, 70

Lew Ta-lao-yieh, Amban of Yarkand, 115; extortionist policy, 118–19; and Petrovsky, 118, 124; replacement, 127; anti-British activities, 257, 259; and opium smuggling, 257, 259; and Afghans, 259

Lhasa, 138; Convention, 141

Liaotung peninsular, 80

Lien, Provincial Governor, downfall, 166

Li Hung-chang, relations with Russia, 115

Li Kuan-tai, Major, murder, 227, 228

Loetsch, M., secretary to Petrovsky, 27, 75, 77

Lop Nor district, 17, 255; Dungan revolt, 86, 87; dismissal of Amban, 154; nuclear weapon site, 264

Macartney (née Borland), Lady Catherine, 158; marriage, 85, 102; character, 85, 102, 209; journies to Kashgar, 102–3, 137; children, 137, 146, 152, 176, 239; and Chinese revolution, 180, 181; in World War 1, 239–40; *An English Lady in Chinese Turkestan*, 261

Macartney, Donald, 176, 180, 181, 200

Macartney, George, first Earl Macartney, 2

Macartney, Sir George, viii; and a Consular Guard, ix, 163, 174–5, 176, 194, 209, 260; Chinese interpreter to Younghusband, 2, 5–6, 14, 15–16, 27, 41; appearance and character, 2, 4, 40, 82–3, 83–4, 123, 209; parentage, 2–3; education, 3, 5; at Yarkand, 6, 33, 54; and Russian aggression in Pamirs, 35–6, 38, 47, 48, 51, 52, 56–7, 60, 61; on Sino/Russian activities, 41, 210, 219; and Hunza crisis, 43–7, 49, 61–2; relations with Chinese, 48, 53, 61–2, 63, 67–8, 76–7, 78, 88, 91, 100, 119–20, 146, 169, 209, 232, 263; and release of British-born slaves, 52, 54, 63, 64, 68–9, 77, 78, 89, 120; and his own position, 62–5, 67, 74, 83, 88, 89, 99–100, 117, 119, 121, 122, 126; pay increases, 68, 113; alleged import of guns, 72; on the Chinese, 81–2; on leave, 84–5, 102, 130–2; 137, 150–1, 152, 239–40; marriage, 85, 102–3; and British prestige, 95–6, 97, 99, 100, 105; five points for settling Indian debt cases, 99, 104, 105; honours, 113, 209, 234; and aftermath of Boxer rebellion, 114–15, 118; appraisal

Macartney, Sir George—*cont.*
  of British position in Kashgaria,
  116–17; and his consular status,
  117, 134–5, 137, 141, 142, 145,
  146, 149, 150, 151, 161, 209;
  achievements, 122–3, 151, 211–12;
  and traders' suits, 139, 145, 148,
  169–70; and registration of British
  nationals, 139–40, 221–2, 223,
  232–4, 236, 237, 238; quells
  Hindu/Muslim riot, 149; suggests
  Sino/Chinese convention, 165–6;
  Consul-General, 168; relations with
  Sokov, 168, 184–5, 204; and
  Chinese revolution, 174, 177, 181,
  183, 184, 186, 197, 217; tribute by
  British Indians, 209; criticisms of,
  209–10, 216; and Chira trial,
  218–20; tour of southern oasis,
  231, 232; legal appointment, 233;
  in World War 1, 238, 239, 242;
  memo on Anglo/Russian spheres of
  interest, 241–2; and counter-
  intelligence, 250–2, 254–61; last
  year in Kashgar, 259–60; local
  farewell, 260; retirement and
  death, 261; assessment, 261–2
Macartney, Sir Halliday, f. of George,
  ancestry and early career, 2–3, 27;
  and Chinese, 5; death, 146
Macdonald, Sir Claude, 111, 112;
  and M.'s position, 98, 99
Macpherson, P. A., at Gilgit, 255,
  256
Manass, 173
Manchuria, Japanese ambitions, 78,
  80, 144; Russian occupation, 115,
  227, 230
Mao Ta-jen, and Dungan rebellion, 87
Maralbashi, 131, 238
Margillan, 32, 35, 45, 49, 52
Ma, Dungan (Kashgar District
  Magistrate), 254
Ma Fu-sin *see under* Titai
Ma Titai, General, ix, 243 n.
Mayo, Earl of, 9, 10
Mestchersky, Prince, succeeds,
  Sokov, 234; in World War 1, 238,
  249, 250; and Turks in Kashgar, 240;
  and German agents, 250, 251, 252;
  relations with Ma Titai, 254;
  pro-Tsarist, 258; post-War fate,
  258 n.

Metentzov, General, in Kashgar,
  203–4, 206, 207; at Chini Bagh, 204
Miles, Capt., stand-in for M., 130,
  132, 133
Mintaka, 65, 129
Misgah, 71
Mongols, Mongolia, 212, 230
Morier, Sir Robert, and Russian
  plans in Central Asia, 48–9
Morrison, Dr, *Times* correspondent in
  Peking, 160, 214
Moscow, 145
Mouravieff, Count, and Raskam
  affair, 111–12
Muhammad Azim Boy, dual agent
  between M. and Petrovsky, 43–6,
  48, 49; and assault on Pamirs, 56,
  58, 72, 73
Muhammadans (Chinese), 18, 19, 79;
  Petrovsky and, 92; conflict with
  Confucians, 236; pilgrims to
  Mecca, 236–7
Muhammad Nazim Khan, Mir of
  Hunza, 53
Mulla Maqsud Gul, opium smuggler,
  257; deportation, 258, 259
Murghabi, 28, 55, 130; Russian
  occupation, 56, 61, 65, 69, 70, 74,
  77, 106, 134, 237
Muslims, x; revolt against Chinese,
  10; border states, 12; appointment
  of leaders, 20; tax-collectors, 20;
  and slave-owning, 64; Dungans
  (*see under*), 79; traders in Yarkand,
  116, 148; anti-Russians, 124;
  disputes with Hindus, 148–9;
  Chinese schools, 162; suspected
  revolt, 203; sympathies in World
  War 1, 238
Mustafa Khan, gs. of Yakub Beg, 202,
  203, 220
Mustagh Pass, 31, 81; Watershed, 241
Muzaffar Khan, s. of Safdar Ali, 129,
  146–7

Nagir, 12, 38; ultimatum from
  government of India, 42–3;
  British annexation, 46–7
Nanking, 2–3; seat of Sun's
  government, 173
Napoleon, and a Franco/Russian
  frontier expedition, 6–7
Naryn, roadways, 143, 147, 152, 168

Index

Nationalism, beginnings in China, 136
Nazar Ali, and Raskam valley, 98, 104
Nilt fortress, 43
Nomal-Gilgit road, 37

Oliver, Capt., in Kashgaria, 162–3
Opium, imperial prohibition, 155;
riots among cultivators, 163;
smoking by Chinese troops, 226;
gamblers and, 235; British
involvement, 238; smuggling, 257;
chief markets, 259
Orenburg-Tashkent railway, 138
Osh, 36, 45, 79, 152; Russian troops
and, 49, 52, 56, 168, 184
Oxus, the, 12, 15, 60; complicated
geography, 8; junction with
Kokcha, 34; Russian territorial
claims, 34, 35, 69, 75, 78;
Afghans and, 76

Pamir, Pamirs, area of unclaimed
territory, 9, 15; and Russian access
to India, 11–12; three-empire
confrontation, 11, 16; Russian
exploration, 12, 13; characteristics,
15, 17; irrigation, 17–18; climate,
18, 52; people, 18–19; oases, 19;
Anglo-Russian interests, 31, 75;
Russia and, 34–5, 51, 61, 69;
Sino/Russian dispute, 55–6, 58, 65,
69; Russian-imposed military
decision, 71; prospect of
settlement, 76, 78, 79
Alai range, 15, 17, 35, 65, 70;
Vrevsky visits, 28, 29; Russian
claims, 69, 74, 75
Alichur Pamir, 14; Chinese and, 16,
27–8, 35, 51, 56; Russia and, 33,
59, 69; Afghan claims, 60–1, 71
Baroghul Pass, 14, 33
Great Karakul, 51, 52, 70
Khorabort Pass, 33
Killik Pass, 13, 34, 46, 117
Kizil Art Pass, alleged identity with
Uzbel, 70
Little and Great Pamirs, 16, 65, 69, 71
Mintaka Pass, 74, 117
Taghdumbash Pamir, 15, 16, 33, 34;
Chinese claims, 55, 140–1;
Russian domination, 61, 71;
Hunza rights, 140–1; British sphere
of interest, 241

Wakham Pamir, 15, 33, 60–1
Uzbel Pass, 56, 70
Pamir (Anglo-Russian) Agreement,
1895, 80, 81
Pamir Boundary Commission, 80,
81–3
Pan, District Magistrate of Yarkand,
77
Pan-Islamism, 157, 248
Panjdeh, 9, 50
Pan-Turanian movement, 248
Peking, Boxer rebellion, 113–14, 115;
centralization, 153; German
agents, 254
Persia, 138, 150, 251; Pan-Turanian
movement, 248
Pescadores Islands, 80
Petrov, Lt. Col., in Kashgar, 184–5
Petrovsky, M., Russian Consul, 23,
81, 83, 210, 262; (virtual ruler of
Kashgar), 24; character and
abilities, 24–5, 94; relations with
Younghusband and M., 26–7, 29,
31–2; diplomatic manoeuvres,
29–30; and the Taotai, 29, 73, 77,
115–16, 124–5, 127, 128–9;
ignorance of China and her
language, 30; and Hunza, 30, 44–6;
and M.'s position, 43, 44, 50, 65,
67–8, 69–70, 72–4, 78–81, 92, 109,
115; and Azim Boy, 44–5, 51; and
Russian aggression in Pamirs, 51,
56, 58, 70, 71, 72, 74–5; and
assault on Loetsch, 75, 77; and
Dungan revolt, 86, 87; on leave, 88;
returns to Kashgar, 92; and
Chinese Muhammadans, 92;
self-opinion, 94; treatment of
Cobbold 94–5; increasing influence,
96–7, 105, 106, 108; undermining
of British prestige and influence,
103, 109, 112, 117–18; and a
Russian occupation of Sinkiang,
106–7, 108, 110–12; modus
operandi, 197; personal vendettas,
107–8, 116; and Sarikol, 112–13,
119, 124–5, 126–7, 130, 133; and
new Amban, 118; appoints Mayor
of Kashgar, 124; and Urumchi, 127,
129; and Raskam valley, 129–30;
last interview with M., 131–2;
departure, 134; retirement, 138;
death, 160

277

Pien Yung-fu, and Kashgar revolution, 178, 181, 185, 200, 201, 206

Polo, Marco, Silk Route to China, 17, 182

Polu, 144; Aksai Chin route, 197, 116

Port Arthur, 80, 141, 144

P'u Yi, successor to Kuang Hsu, 160

Quili Beg, and crown of Kashgar, 27, 202, 203

Rangkul, Chinese base, 49, 51, 55, 56, 70; Russian troops, 59, 65, 69, 77; Afghan withdrawal, 61

Raskam valley, 14, 82; Hunza rights, 92, 93, 98, 240; M./ Petrovsky contest, 92, 93–4, 96, 104, 105 ff., 129; British interests and policy, 117, 119, 122, 141, 240–1; Chinese alienation, 117; German agents, 254–5

Robertson, Surgeon-Major, British agent, 63, 64–5

Roerich, G. N., on Yang Tseng-hsin, 211

Romanoff, Consular secretary, on Russian annexations, 241

Rosebery, Lord, 75

Roshan principality, 8, 9, 12; Russian claims, 34, 35, 75, 76; Afghan evacuation, 76

Russia, strategy against India, 6–7; drive into Central Asia, 7, 21; conquest of khanates, 7; trade relations with China, 10, 159–60, 164; commercial domination of Sinkiang, 11, 25, 127, 131; access to the Pamirs, 11–12, 14, 16; threat to Sinkiang, 23–4. 25, 90, 119–20; road and rail-building programmes, 25, 50, 143, 144, 147; trans-Siberian railway, 78, 79; Japanese threat, 79, 80; aid to China, 80, 87; and a British consul in Kashgar, 121, 137, 138, 142, 145, 151, 158; effect of Japanese victory on Asian prestige, 135, 139; attempted revolution (1905), 144–5; convention with Japan, 150, 167; agreement with Britain, 150; manipulation of Chinese revolution, 183, 184, 193–5; and registration

question, 220–1; and Chira Incident, 227; alleged policy in Kashgar, 230; withdraws troops for World War 1, 237; contempt for Chinese rule, 263 *see also* Petrovsky

Russian government, control of Consular decisions, 25; acquiescence in acts of aggression, 36; relations with Britain over Pamir, 60; and Chira Incident, 192; threatened by Turki nationalism, 248

Russian Revolution, repercussions in Kashgar, x, 258; effect on Anglo/ Russian prestige, 258; Bolshevik rule, 259

Russian troops (Cossacks), at Karakul, 51, 52; and assault on Pamirs, 56, 58, 61, 65; at Rangul, 59, 65; further moves, 69, 73, 74, 75, 77–8; Consulate Guard, 89, 91, 138, 168, 174; and Raskam Valley dispute, 106; and Sarikol, 110, 124–5, 134; Muslim dislike, 124; Central Asian activities, 138; provocative movements, 168, 169; and fuel dispute, 170; and Chinese revolution, 177, 180, 184, 196; arrival of European-trained units, 184; leave Kashgar, 203; threatened reinforcements, 223–4, 231; withdrawals in 1914, 237

Russian Turkestan, 36, 162; Governor-General and the Alai, 75; unknown area, 120; transport monopoly with Kashgar, 121; army mobilization, 138; effect of defeat by Japan, 149; return of Cossack troops, 203; escaped prisoners of war, 249; autonomous sentiments, 259

Russo-Chinese Bank, 113, 121, 147; and economy of Kashgaria, 131, 134; import of silver, 132; transport monopoly, 147–8

Russo-Japanese War, 139, 141; effect of Japanese victory, 135–6, 157; Russian concessions, 144

Safdar Ali Khan, Mir of Hunza, 12, 37; relations with Russians, 13, 37–8, 126, 129; and India, 14; and Chinese, 42, 47; defies British ultimatum, 43, 45; imprisonment, 54; subsequent fate, 126, 129–30, 146, 147, 165

St Petersburg, Bloody Sunday (1905), 144; Soviet, 145

Sakhalin island, 144

Salisbury, Lord, 58–9

Samarkand, railway to Andijan, 79

Sanju, trade route, 91, 94, 95–6, 120

Sarikol, Chinese border district, 14, 15, 34, 35, 46, 90, 96, 240; Gilgit slaves, 48; Russian plans and activities, 58, 61, 69–70, 71, 103–4, 110, 112, 124 ff., 130, 134, 142, 168, 170, 171; and Pamir dispute, 60; treatment of M., 68; Chinese defence, and Raskam valley, 104; British position, 129; census, 162; fuel dispute, 169–70; in World War 1, 256; opium market, 259

Sarikolis, 117, 130

Satow, Sir Ernest, 135

Sayad Bahadur Ali Shah, Munshi, 103, 108

Sayad Yusif, Haji, 108

Sazanov, M., 195, 229–30

Scott, Sir Charles, and Raskam affair, 111–12

Semiretchia, 92

Shahidulla, 82

Shamshal Pass, 117

Shanghai, 233; German agents, 255

Shantung, Boxers, 113

Shensi province, Chinese revolution, 172, 186, 187

Shibos, 213

Shignan principality, 8, 9, 12, 50; Afghans and, 28, 74, 76; Russian claims and aggression, 34, 35, 56, 61, 74, 75; Anglo-Russian agreement, 50; withdrawal of Russian troops, 1914, 237

Shikarpuri Hindus (money-lenders), 116, 140, 148; M. and, 148, 174; return to India, 159

Shimshal Pass, 141

Shuttleworth, Capt., 151, 152, 157, 160; Consular recognition, 158; and Shikarpuris, 159; and Yarkand famine, 161

Sian, Ko-Lao-Hui rising, 186

Sikkim, 5, 11, 31, 138

Sining, 87

Sinkiang, impact of Chinese revolution, ix, 173, 182, 186; Russian occupation and involvement, 23, 24, 25, 159, 164, 167, 168, 169, 170–1, 182, 234, 263–4; Chinese province, 9, 11, 21–3, 86–7, 163, 263; gap in frontier line, 9, 11–12; M.'s aims, 41, 119, 121; and trade with India, 90; and Boxer rebellion, 114; financial plight, 130–1, 167, 214, 234–5; government lotteries, 133; military reforms, 152, 156; British trade, 158; prohibition on mixed marriages, 163–4, 167; customs abuses, 171; registration of British and Russian subjects, 171, 197, 233; triangular contest for control, 188 ff., 208; worsening economic and political situation, 234–5, 248; Anglo/Russian spheres of interest, 241; stability under Governor Yang, 248; opium smuggling, 257

Sinkiang Provincial Governor, and Russian aggression in Pamirs, 48; and M.'s official position, 67, 68, 74, 137; and release of British-born slaves, 69, 77; and Raskam valley dispute, 93, 98, 104, 106, 109; and soldiers' pay, 118; and Japanese indemnity, 127, 130; and Huang's degradation, 128; and Russian position in Tashkurghan, 133–4 *see also* Yeng Tseng-hsin

Slave trading, 12, 37; M. and, 48, 52, 54; unlawful in Kashgaria, 89–90

Sokov, M., successor to Kolokolof, 161; and prohibition of sale of land and mixed marriages, 163–4, 167; relations with Chinese, 163–4, 170, 216; and Taotai, 168, 170; and Chinese revolution, 174, 177, 180, 182–3, 184, 187, 199–200, 262; and Chira Incident and trial, 191–2, 192–3, 198, 208, 210, 217–20, 224–6, 230–1; relations with Bobrov, 197, 200, 203, 206; accusations against, 206; and registration question, 222–3, 224, 225; departure, 231, 234

Somatash, 14–15, 16, 28; Chinese 'stone', 14, 35, 47; Chinese

Somatash—*cont.*
  involvement, 27–8, 48, 50, 56;
    Afghan claims, 42, 50, 54–5;
    Russian/Afghan clash, 59–60, 61
Stein, Sir Aurel, 115–16, 209
Srinagar, roadway to Gilgit, 13
Suchow, 2
Sun Yat-sen, 173, 175, 214
Swedish missionaries, 158, 252; at
  Chini Bagh, 39, 103, 108, 146, 174;
  and Von Hentig, 253; and
  Afghanistan, 258
Syed Haji, and Chira Incident,
  188–9, 190–1, 192–3, 198; trial,
  208, 218–19, 222–3, 224; sentence,
  231
Syed Hamza, German agent, 249,
  256, 257
Sykes, Brig. Sir Percy, 239, 240;
  talks with Romanoff, 241
Szechuan, 186

Tagharma, 71, 75, 106, 130
Taghdumbash, 255, 256; Chinese/
  Russian claims, 55, 75, 130
Taiping rebellion, 2
Ta-lao-yieh, Amban of Yarkand, 115,
  118, 127
Tang-Ta-jen, Chifu of Khotan, on
  trial, 218, 222
Taotai, the, position in hierarchy, 22;
  suggested abolition of post, 155,
  160; becomes Taoyin, 237
Taotai Huang, 20, 22, 23;
  subordination to Petrovsky, 23, 25,
  29–30, 51, 94, 97, 100, 110, 111;
  relations with Younghusband and
  M., 27, 28, 30; and possible
  Russian aggression, 28–9, 51;
  frontier limitation, 31; and Mir of
  Hunza, 42, 43, 45–6, 53, 54; and
  British occupation of Hunza, 47;
  repatriation of British-born slaves,
  48, 54, 64, 68–9; and Pamir
  dispute, 55, 56–7; personal
  relations with M., 57–8, 60, 68–9,
  77, 128; character, 85, 105; and
  safety of British subjects, 88–9, 91,
  103; and Raskam valley, 93, 98,
  104, 106; becomes Provincial
  Treasurer, 115; death, 127–8;
  degradation, 128

Taotai Chu Ta-jen, succeeds Huang,
  128; successor, 133
Taotai Yuen Wung-fu, and
  Petrovsky, 133; relations with
  Kolokoloff, 142–4; and M., 148,
  166; and economic reform, 153–7;
  charges against, 160–1, 162; and
  sale of land to Russians, 167;
  relations with Sokov, 168, 170; and
  Chinese revolution, 176; death,
  177–8, 181, 228
Taotai Wang, succeeds Yuen Wung,
  179, 184–5, 228; and Chira
  Incident, 191–2, 192–3, 198, 202,
  218, 220; and nationality question,
  220, 222; object of disrespect, 225,
  226; dismissal, 228, 229, 231;
  Russia and, 227
Taotai Chang, 229; and British
  nationality question, 237, 238;
  becomes Taoyin, 237; relations
  with M., 238; and Turks in
  Kashgar, 239, 240; anti-foreign
  views, 240, 242, 244; power
  struggle with Ma Fu-sin, 244–5;
  dismissal, 245–6
Taoyin Hsu, and Von Hentig, 240,
  250, 252; replacement, 253
Taoyin Yang, replaces Hsu, 253;
  character, 253–4; and German
  intrigue, 255; dismissal, 255–6
Taoyin Chu, succeeds Yang, 254,
  257; relations with M., 258–9
Tarbagtai, 241
Tarim river, 15; Basin, 16, 17;
  toured by Behrens, 170, 171, 183
Tashkent, Russian General Staff, 12,
  36, 45, 202; internal disputes, 144,
  147; communist training centre, 259
Tashkurghan, 15, 60, 65, 90, 103–4;
  and Pamir dispute, 73; Russian
  involvement, 124–6, 129, 130, 132,
  133, 240, 256; new fort, 134; fuel
  dispute, 169–70, 238; in World
  War 1, 256
Teichman, Sir Eric, on Ko-Lao-Hui,
  186–7
Terek Pass, 184, 223
Tibet, 5, 31, 141, 150, 194; exclusion
  of Russian influence, 138–9, 230
Tien Shan, 17, 23–4, 175, 213; limit
  of British sphere, 241; Dungan
  area, 243

Titai Chang, 127, 128
Titai Chiao, and Dungan revolt, 86, 87; 'European' type dress, 158; and Chinese revolution, 176; to succeed Provincial Governor, 179; and Chira Incident, 191, 202, 213; to command New Regiment, 199, 201; replacement, 213
Titai Ma Fu-sin, 243, 246; power struggle with Taotai Chang, 244–5; policy, 246; and Chinese neutrality, 251; and Von Hentig, 252, 253; relations with M., 254; traffic in arms, 257
Titai Yang, judge at Chira inquiry, 218, 222–3, 224, 227, 230; resignation, 229, 235
Transcarpia, 8, 36
Treaty of Livadia, 24, 69
Treaty of St Petersburg, Russian concessions, 23–4, 25, 27, 51, 142, 158, 163–4; negotiations for renewal, 164–5, 167, 170, 183, 201, 207, 208, 234
Tseng, Marquis, 27
Tsinghai province, 86
Tsitsihar, Governor of, 227, 228
Tsou, Amban of Yangi Hissar, 182; nominated Prefect, 195–6, 199
Tsu Hsi, Empress Dowager, 153, 160
Turcomans, 8
Turfan, 17, 19, 258
Turgat Pass, 143, 144, 147
Turkey, Turks, Muslims and, 238; in Kashgar, 238–9; pan-Islamism, 248–9
Turki people, 18, 20, 82, 89, 242, 251; called 'turban heads', 20; official corruption, 22; discontent, 52, 155; European and pan-Islamic influences, 157; and Chinese revolution, 174, 177, 182, 185, 213, 215; nationalism, 248; fostering of future leaders, 264
Tzaichenko, Capt., replaces Kornilov, 126

Upper Burma British annexation, 30–1
Urumchi, ix, 19; capital of Sinkiang, 17; seat of Provincial Governor (*see under* Sinkiang), 17; garrison commander, 162; riots among opium producers, 163; violence among foreign-drilled troops, 163; manufacture of paper currency, 167; and the revolution, 173, 174, 175, 186; arrival of New Regiment, 200–1; distance from Kashgar, 210–11; censorship of German letters, 258; opium market, 259
see also Yang Tseng-hsi
Urak, 109–10
Uspensky, secretary to Mestchersky, 258

Vagin, Capt., 196–7
Vannovsky, Capt., 76, 77
Von Hentig Mission, 250–1, 257; in Kashgar, 252–4; influence on officials, 255
Vrevsky, General, Gov.-Gen. of Turkestan, 25, 29, 32, 34

Wakhan, Wakhanis, 7, 55, 61, 140, 251, 255; Anglo/Russian agreement, 50; Afghan suzerainty, 76, 233, 240
Wakhan river, north bank boundary, 81
Wakhjir Pass, 255
Wang, General, and M., 39
Wazir Dadu, in Hunza, 43, 53; sent to Hami, 54
Wei, and Chinese revolution, 178, 181, 185, 206
Wei-Hai-Wei, British lease, 99
Witte, Count, 115, 144
World War 1, impact on Kasgaria, 237, 238–9; Sino/Russian preoccupation, 248
Wu, A. K., on Governor Yang, 211–12
Wuhan, revolution by Chinese troops, 172, 173

Yakub Beg, 10, 11, 18, 220; treaty with Russian 10; death, 11; stops Hunza raiding, 12; reconquest, 21; expels Chinese from Kashgaria, 23–4; defeat, 24; and Ili, 183, 187
Yangi Hissar, 154; coal mines, 153; and revolution, 182; Prefecture, 196, 199
Yang Hsietai, and Chinese revolution, 177, 178–9, 180–1, 228; and foreign nationals, 182; fear of

Yang Hsietai—*cont.*
Russia, 184, 197; and departure
of New Regiment, 200–201;
character, 228; promotion, 229
Yang Tseng-hsin, Governor of
Sinkiang, ix, 188, 196; statecraft, x,
201, 211–12, 213, 260; and the
revolution, 174; integrity, 175; and
battle for power, 189, 208, 246;
and New Regiment, 199, 201–2;
assessments, 211; task in Sinkiang,
212; use of Dungan troops, 212–13,
236, 244–5; financial problems,
213–14, 221; relations with Peking,
214, 220, 221; and foreign
nationality certificates, 221–2, 233;
suppresses Khaghalik gamblers,
235–6; reaction to foreign pressure,
244–5; and rebel Yunnanese, 246;
and Turki nationalism, 248–9;
and German agents, 251, 252;
nepotism, 253–4, 257
Yang Tsuan-hus, Brig., 212; and
revolution in Ili, 173, 214; Titai
of Kashgar, 214–17, 228;
Europeanization, 215–16; and
Russian demands, 217; and Chira
inquiry, 217, 228; and Taotai
Wang, 225, 226; disappoints M.,
225–6; personal struggle for power,
226–7; downfall, 227; murders his
subordinate, 227, 228; Presidential
adviser, 254
Yarkand, 1, 73; Younghusband M.,
expedition, 5–6; trade route, 10;
Chinese conquest, 11; Hunza
landholdings, 12; and Pamir gap,
14–15, 17; population, 19; trading
disputes, 95–6, 98, 100, 119, 148–9;
post of Aksakal, 109, 120, 127;
British interests, 116; famine, 161;
registration of British subjects, 221,
232–3, 237, 238; anti-foreign
campaign, 245; German agents,
250, 252; and opium smuggling, 257
Yarkand Amban, 1, 22, 23; and
release of slaves, 78; and Raskam

valley dispute, 93, 98, 104, 109, 112;
and trade routes, 94; and Indian
traders, 95–6, 99, 104–5;
confrontation with M., 99, 100;
fear of Petrovsky, 104, 109, 115–16;
replacement, 115, 118; new
extortionist policy, 118–19;
petition from Sarikol, 125; and
British nationality, 140; and
traders' suits, 148; denunciation,
166; anti-British activities, 257
Yarkand-Leh frontier, 90, 91, 94
Yarkand river, 14, 17
Yarkhalik, 166
Yasin, 11, 33
Yonoff, Col., expedition to Pamirs,
33–4, 36, 51, 59; and
Younghusband, 33–4, 36; in
Roshan, 76
Younghusband, Capt. Francis, 6, 24,
149, 152; appearance, 1; in
Yarkand, 2, 5; debt to M., 5–6,
40–1; meetings with Gromchevsky,
6, 14; mission to Sinkiang, 10, 27,
41; explores Hindu Kush, 13–14;
and the Pamir dispute, 14–16,
27–8, 36–7; on Turkis, 18; on
Chinese, 20, 55; and Russian threat
to frontier, 28, 31; relations with
Petrovsky, 29–30, 31–32; return
journey to India, 32, 33–4, 37;
expulsion, 33, 34, 35
Yuan Shih-k'ai, President of Chinese
Republic, 175, 185, 187; on
Governor Yang, 211; need to pay
his troops, 213; imperial
ambitions, 214, 243; and Russian
demands, 227; and Chira affair,
228–9; proclaimed Emperor, 244;
and Taoyin Chang, 245;
unmourned death, 246–7
Yuan Ta-hua, Governor of Sinkiang,
and the revolution, 174, 175, 179,
212; pro-Manchu, 175;
replacement, 188, 211
Yunnan, 212; murder of Yunnanese
by Governor Yang, 246

*Some other Oxford Paperbacks for readers interested in Central Asia,
China and South-East Asia, past and present*

CAMBODIA

GEORGE COEDÈS
Angkor

CENTRAL ASIA

PETER FLEMING
Bayonets to Lhasa

LADY MACARTNEY
An English Lady in
Chinese Turkestan

C. P. SKRINE AND
PAMELA NIGHTINGALE
Macartney at Kashgar*

ALBERT VON LE COQ
Buried Treasures of
Chinese Turkestan

AITCHEN K. WU
Turkistan Tumult

CHINA

All About Shanghai:
A Standard Guide

HAROLD ACTON
Peonies and Ponies

VICKI BAUM
Shanghai '37

ERNEST BRAMAH
Kai Lung's Golden
Hours*

ERNEST BRAMAH
The Wallet of Kai Lung*

ANN BRIDGE
The Ginger Griffin

CHANG HSIN-HAI
The Fabulous Concubine*

CARL CROW
Handbook for China

PETER FLEMING
The Siege at Peking

CORRINNE LAMB
The Chinese Festive Board

W. SOMERSET MAUGHAM
On a Chinese Screen*

G. E. MORRISON
An Australian in China

PETER QUENNELL
A Superficial Journey
Through Tokyo and
Peking

OSBERT SITWELL
Escape with Me! An
Oriental Sketch-book

J. A. TURNER
Kwang Tung or Five
Years in South China

HONG KONG

The Hong Kong Guide
1893

INDONESIA

S. TAKDIR ALISJAHBANA
Indonesia: Social and
Cultural Revolution

DAVID ATTENBOROUGH
Zoo Quest for a Dragon*

VICKI BAUM
A Tale from Bali*

MIGUEL COVARRUBIAS
Island of Bali*

BERYL DE ZOETE AND
WALTER SPIES
Dance and Drama in Bali

AUGUSTA DE WIT
Java: Facts and Fancies

JACQUES DUMARÇAY
Borobudur

JACQUES DUMARÇAY
The Temples of Java

GEOFFREY GORER
Bali and Angkor

JENNIFER LINDSAY
Javanese Gamelan

EDWIN M. LOEB
Sumatra: Its History and
People

MOCHTAR LUBIS
Twilight in Djakarta

MADELON H. LULOFS
Coolie*

COLIN McPHEE
A House in Bali*

HICKMAN POWELL
The Last Paradise

E. R. SCIDMORE
Java, Garden of the East

MICHAEL SMITHIES
Yogyakarta: Cultural
Heart of Indonesia

LADISLAO SZÉKELY
Tropic Fever: The
Adventures of a Planter
in Sumatra

EDWARD C. VAN
NESS AND SHITA
PRAWIROHARDJO
Javanese Wayang Kulit

MALAYSIA

ABDULLAH ABDUL KADIR
The Hikayat Abdullah

ISABELLA L. BIRD
The Golden Chersonese:
Travels in Malaya in 1879

PIERRE BOULLE
Sacrilege in Malaya

MARGARET BROOKE
RANEE OF SARAWAK
My Life in Sarawak

C. C. BROWN (Editor)
Sejarah Melayu or Malay
Annals

K. M. ENDICOTT
An Analysis of Malay
Magic

HENRI FAUCONNIER
The Soul of Malaya

W. R. GEDDES
Nine Dayak Nights

JOHN D. GIMLETTE
Malay Poisons and
  Charm Cures

JOHN D. GIMLETTE AND
H. W. THOMSON
A Dictionary of Malayan
  Medicine

A. G. GLENISTER
The Birds of the Malay
  Peninsula, Singapore
  and Penang

C. W. HARRISON
Illustrated Guide to the
  Federated Malay States
  (1923)

TOM HARRISSON
World Within: A Borneo
  Story

DENNIS HOLMAN
Noone of the Ulu

CHARLES HOSE
The Field-Book of a
  Jungle-Wallah

SYBIL KATHIGASU
No Dram of Mercy

MALCOLM MacDONALD
Borneo People

W. SOMERSET MAUGHAM
Ah King and Other
  Stories*

W. SOMERSET MAUGHAM
The Casuarina Tree*

MARY McMINNIES
The Flying Fox*

ROBERT PAYNE
The White Rajahs of
  Sarawak

OWEN RUTTER
The Pirate Wind

ROBERT W. C. SHELFORD
A Naturalist in Borneo

J. T. THOMSON
Glimpses into Life in
  Malayan Lands

RICHARD WINSTEDT
The Malay Magician

PHILIPPINES

AUSTIN COATES
Rizal

SINGAPORE

PATRICK ANDERSON
Snake Wine: A Singapore
  Episode

ROLAND BRADDELL
The Lights of Singapore

R. W. E. HARPER AND
HARRY MILLER
Singapore Mutiny

JANET LIM
Sold for Silver

G. M. REITH
Handbook to Singapore
  (1907)

J. D. VAUGHAN
The Manners and Customs
  of the Chinese of the
  Straits Settlements

C. E. WURTZBURG
Raffles of the Eastern Isles

THAILAND

CARL BOCK
Temples and Elephants

REGINALD CAMPBELL
Teak-Wallah

MALCOLM SMITH
A Physician at the Court
  of Siam

ERNEST YOUNG
The Kingdom of the
  Yellow Robe

Titles marked with an asterisk have restricted rights

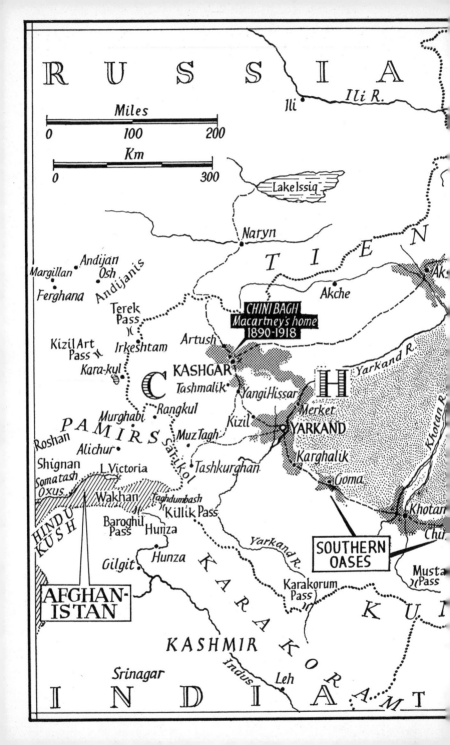